Graphic Design Studio Procedures

Graphic Design Studio Procedures

by David Gates

Lloyd-Simone Publishing Company

Copyright © 1982 by David Gates

First published 1982 in the United States by
Lloyd-Simone Publishing Company
32 Hillside Avenue, Monsey, New York 10952

Distributed by Library Research Associates
Dunderberg Road R.D. #5, Box 41
Monroe, New York 10950

Library of Congress Cataloging in Publication Data
Gates, David, 1927–
   Graphic design studio procedures.
   Bibliography: p.
   Includes index.
   1. Printing, Practical. 2. Graphic arts.
I. Title.
Z244.G29   1982   686.2'24   82-13023
ISBN 0-912526-30-0

Manufactured in U.S.A.

First printing, 1982

Dedicated to
EDGAR LEVY
1907-1975

Contents

Section One:
Graphic Arts Production Technology

Section Two:
Graphic Design Studio Procedures

Acknowledgments

Of many years in the making, this book has involved innumerable people and organizations. I would therefore like to express my gratitude to all those who have contributed to it, either directly or indirectly.

At Pratt Institute, I am particularly indebted to the students who contributed design work to the book, and to my colleagues Gerry Contreras, Ray Barber, Dale Clark, Peter Fiore, Charles Goslin, George Klauber, Herb Young, John Snyder, John Camejo, and Steve Cieslawski for their advice, assistance, and encouragement.

Among the innumerable contributors in the visual communication profession and the graphic arts industry, I would particularly like to thank Charrette Corporation for their permission to use illustrations from their art materials catalog; Grieco Printing Company for their technical information and advice; and Schaedler/Pinwheel for their line conversion examples.

Above all, I would like to thank my wife, Frieda, for her advice and encouragement, as well as for her invaluable assistance in editing, design, and production.

Introduction

This book is specifically intended for graphic design students, as well as for beginners in the graphic design profession. While its major emphasis is on the equipment, materials, techniques, and procedures of the graphic design studio, it also describes those aspects of the graphic arts industry that the designer must be familiar with in order to prepare art and copy for reproduction.

In writing this book, I tried to avoid taking anything for granted on the part of the reader. In my many years as a graphic design teacher, I have observed that too many authors and teachers fail to adequately cover the craft aspects of the profession. Either they assume that the student has already acquired this experience, or they believe that it is too insignificant, in comparison to creative aspects, to be worthy of discussion. Consequently, while the student is desperately trying to figure out, on his own, how to rule a line without smearing it, the teacher or author is airily probing the outer reaches of creativity.

This serves neither aspect of the profession well. Not only does the student fail to develop the necessary level of craftsmanship, but he is so distracted and frustrated by problems of execution that he is unable to pay proper attention to the larger problems of creativity. In any creative endeavor, a mastery of the craft is essential for masterly creative expression.

There have been many important technological developments in the graphic design profession and the graphic arts industry in recent years. However, although these new technologies have resulted in important changes in professional studio practices, their use in the learning process (and sometimes even in the one-man professional studio) is not always either practical, necessary, or desirable. Frequently, a new technology is simply a means of doing something easier or faster. While this may be of great value professionally (time is money), it sometimes robs the student of a valuable learning experience. Also, the new technology is almost always more expensive than the one it replaces, which additionally robs the student of money.

Consequently, while this book thoroughly covers all techniques and technologies, both conventional and new, it stresses those that are best suited to the beginner's educational needs and budgetary situation. It is important to understand that the graphic designer is first and foremost an artist/communicator, and that his hand, eye, and mind are his essential tools. Once he has fully developed the capabilities of these tools, he can easily apply them to any new technology that might come along.

Of prime importance to the beginner is the setting up of a personal studio. Such a studio should be regarded as a permanent investment, not just a temporary arrangement to be used while at school. Not only is a personal studio a necessity for free-lance work, but even staff designers need a home studio for night and weekend work.

Since the outfitting of a studio can be quite expensive, the beginner must spend his money wisely. As a general rule, precision tools that are used frequently should be of first quality, while non-precision tools, tools that are not used frequently, and large equipment may be of lower quality or even makeshift. Special-purpose tools should be avoided if there are general-purpose tools available that will accomplish the same task, as well as others, with reasonable success. In any event, it is better to have a completely outfitted studio, even though some of the tools and equipment are a temporary expedient, than to have a studio that is incomplete.

Expendable materials, such as paper, board, pencils, and color mediums, should be of as high a quality as possible, and a complete stock should be kept in the studio. Bear in mind that once a job is started, it is usually inconvenient, if not impossible, to run to an art supply store for a needed material, and that the want of even a simple material, such as tracing paper, can make an easy job difficult.

The section on studio equipment and material thoroughly describes the outfitting of the personal studio, and places particular emphasis on the tools, materials, and equipment that are within the budget of the beginner. In addition to describing workable substitutes for professional equipment, it stresses the use of tools and materials which have the widest variety of applications.

This book contains two sections: graphic design studio procedures and graphic arts production technology. For the reader who has little or no knowledge of either subject, the best approach is to read both sections in their entirety, without concern for detailed descriptions or procedures. After a general understanding of these subjects has been acquired, he will then have an adequate background to knowledgeably follow the detailed procedure necessary for any one of the graphic design operations. At that time, as he comes upon references to other sections of the book, he should immediately refer to those sections to acquire any additional information that he may have missed or misunderstood in the first reading.

While this book covers graphic design studio procedures thoroughly, the reader should be aware that it is necessarily concise in all related areas. For more information regarding art materials, the reader can acquire, at little or no cost, an art supply catalog from one of the many large art supply dealers, and for more information regarding graphic arts production, the reader should refer to such books as *Pocket Pal* or *Production for the Graphic Designer*. All of these books, plus many more, are listed in the bibliography.

Typesetting Methods

There are three basic methods of type-setting: hand-set, machine-set, and photographic. The hand-set method, invented by Gutenberg around 1450 AD, was the only method employed until the late 19th century, at which time the Linotype and Monotype machines were invented. These machines, which could set text sizes of type by keyboard control, eventually became the predominant method of setting text matter. A machine for setting display sizes (Ludlow) was introduced in 1906, but it never became very popular. Consequently, metal display type is still largely hand-set.

During the 1930's, a manually-operated machine for photographically setting display sizes of type was introduced (photo-lettering), and during the 1950's, keyboard-operated machines for photographically setting text sizes of type were introduced (phototypesetting). While both of these photographic typesetting methods are still undergoing rapid technological development by numerous manufacturers, they have already surpassed metal typesetting methods in quality, speed, economy, and versatility. Hand-set display composition has already largely been replaced by photolettering, and machine-set text composition, although still commonly used, is rapidly giving way to phototypesetting.

Other recently-introduced methods of typesetting are typewriter composition and printed alphabet sheets. Both of these methods are limited in quality, and are therefore used primarily for low-budget jobs.

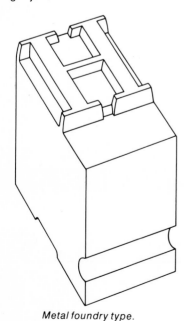

Metal foundry type.

HAND-SET COMPOSITION

In hand-set (or foundry type) composition, the type characters are cast in relief on separate pieces of metal at the type foundry (thus the name, foundry type). They are purchased by the printer or typographer and stored in a partitioned tray called a type case. The typesetter, or compositor, picks the type from the case and assembles it, character by character, in a hand-held composing stick that has been set to the desired column width. Pieces of metal called quads and spaces are used to adjust letter and word spacing, and strips of metal called leads (pronounced ledds) and slugs are used to adjust line spacing. As the composing stick fills up, the assembled type is transferred to a flat tray called a galley. When the typesetting is completed, the type is tied up in the galley and proofed on a proofing press. After the galley proof has been proofread and corrections have been made, the type is locked up in a metal frame called a chase. The locked-up type can then be used to make reproduction proofs for use in offset or gravure; to make a printing plate (such as an electrotype or stereotype) for letterpress; or for direct production printing on a flat-bed letterpress press. After use, the type is cleaned and distributed back into the type case.

Setting foundry type.

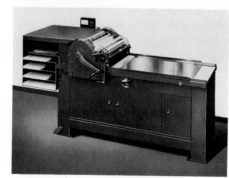

Vandercook SP20 proofing press.

Type form in a proofing press (Vandercook).

MACHINE-SET COMPOSITION

In machine-set composition, the type characters are molded into brass dies, or matrices. These matrices are used by the printer or typographer to compose and cast printing type more or less automatically, depending on the system employed.

Linotype and Intertype. In these systems, the matrices are contained in a machine that is operated by keyboard. As the copy is "typed," the matrices fall into assembly, with a wedge, or spaceband, inserted between each word. At the end of the line, the spacebands are wedged between the words, thus justifying the line (making it the full width of the column). The composed line of matrices is then cast in molten metal, thus forming a "line o' type" slug with the characters in relief on one edge. Leading (line spacing) is automatically achieved by increasing the thickness of the slug. The matrices are then returned to their original position in the machine, and the slugs are assembled in a galley, for use in the same way as hand-set type. Apart from keyboard control, these operations are largely automatic. After use, the slugs are melted and the metal is returned to the caster.

Type matrices are available in sizes from 5 to 18 point, and type can be set as wide as 30 picas (some machines can set up to 42 picas wide). Wider columns are possible by butting slugs, but being a hand operation, this usually costs more.

Some linecasting machines are automatically operated by perforated tape. The tape is perforated on a separate machine, either by keyboard or by wire service from another location.

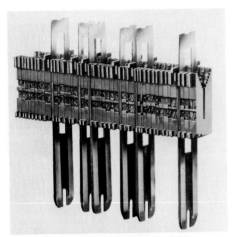

Linotype matrices with spacebands.

Linotype slugs being assembled.

Monotype. In this system, the copy is punch-coded, by keyboard, in a roll of paper tape. All information for typesetting is contained in the tape, including the amount of wordspacing required to justify the line, indentations, linespacing, etc. The perforated tape is then inserted in an automatic typecasting machine, where the characters are cast individually (not in lines) and then composed. Type matrices are available in sizes from 4½ to 14 point, and type can be set up to 36 picas wide. Monotype is commonly used for setting complicated tables and charts, as well as for books. As with linecasters, "dead" type is melted for re-use.

Ludlow. In this system, individual type matrices are hand-selected from a case and assembled in a special composing stick. As each line is completed, the stick is clamped in the casting machine, the line is cast, and the matrices are distributed back into the case. This system is no faster than hand-set composition, but its advantage is an unlimited supply of type from a limited font of matrices. It is primarily intended for setting display copy, and type matrices are available in sizes from 6 to 144 point.

Monotype keyboard.

Monotype typecaster.

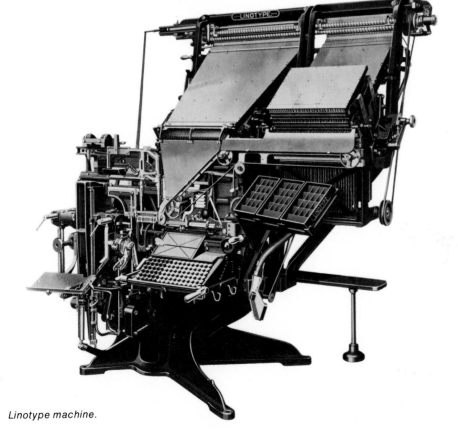

Linotype machine.

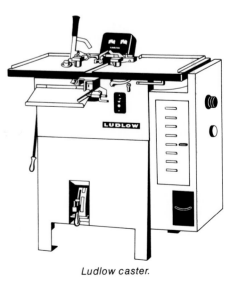

Ludlow caster.

PHOTOTYPESETTING

Since its introduction in 1950, photo-typesetting has undergone three stages, or generations, of development. The first-generation systems are adaptations of the Intertype and Monotype machines. The matrices contain negative character images instead of molds, and are photo-graphed instead of cast.

The second-generation systems are entirely unique in design, and have little or no relationship to earlier systems, either metal or photo. These systems, which utilize photographic, electronic,

First generation. This Intertype Fotosetter can set 15 lines per minute.

Second Generation. This Mergenthaler V-I-P system can set 50 lines per minute. Twenty-two type sizes are on machine from 6 to 72 point.

Third generation. This Mergenthaler Linotron 505 CRT system can set a complete newspaper page in about 4 minutes (over 400 lines per minute). Twenty-two type sizes are on machine from 4 to 72 point.

and mechanical components, are available in over 100 models from more than a dozen manufacturers. While they all differ in design and capabilities, they use a similar method of imaging: the type characters are stored in negative form on a drum, disc, or grid, and as each character is selected for setting, a lens and light system projects it on to photographic film or paper.

The third-generation systems employ a cathode-ray tube (CRT) in the imaging process. The type characters are stored either in negative form (as in second-generation systems) or in digital form on magnetic tape. As each character is selected for setting, it is converted into a vertical scan-line pattern on the cathode-ray tube and projected onto pho-tographic film or paper. The ragged edges created by the scan lines are too fine to be

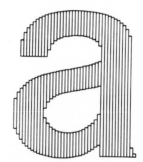

The imaging of a letter on a cathode-ray tube (simplified scan-line pattern).

visible with the naked eye. CRT type-setters are capable of extremely high speed, and are ideally suited for high-volume applications.

Phototypesetting has many advantages over metal typesetting. It is much faster, less expensive (especially in high-volume applications), and the type characters are sharper. Also, because the characters are on film rather than on metal bodies, the letterspacing is not only more consistent, but it can be adjusted to any degree of openness or tightness, including overlapping.

Enlarged metal type   *Enlarged phototype*

Just look at the diversity... +1

Just look at the diversity... 0

Just look at the diversity... -1

Just look at the diversity... -2

Just look at the diversity... -3

Diatronic 64-unit system permits spacing as tight as −4 or as loose as +11.

Because of the great variety of photo-typesetting systems available, it would require an inordinate amount of space to describe the features and operation of each system individually. Therefore, the basic operations in the phototypesetting process will be listed, along with a general description of how these operations are performed in various systems. The systems described are largely second-generation, which is the category most frequently encountered in general graphic design work.

The Unit System of Measuring. The unit system is a method of measuring the width of characters and spaces in a line. A unit is a subdivision of the em measurement, which is the square of the typeface height. For example, in 12 point type the em is 12 points wide, in 8 point type the em is 8 points wide, etc. (see Copyfitting, page 127). Most phototypesetting systems employ 18 units to the em, while others employ anywhere from 4 to 64.

A counting mechanism in the keyboard, computer, or typesetter totals the number of units used in a line and determines when the line is ready to be justified. The unit system is also used to control letterspacing. In addition to overall normal, tight, or open letterspacing, individual letter combinations can be adjusted for a better fit.

Em divided into 18 units.

16 UNITS   10 UNITS   15 UNITS

Keyboard Unit. In a few systems, the keyboard is connected directly to the typesetting unit. The operator determines hyphenation and justification, and typesetting speed is determined by the input speed of the operator. This is called direct entry or direct input.

CompuWriter II is a direct entry system with keyboard and photounit combined.

In the majority of systems, the keyboard produces a magnetic or perforated paper tape. There are two types of keyboards for tape recording; counting and non-counting. With the counting keyboard, the operator determines hyphenation and justification, thus producing a justified tape that can be used directly in the typesetter. With the non-counting keyboard, the operator makes no end-of-line decisions, thus producing an unjustified, or idiot, tape. Hyphenation and justification decisions are later made by a computer, which may be a separate unit or part of the typesetting unit.

With the use of an optical character recognition (OCR) system, the keyboard unit and operator are eliminated entirely. In this system, the original manuscript copy is put into a scanner, which reads the copy and produces a tape. OCR systems require the use of a specially designed typewriter face with which to type the original copy.

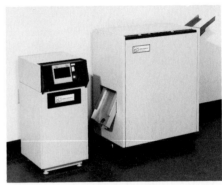

Graphicscan OCR input system.

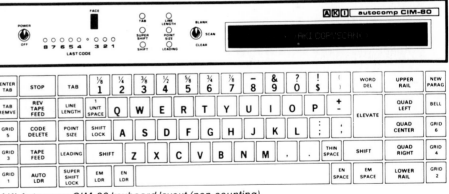

AKI Autocomp CIM-80 keyboard layout (non-counting).

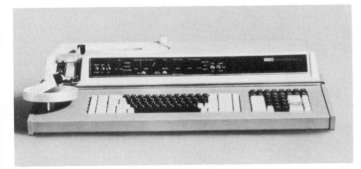

AKI Autocount MPM-6 counting keyboard.

AKI Automite CIT-70 non-counting keyboard.

Phototypesetting Unit (Photounit).
The typeface characters are carried in negative form on an image master, which may be a drum, disc, grid, or film strip. Depending upon the machine, each image master contains from 1 to 16 fonts, and from 1 to 18 image masters are held in the machine. Typefaces and type sizes can usually be mixed within a line, and font changes are usually automatic for those that are held in the machine.

Some machines use a different font for each type size, while others use one font and a lens system to achieve different sizes. The maximum type size varies greatly among machines, ranging anywhere from 12 to 72 point. The maximum line length generally ranges from 30 to 50 picas, but some machines can set wider.

The typesetting speed of most second-generation machines ranges from 30 to 150 lines per minute, while third-generation CRT machines are capable of over 1,000 lpm. (The line used for this measurement is 8 point type set 11 picas wide, or approximately 30 characters.)

Monotype 600 phototypesetter.

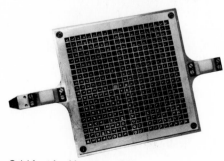

Grid font for Monotype 600.

Editing and Correcting. To enable the operator to see the words being recorded on tape, some keyboard units have a visual display, and others produce typewritten (hard) copy. If an error occurs, the type can then be corrected immediately. Some keyboards have neither of these features, and are called blind keyboards.

After keyboarding, the tape can be edited on a video display terminal (VDT), which has a screen for viewing the copy and a keyboard for making changes or corrections. The unit produces a new, corrected tape.

Another method of editing a tape after keyboarding is to make a printout on a machine called a line printer. Corrections are made by punching a new tape and merging the two in a computer.

After typesetting, corrections can be made by either method described previously, or, if the corrections are minor, by patching the film or paper proof.

The Graphic Ediset editor.

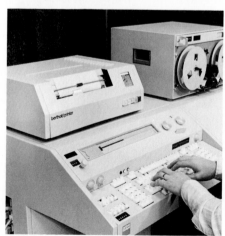

Berthold line printer connected to keyboard unit.

Video Layout Systems. Video layout systems, also called photocomposing systems or composition and makeup terminals, permit the keyboard operator to lay out a complete ad or page of type without marking up the copy, and without the need to later paste up the various typographic elements. The copy is first keyboarded on tape in the usual manner, and then fed into the layout terminal, where it appears on the video display screen ready for layout. Using a keyboard-directed cursor and copyfitting keys, the operator sizes and positions the copy according to the designer's layout. With merely the press of a key, the operator can set copy in any column arrangement and width, change type sizes and styles, delete or add copy, etc. When the layout is correct, the operator presses a key, and the copy and layout instructions are coded in a tape which is then used to drive the typesetter. The result is a one-piece paper proof which can be pasted in the mechanical, or a film proof which can be used directly for platemaking.

Video layout systems are becoming popular for newspaper editorial and advertising layout, telephone directories, etc. They are not yet well-suited for high-quality graphic design applications, however.

Harris 2200 Video Layout System.

MAVERICK 1970
Auto. Transmission.
Best Buy $1295

MONACO 1965
Hardtop, See Try and
Buy at Only $175

'66 PONTIAC
4-door Hardtop, ''Loaded'', Air
JENSON'S PRICE ONLY $695

'65 MONACO
Hardtop
QUICK SALE PRICE
$275

Layout on video display screen.

PHOTOLETTERING

Photolettering, also called photodisplay, is an inexpensive method of setting display type photographically. There are more than 20 photolettering machines available, some of which are sufficiently uncomplicated and inexpensive to be suitable for studio purchase and operation. While the machines vary greatly in design and capabilities, the general operating procedure is as follows: the type font, which is on a film strip, disc, or slide, is inserted in the machine. It is then adjusted to bring the selected character into exposure position, and a light is flashed to expose the character on to photosensitive paper or film. The next character is then brought into exposure position, and the paper or film is advanced to achieve proper letterspacing. In some machines, the characters are developed as soon as they are exposed, and in others, developing is a later, out-of-machine operation. With immediate development, it is possible to see the characters being set, and letterspacing can therefore be adjusted by eye. With out-of-machine development, letterspacing must be done by mechanical means, such as spacing marks on the type font. Visual spacing is more accurate, but it requires a trained eye.

On most machines, the foregoing operations are manually performed, but a few machines employ a keyboard for character selection and other operations. Also, most machines set type in a single line on a strip of paper or film about 2″ wide, which means that for consecutive lines, the strips must be trimmed and pasted up. A few machines employ wide paper, and can set consecutive lines on one sheet.

Photolettering is faster and less expensive than the handsetting of foundry type, and also permits very accurate letterspacing with any degree of openness or tightness, including overlapping. Through the use of special lenses and devices, some machines can expand, condense, italicize, backslant, and screen letters, as well as set curved lines. Some phototypesetting machines can set display sizes completely automatically, but for the typical short headline or caption, photolettering is usually faster, less expensive, and more versatile. It is also usually more accurate in regard to letterspacing.

Photolettering fonts are relatively inexpensive, and the majority of machines offer anywhere from 100 to 5,000 typefaces and sizes, including many designs that are not available in other typesetting systems. Some machines can enlarge or reduce a typeface to any size desired. For those that cannot, typefaces are generally available in a number of standard point sizes. In-between sizes, of course, can be achieved by photostatting.

Photo Typositor 3000.

VariTyper Headliner 860.

Typography
TOUCHING

Typography
VERY TIGHT

Typography
TIGHT

Typography
NORMAL

Typography
TV SPACING

Helvetica Medium with various letterspacing (Photo Typositor).

Typography
CONDENSED 24%

Typography
CONDENSED 8%

Typography
EXPANDED 24%

Typography
EXPANDED 8%

Typography
OBLIQUE

Helvetica Medium reproportioned on the Photo Typositor.

TYPEWRITER

Typewriter composition, also called strike-on or direct-impression composition, is an inexpensive method of setting text copy. There are various systems in use, the most common being the Vari-Typer and IBM Selectric Composer. Unlike conventional typewriters, composition typewriters have interchangeable type fonts, characters that vary in width and spacing, a wordspacing system to achieve justified lines, and variable linespacing (leading) that is measured in points. A carbon ribbon is used to achieve sharp, clean impressions, and the copy is typed directly on reproduction-quality paper. While the quality is not as high as in machine setting or phototypesetting, it is usually adequate for low-budget jobs.

There are two methods of justification: manual and automatic. In manual justification, the copy must be typed twice. In the first typing, standard wordspacing is used and the lines are unjustified. In the second typing, justification is achieved by adjusting the wordspacing for each line. This is done either automatically or by keyboard control, depending on the system. (By employing a flush left/ragged right column arrangement, the second typing can be eliminated, thus substantially reducing the typesetting cost.)

In automatic justification, as the copy is typed it is recorded on magnetic or perforated tape. The tape, which contains all information regarding justification, indentations, linespacing, etc., is then put in a separate machine to automatically compose the copy. Thus, only one manual typing operation is necessary.

Most typewriter composition systems employ a unit system for measuring line length. Each typeface character has a specific unit width (for example, in the IBM 9-unit system, the characters range in width from 3 to 9 units). As the line is typed, the character units, plus wordspacing units, are automatically counted. If the line is to be justified, the total number of units used in that particular line is compared to the total number of units in the desired column width, and the difference is divided equally among the number of wordspaces in the line. The wordspacing is then adjusted by either manual or automatic justification methods, as described previously. The unit system is also used in phototypesetting, and is further described in that section.

IBM Selectric Composer. In the Selectric Composer (called the SC), the characters vary in width and spacing, and are based on a 9-unit system. There is a good selection of typefaces, in sizes ranging from 6 to 12 point, and maximum column width is 76 picas. The machine holds only one font, which is ball-shaped. While font changing is not difficult, it can be very time-consuming if frequent changes are necessary. The Selectric Composer can be used by itself to type and compose in the same operation (double typing is necessary for justification), or it can be used as part of a magnetic tape system for automatic composition.

In the magnetic tape system, the copy is typed on a Selectric Typewriter, which is a conventional office-model electric typewriter. The typewriter is connected to a magnetic tape input unit, which is programmed with all instructions regarding column arrangement (justified, flush left, flush right, centered), indentations, typeface style, etc. This input aspect of the system is called the MT/ST (Magnetic

IBM Selectric Composer (SC).

IBM Magnetic Tape Selectric Typewriter connected to Recorder Unit (MT/ST).

IBM Magnetic Tape Selectric Composer connected to Reader Unit (MT/SC).

IBM Selectric fonts.

Tape/Selectric Typewriter).

The completed tape is inserted in a small computer, or reader, which is connected to the Selectric Composer. The operator sets the composer for column width and line spacing, inserts the correct type font, and the tape automatically composes the copy. The composer stops when operator assistance is needed, such as for the hyphenation of words at the end of lines, changes in typeface size or style, and changes in leading. This output aspect of the system is called the MT/SC (Magnetic Tape/Selectric Composer).

VariTyper. There are two VariTyper models. In one, the characters are all equal in width as in a conventional typewriter. In the other, the characters vary in width and spacing and are based on a 4-unit system. Both models employ manual justification and require double typing. Over 1,200 typefaces are available, in sizes ranging from 3½ to 13 point. The machines are designed to hold two type fonts, which makes it possible to combine two typefaces without changing fonts.

VariTyper Model 1010.

PRINTED ALPHABET SHEETS

For small and/or low-budget typesetting jobs, it is frequently possible to use printed alphabet sheets. There are two kinds of sheets: dry transfer and cut-out. Both are available in hundreds of typefaces. Sizes usually range from 12 to 72 point, but some typefaces are available in sizes as small as 8 point or as large as 3". Most typefaces are available in either black or white, and some dry transfer typefaces are also available in basic colors for use on comps and presentations.

Cut-out Lettering. The letters, which are printed on a clear acetate sheet that is backed with low-tack adhesive, are cut out, peeled from the protective backing sheet, positioned on the working surface, and burnished firmly. The advantage of cut-out lettering is that the letters can be very accurately positioned before final burnishing. The disadvantage is that the pieces of film surrounding each letter make it unsuitable for comps and presentations.

Cut-out letters being cut and lifted from backing sheet (Formatt).

Cut-out letters being applied to artwork (Formatt).

Dry Transfer Lettering. The letters are printed with a special ink on the back of a transparent carrier sheet. The sheet is placed on the working surface and the selected letter is positioned. The sheet is then rubbed with a ballpoint pen or similar stylus tool, which transfers the letter to the working surface. In the event of an error, letters can be removed with either a soft eraser, a rubber cement pickup, or masking tape. A special spray coating is available to protect the lettering from damage in later handling.

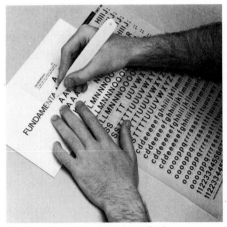

Dry transfer letters being applied.

HAND LETTERING

Although hand lettering is not a typesetting method, it is frequently used in place of type for custom design applications, such as logos, trademarks, titles, product names, etc. Also, of course, the original designs for typefaces are hand lettered.

The execution of finished lettering for reproduction requires a good amount of training and experience. For that reason, it is frequently done by a lettering specialist, who either initiates the design or works from a layout or comp provided by an art director or designer. After the lettering design has been fully resolved through a series of pencil sketches on layout paper, it is transferred to bristol board, bond paper, or vellum for rendering in ink. Finished lettering is usually executed 20 to 50 percent larger than reproduction size. When reduced to reproduction size, such a reduction range eliminates minor imperfections but still retains details.

Hand lettering by Ray Barber.

Printing Processes

There are three major printing processes: letterpress, gravure, and offset lithography. Each employs a different method of platemaking and printing, and each, consequently, has unique characteristics with which the designer must be familiar. In addition to selecting the process that is best suited for a particular job, he must also know how to prepare the artwork for that process.

There are a number of minor printing processes with which the designer must also be familiar, even though they may not be frequently encountered. Some of these, such as flexography, letterset, and thermography, are modifications of major processes, while others, such as screen printing, collotype, and engraving, are entirely different.

LETTERPRESS

Letterpress is a relief method of printing. In this method, the printing area, or image, is raised, and the non-printing area is depressed. Ink is applied to the raised surface, and when paper is pressed against it, the image is transferred to the paper. This is the simplest and oldest method of printing, and there is evidence of its use, in primitive form, as far back as 1500 BC. However, it was not until Gutenberg invented movable type, around 1450 AD, that it began to be used as we know it today.

Letterpress is a high-quality printing process that is suitable for both short and long run work of many kinds. Printing can be done from cast metal type, wood type, wood cuts and engravings, and linoleum blocks, as well as from metal, plastic, and rubber plates that have been relief-imaged by a photomechanical process. It is the only printing process that permits the direct printing of metal and wood type.

There are three types of presses for letterpress printing: platen, flat-bed cylinder, and rotary. The platen, or job, press employs two flat surfaces that open and close with a clamshell movement. One surface, called the bed, holds the printing form, and the other, called the platen, presses the paper against the form. The paper is sheet fed, either by hand or automatically. Platen presses are also used for embossing, die-cutting, and scoring.

The flat-bed cylinder press holds the printing form on a flat bed that moves back and forth beneath an impression cylinder. Presses are generally sheet-fed, but some are web-fed (a web is a continuous roll of paper). The paper is

Letterpress plate.

gripped on the cylinder to make rolling contact with the form as it passes beneath.

The rotary press has two cylinders: a printing plate cylinder and an impression cylinder. The printing plate must either be molded to fit the curve of the cylinder (such as a stereotype or electrotype plate), or it must be made of a flexible material that can be wrapped around the cylinder (such as a photopolymer plate). Presses are either sheet-fed or web-fed. Web-fed presses operate at very high speed and are used for printing newspapers, magazines, catalogs, and the like.

In the conventional letterpress process, metal type and/or photoengraved line cuts and halftones are locked up in a metal frame called a chase. Printing can be done directly from the locked-up form on a platen or flat-bed rotary press. Frequently, however, the form is used to make a mold from which a duplicate plate (either flat or curved) is cast in metal, plastic, or rubber. Examples of duplicate

plates are stereotypes and electrotypes. A duplicate plate is necessary to convert the flat form into a curved plate for use on a rotary press, and is highly desirable, in flat-bed printing, to avoid wear on the original type and engravings in long press runs.

The line cuts and halftones used in the conventional letterpress process are called photoengravings, and are usually made by a company that specializes in platemaking. Because they are relatively difficult and expensive to make, letterpress is more expensive than offset lithography when much illustrative matter, either line or continuous-tone, is involved. Photoengravings are made by placing a line or halftone negative in contact with a zinc, magnesium, or copper plate that has a light-sensitive coating, and exposing it to light in a vacuum frame. This hardens the coating in the light-exposed areas, making it acid-resistant. The plate is then dipped in acid, which etches, or eats into, the unprotected areas of the metal, thus producing a relief image. After the plate has been relief-imaged, it is mounted on a block of wood to make it type-high, and then proofed and sent to the printer. Each piece of illustrative copy is a separate engraving, or cut, and the printer must assemble the

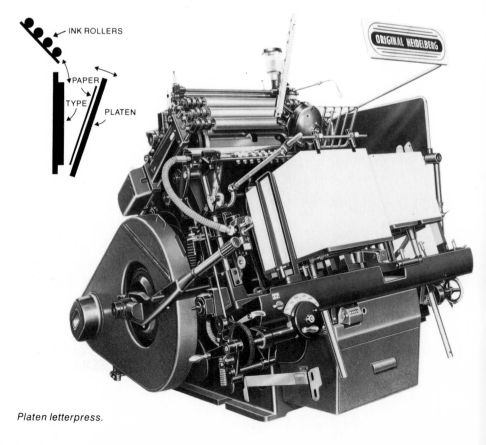

Platen letterpress.

engravings, along with the type matter, in a chase. Furniture (pieces of wood or metal) and quoins (steel wedges) are used to lock up the elements in printing position. A proof is then made of the completed assembly for client approval.

Since the printer composes the type and assembles all layout elements, the designer merely needs to provide him with a layout, manuscript copy (with type specifications), and finished art of illustrations and photographs. While this greatly simplifies the job of the designer, it also denies him the opportunity to make the sort of adjustments and changes that are possible on a mechanical. Only after the proof is pulled does the designer see the finished art in exact printing position, and by that time, of course, alterations are both difficult and expensive to make.

A new method of platemaking has recently been developed for letterpress. In this method, all copy is relief-imaged on a photopolymer direct-relief printing plate. Photopolymer plates are not only easier and faster to make than conventional photoengravings, they eliminate lock-up time and simplify press makeready operations. Also, since the copy is assembled on a mechanical (as in offset), the designer is in complete control of all graphic decisions.

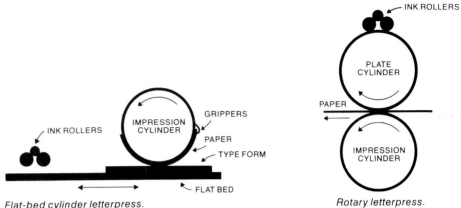

Flat-bed cylinder letterpress.

Rotary letterpress.

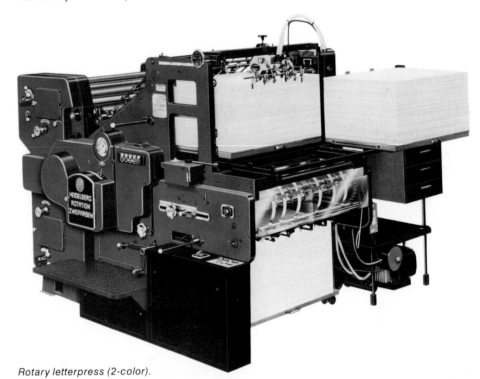

Rotary letterpress (2-color).

Flat-bed cylinder letterpress.

Rotary newspaper letterpress.

GRAVURE

Gravure is an intaglio method of printing, which is exactly the opposite of relief printing. That is, the printing area, or image, is depressed, and the non-printing area is raised. In the gravure process, the image is chemically etched into the plate, and the plate is inked and then wiped clean with a device called a doctor blade. This removes the ink from the raised surface but not from the depressions. When paper is pressed against the plate, the ink in the depressions is transferred to it. The deeper the depression the thicker the deposit of ink, and consequently the darker the printed tone. Gravure is printed by rotary press, either sheet-fed (uncommonly called photogravure) or web-fed (commonly called rotogravure).

Because of the varying depth of the ink cells in the screened printing plate, gravure is capable of reproducing continuous-tone copy with exceptional subtlety and richness. On the other hand, line copy must also be screened, which makes gravure less accurate for line reproduction than letterpress or offset printing. However, the screen used in gravure printing is usually so fine (generally 150-line or finer), that the screened edges of the line copy are not discernible to the naked eye. (It is a good policy, nevertheless, to avoid very small type with fine hairlines.)

Gravure printing plates are very difficult and expensive to make. However, they are long lasting, require minimum press makeready, will print on virtually any surface with a minimum of press control, and use fluid ink that is extremely fast drying. For these reasons, rotogravure is commonly used for such high-speed, long-run applications as packages (paper, cellophane, foil), Sunday newspaper supplements, magazines, catalogs, and wallpaper. Because of the high platemaking costs, short-run, sheet-fed gravure printing is generally limited to applications where high-quality reproduction of continuous-tone copy is of prime importance, such as fine art reproductions, calendars, and annual reports.

There are three types of gravure printing plates: variable depth (conventional), variable area/variable depth, and variable area. In variable depth or conventional plates, the etched ink cells are equal in size and shape but vary in depth. Printing tones are achieved by the thickness of the ink deposits, not by the optical mixing of black and white dots as in letterpress and offset halftone printing. In

INK

Gravure plate.

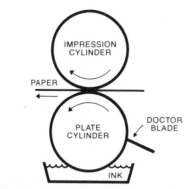

IMPRESSION CYLINDER

PAPER

PLATE CYLINDER

DOCTOR BLADE

INK

Gravure press.

fact, the screen lines that separate the ink cells in gravure are so fine that they usually fill in during printing, thus resulting in virtually screenless reproduction of very high quality.

In variable area/variable depth plates, the ink cells vary in size and shape as in letterpress and offset halftones, and also vary in depth as in conventional gravure. The advantage to this method is that it retains tones and shadow detail lost in conventional gravure, and extends the life of the printing plates. It is particularly well suited for long-run, full-color reproduction, and is commonly used for Sunday newspaper supplements, magazines, and catalogs.

In variable area plates, the ink cells vary in size and shape but are equal in depth. As with letterpress and offset

Rotogravure printing press (Motter).

halftones, tones are achieved by the optical mixing of black and white dots, not by the thickness of ink deposits. The range and richness of tones is therefore limited. Variable area plates are mainly used for printing packages.

The preparation of copy for gravure printing is the same as for offset printing, but the platemaking process is entirely different. In conventional gravure, a sheet of paper coated with light-sensitive gelatin (called carbon tissue) is placed in contact with a gravure screen (an opaque film with transparent grid lines) and exposed to light, which hardens the gelatin where the grid lines occur. The carbon tissue is then placed in contact with a continuous-tone film positive of the original copy and again exposed to light, which hardens the gelatin squares between the grid lines in proportion to the amount of light admitted through the film. Finally, the carbon tissue is adhered to the printing plate cylinder, gelatin side down, and processed. Processing removes the paper backing as well as varying amounts of gelatin (the harder the gelatin, the less that is removed; the softer the gelatin, the more that is removed). When the printing plate is subsequently etched with acid, the gelatin acts as an acid resist. The thicker the gelatin coating, the shallower the etch, and the thinner the gelatin coating, the deeper the etch. In this process, it is important to note that the gravure screen

merely serves as a means of providing plate-high partitions for the doctor blade to ride on. The screened dots do not vary in size or shape, and consequently have nothing to do with printing tones.

In variable area/variable depth gravure, the platemaking process is basically the same as described above, the major difference being that a halftone film positive is used in conjunction with the continuous-tone film positive and gravure screen to expose the carbon tissue.

Thus, the screened dots vary in size and shape as well as depth.

In variable area gravure, the gravure screen and carbon tissue are omitted entirely, and a halftone film positive is exposed directly to a gelatin-coated printing plate cylinder. Thus, the screened dots vary in size and shape but not in depth.

There is no preliminary proofing operation in gravure printing. Proofs are made on the production press at the beginning of the press run.

Gravure printing cylinder (Motter).

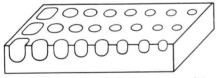

Variable depth (conventional) gravure plate.

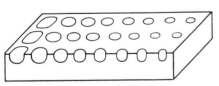

Variable area/variable depth gravure plate.

Variable area gravure plate.

Rotogravure printing press (Motter).

OFFSET LITHOGRAPHY

Offset lithography, commonly referred to simply as "offset," is a planographic method of printing. The printing plate is chemically treated so the non-printing area is receptive to water, and the printing area, or image, is receptive to ink. There is no difference in height between the printing and non-printing areas; both are on the same level or "plane."

In the printing operation, the printing plate is dampened and then inked with each revolution of the printing cylinder. The inked image is transferred to a rubber blanket cylinder, and from the rubber blanket cylinder to the paper. The advantage to this "offsetting" procedure is that the rubber blanket, being resilient, requires less printing pressure and ink, is capable of printing on a wide variety of paper surfaces, and increases plate life. Also, the printing plate is right reading, not reverse reading as in other printing processes, which makes it easier to work with.

Offset is a high-quality printing process that is suitable for both short- and long-run work of many kinds. Presses are either sheet-fed rotary or web-fed rotary. Web offset is used for printing newspapers, catalogs, books, magazines, and other high-speed, long-run jobs.

Offset lithography plate.

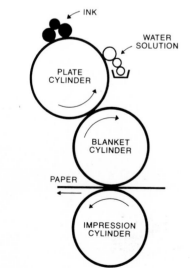

Offset lithography press.

Printing plates for offset are relatively inexpensive and easy to make. Also, they allow extensive use of illustrative matter, both line and halftone, at little or no extra cost. For these reasons, unless another method of printing offers a distinct advantage, offset is the preferred choice. (Most printers make their own offset plates. Letterpress and gravure plates, however, as well as process color offset plates, are usually made by companies that specialize in platemaking.)

As described in the section on Preparing the Mechanical (page 154), all line copy is assembled in position on a mechanical. The size and position of continuous-tone copy is indicated on the mechanical, but the original art itself is submitted to the platemaker as separate shooting copy. The platemaker makes a

One-color offset press.

Two-color offset press.

line negative of the mechanical, and a halftone negative for each piece of continuous-tone copy. He then tapes all the negatives (plus screen tints, if any) in position on a sheet of lightproof yellow/orange paper called goldenrod, and cuts openings in it for the negatives. This process is called stripping, and the completed assembly is called the flat. A photographic blueprint or brownprint proof is then made from the flat and submitted to the client for approval. (For multicolor proofs, see Color Printing, page 32.) After the proof has been approved, the flat is used to make the printing plate.

The printing plate is made by placing the flat in contact with a printing plate that has a light-sensitive coating, and exposing it to light in a vacuum frame. This prepares the coating for chemical treatments that render the non-printing areas water-receptive/ink-repellent, and the printing areas ink-receptive/water-repellent.

Multilith 1850 offset press.

Goss Metro-Offset web-fed newspaper press.

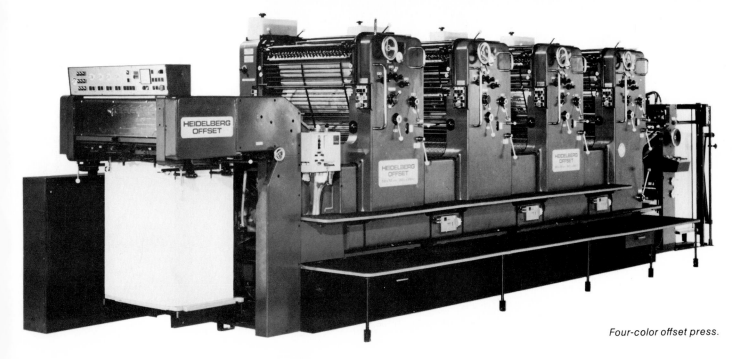

Four-color offset press.

SCREEN PRINTING

Screen printing, also called silkscreen printing, is a printing method that employs a stencil adhered to a fine-mesh screen. The screen can be made of silk, nylon, Dacron, or metal, and is stretched on a frame. The stencil is a specially prepared film that, in one type, is cut by hand, and in another, is photomechanically imaged. In the printing operation, the screen is pressed against the printing surface, and heavy, paint-like ink is forced through the open, or image, areas of the mesh with a rubber squeegee. Presses range from simple, hand-operated devices to semi- and fully-automatic machines. Also, rotary presses have recently been introduced. Even at its fastest, however, screen printing is much slower than letterpress, gravure, or offset printing.

The unique advantage to screen printing is that just about any material, in just about any size, shape, or thickness, can be printed. Materials include wood, glass, metal, plastic, fabric, cardboard, and paper, and applications include bottles, boxes, banners, posters, billboards, signs, dials, wallpaper, and draperies.

Because the ink is heavy-bodied and opaque, it is the only printing process in which white or light colors can be printed on dark surfaces. A great variety of ink types are available, including matte, glossy, metallic, and fluorescent.

The copy for a photographic stencil must be assembled entirely in line form on a mechanical. Screen tints can be achieved with shading sheets, and half-tones can be achieved with veloxes. It is generally not advisable to make screen tints and veloxes finer than 85-line, or to use extremely small or delicate type. To image the stencil, the mechanical must be converted to a film positive. (Copy preparation for a photographic screen stencil is exactly the same as copy preparation for super comps, as described on page 111.)

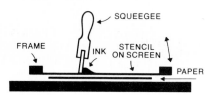

Screen printing.

Cylinder screen printing press (Lawson Aladdin).

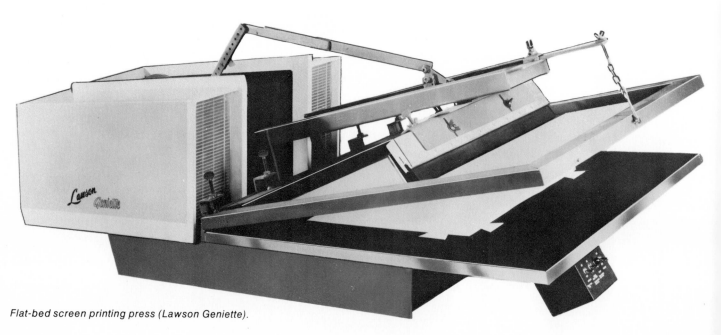

Flat-bed screen printing press (Lawson Geniette).

FLEXOGRAPHY

Flexography is a form of relief or letterpress printing in which the printing plate is made of rubber, and the ink is liquid (not paste as in conventional letterpress) and quick-drying. Printing is done with rotary, web-fed presses.

Flexographic printing is used extensively in the packaging industry for bread wrappers, candy bar wrappers, cellophane and paper bags, milk cartons, corrugated cartons, etc. It is also used for wallpaper, gift wrapping paper, shower curtains, and other decorative applications.

Because of the thinness of the ink and the distortion of the rubber plate, flexography is not capable of reproducing fine detail or maintaining hairline register. For this reason, type should not be smaller than 6 point, and reversed type should not be smaller than 8 point. Also, faces with fine hairlines should be avoided, especially when reversed.

LETTERSET

Letterset, also known as dry offset or indirect letterpress, is a printing method that employs a letterpress printing plate on an offset press (thus the acronym letterset). Since the printing image is in relief, no dampening system is required, which simplifies press makeready and operation.

Letterset combines some of the advantages of letterpress, such as the ability to use quick-drying, glossy, or other special inks, with some of the advantages of offset lithography, the most important being the ability to print on many types of surfaces. It is commonly used for printing plastic containers.

COLLOTYPE

Collotype, also known as photogelatin, is the only printing method in which continuous-tone copy can be reproduced without the use of a halftone screen. The printing plate is a thin metal sheet that has been coated with light-sensitive gelatin. When placed in contact with a continuous-tone negative and exposed to light, the gelatin becomes moisture-repellent (and therefore ink-receptive) in proportion to the amount of light exposure. In the printing operation, the plate is first dampened and then inked as in lithography. Unlike offset lithography, however, the inked image is transferred directly from the printing plate to the paper. Either flat-bed or rotary presses can be used.

Collotype reproduces tones and details with remarkable accuracy. It is commonly used for fine art reproductions, posters, point-of-purchase displays, and giant, back-lighted transparencies. It is also used to simulate photographic prints, such as autographed photos of celebrities.

Collotype is a comparatively inexpensive method of reproducing continuous-tone copy (either one-color or full-color), especially in large sizes and/or short runs. It is used in sizes up to about 4' x 5', and in runs up to about 5,000. (The gelatin-coated plate wears out after about 5,000 impressions.)

ENGRAVING

Engraving, also known as steel-die or copperplate engraving, is an intaglio method of printing in which the image is hand cut, machine cut, or chemically etched into the surface of a steel or copper plate or die. (A plate is made of thin copper or steel, and a die is made of thick steel. The choice of metal and/or thickness depends on printing pressure, length of press run, etc.) In the printing operation, which employs a die-stamping press, the plate is inked and wiped clean, leaving ink in the depressed areas. Dampened paper is then pressed against the plate to transfer the image. Depending on the amount of printing pressure and other production factors, the image may or may not emboss the paper. Embossed printing is usually used for letterheads, greeting cards, and invitations, while smooth printing is used for paper money, postage stamps, stock certificates, etc.

Engraved printing is very fine and sharp in detail, and very rich in tone. When further enhanced by embossing and high-quality paper, it connotes the ultimate in richness and refinement.

THERMOGRAPHY

Thermography is not a printing process; rather, it is an inexpensive method of achieving engraved-like embossing in letterpress and offset printing. In the printing operation, the image is printed with a special heat-drying ink, dusted with a special wax powder, and then heated. This fuses the ink and powder, thus producing a raised image. Printing can be done in matte and glossy colors, including copper, gold, and silver. It is frequently used for invitations, greeting cards, and business cards.

Printing Paper

Paper usually represents 25 to 50 percent of the total cost of reproduction. Also, the printing quality of the paper, as well as the functional and esthetic qualities of the paper itself, are frequently as important as the quality and content of the graphic imagery. For these reasons, the designer must be thoroughly familiar with paper characteristics, grades, and finishes.

While this section provides basic information on paper and papermaking, the designer should also have an up-to-date library of paper samples and specifications from the various manufacturers. Some sample books are so expensive that they are available only to regular customers, but most manufacturers also have inexpensive sample folders and books that are available to anyone for the asking. A few manufacturers, such as Champion and Strathmore, sell kits of their printing papers in sizes large enough to be used for comps and dummies.

Although the designer usually chooses the printing paper, he must discuss his choice with the printer and/or paper merchant to ascertain that it meets all technical requirements for the job.

PAPERMAKING

Pulping. Most papers are made from wood, but expensive papers may be made either partly or entirely from cotton and/or linen "rag." There are two methods of converting wood into pulp: mechanical and chemical. In mechanical pulping, the cleaned and de-barked logs are reduced to fiber by grinding. This is called groundwood pulp. In chemical pulping, wood chips are reduced to fiber by cooking them with chemicals in either a sulfite or sulfate solution.

Mechanical pulping produces the highest yield, but the pulp is short-fibered and contains many impurities, which weakens and discolors the paper. It is therefore used primarily for newsprint. Both of the chemical pulping processes produce high-quality paper, but sulfate (also called kraft) paper, which is made from a variety of both hard and soft woods, is stronger. There is also a semi-chemical process in which hardwood is first ground into pulp and then chemically cooked. This produces a high yield of high-quality pulp that is usually blended with chemical pulp.

Bleaching, Refining, and Additives. After the pulping process, the pulp is washed, screened, and bleached. It is then beaten or refined, which crushes and frays the fibers so they will bind together properly when formed into paper. The amount of beating depends on whether the paper will be soft, rough, and bulky, or hard, smooth, and thin. Finally, additives such as fillers, sizing, and dyes are mixed with the pulp. Fillers are used to increase opacity, improve printability, and make a smoother surface. Sizing helps to bind the fibers together and controls the penetration of water and ink. The completed mixture of pulp and additives is called stock, and is stored in a tank in front of the paper machine.

The Paper Machine. There are four sections to the paper machine: (1) the paper-forming section, known as the Fourdrinier or wet end; (2) the press section, which removes the water; (3) the drying section, which reduces the moisture content to atmospheric level; and (4) the calender section, which smooths and compacts the paper.

Forming. The stock is diluted with water and pumped into a distribution box at the head of the machine, from where it is discharged on to a moving wire screen belt. The excess water drains through the screen, and the screen passes beneath a cylinder covered with a fine wire mesh, called a dandy roll. The dandy roll compresses and distributes the fibers evenly, and imparts an almost imperceptible "wove" texture to the paper. The dandy roll can also be overlaid with a pattern of closely spaced wires in one direction and widely spaced wires in the other direction, and will impart a clearly visible "laid" texture to the paper. The laid texture simulates the texture of hand-made paper. The dandy roll may also contain raised letters or designs. The resulting impressions (thin areas) in the paper are called watermarks. (A laid texture is also a watermark.)

Pressing. The paper, which is still about 80 percent water, is carried through the press section on a felt belt, and is pressed between a series of rollers. This squeezes out a good amount of water, and further compacts and levels the paper.

Chips being conveyed into digester (Westvaco).

Digester converts wood chips into pulp with steam and chemicals (Warren).

Drying. The paper, which is now about 70 percent water, is carried through the drying section on an asbestos-felt belt. Both sides of the paper come in contact with a series of large, steam-heated drums, which reduces the moisture content of the paper to the relative humidity of the atmosphere.

Calendering. The calender section is comprised of a vertical stack of polished steel rolls, called calenders. The more calenders the paper is pressed between, the smoother and more compacted it becomes.

Slitting and Sheeting. After calendering, the paper is wound in a roll. It is later slit and re-wound in narrower rolls, which can be used directly on web-fed presses, or can be cut into sheets for use on sheet-fed presses.

While this section describes the basic papermaking process, every paper finish involves some variation in this basic process. Additionally, some finishes involve special, "off-machine" operations. These variations and special operations are described under Finish (page 28).

Fourdrinier or "wet end" of paper machine. Dandy roll is in foreground (Warren).

Control panel for paper machine (Westvaco).

Calender section of paper machine (Warren).

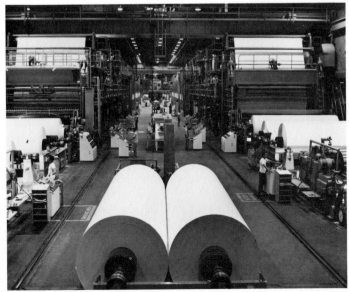

Dry end of paper machine (Westvaco).

Slitting and sheeting rolls of paper (Westvaco).

PAPER CHARACTERISTICS

Grain. During papermaking, the paper fibers tend to align themselves in one direction, thus creating a grain in the paper. Grain direction influences printing and folding, and must therefore be taken into account when planning press sheet layout. For example, paper is stiffer and folds more smoothly in the grain direction, which means that in pamphlets, books, etc., the binding should be parallel with the grain.

If the grain runs the long dimension of the sheet, the paper is called grain-long. If it runs the short dimension, the paper is called grain-short. Most printing papers can be purchased either grain-long or grain-short. A common method of determining grain direction is to tear or fold the paper: it will tear straighter and fold more smoothly with the grain than across it. Another method is to cut two 1″ x 6″ strips of paper, one grain-long and one grain-short. When held at one end, the grain-long strip will bend less than the grain-short strip. Also, when wetted on one side, the grain-long strip will curl in the short dimension, forming a trough-like shape, while the grain-short strip will curl in the long dimension.

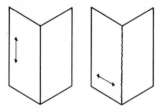

Paper folds more smoothly with the grain than across it.

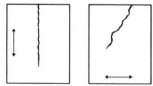

Paper tears straighter with the grain than across it.

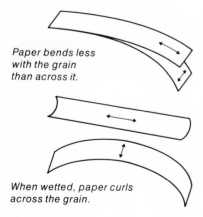

Paper bends less with the grain than across it.

When wetted, paper curls across the grain.

Basis Weight. Basis weight, also called substance, is the weight of 500 sheets (1 ream) of paper of a basic size. The basic size is different for each grade or type of paper. For example, book paper is 25″ x 38″, bond paper is 17″ x 22″, and cover paper is 20″ x 26″. Therefore, 80 lb. book paper, 31 lb. bond paper, and 44 lb. cover paper are all equal in weight per square inch. Each grade of paper is made in many weights, and in many standard sizes in addition to the basic size.

While basis weight refers to 500 sheets, paper is usually listed in size and price tables in 1,000 sheet lots (M is the abbreviation for 1,000). For example, 25 x 38 – 160M is the designation for 80 lb. book paper.

Paper may also be listed in metric weight or grammage. Grammage refers to grams per square meter (gsm).

EQUIVALENT WEIGHTS
In reams of 500 sheets.
Basis weights in bold type.

	BOOK 25 x 38	BOND 17 x 22	COVER 20 x 26	INDEX 25½ x 30½
BOOK	**30**	12	16	25
	40	16	22	33
	45	18	25	37
	50	20	27	41
	60	24	33	49
	70	28	38	57
	80	31	44	65
	90	35	49	74
	100	39	55	82
	120	47	66	98
BOND	33	**13**	18	27
	41	**16**	22	33
	51	**20**	28	42
	61	**24**	33	50
	71	**28**	39	58
	81	**32**	45	67
	91	**36**	50	75
	102	**40**	56	83
COVER	91	36	**50**	75
	110	43	**60**	90
	119	47	**65**	97
	146	58	**80**	120
	164	65	**90**	135
	183	72	**100**	150
INDEX	110	43	60	**90**
	135	53	74	**110**
	170	67	93	**140**
	208	82	114	**170**

Bulk. Bulk, or paper thickness, can be measured in two ways. One way is to measure the thickness of the sheet with a micrometer. This measurement is called the caliper, and is expressed in mils or thousandths of an inch (mils are called points in the paper industry). The other way is to convert the caliper measurement into the number of pages per inch (PPI). This is the more useful of the two measurements, especially for book printing.

Opacity. There are two kinds of opacity: printed and visual. Printed opacity relates to the "show-through" of the printed image from the reverse side of the sheet, and visual opacity relates to the "show-through" of the printed image from the succeeding sheet. Opacity is affected by the weight and bulk of the paper, as well as by fillers, dyes, and coatings. Printed opacity is also affected by the absorbency of the paper. The less absorbent the paper, the better the ink "holdout," and therefore the greater the printed opacity.

Color. In addition to being available in a wide variety of colors, printing papers are also available in various degrees of whiteness, ranging from warm to neutral to cool. Warm (creamy) white is commonly used for lengthy text matter because it is easy on the eyes; neutral white is commonly used for process color reproduction because it doesn't alter colors; and cool (bluish) white is commonly used to achieve brilliant contrast or sparkle in black and white and flat color reproduction.

Finish. Paper finishes can be divided into two basic categories: uncoated and coated. Within each category, there are various kinds of finishes and/or various degrees of smoothness.

Uncoated. Smoothness and bulk is determined by the number and type of rollers that the paper passes between. Paper that comes directly from the drying section of the papermaking machine has the roughest surface and highest bulk and is called uncalendered paper. Uncalendered paper can be either wove or laid (see Forming, page 26). Also, each side of the paper usually has a slightly different texture. The side that was in contact with the wire screen is called the wire side, and the other side is called the top or felt side. The felt side usually has a slightly smoother finish.

A smoother surface and less bulk can be obtained by subsequently pressing the paper between a stack of polished steel rolls called calenders. The more calenders employed, the smoother and less bulky the paper. Because calenders are a part of the papermaking machine, calendered paper is called machine-calendered or machine-finished.

An even smoother surface can be obtained by super-calendering, which is a separate, or off-machine, process that employs alternate steel and fiber calender rolls. Paper that is finished by this process is usually called super or SC.

Paper can be embossed with various textures and patterns, such as linen, tweed, and pebble. This is an off-machine process that involves the use of a rotary embosser.

Coated. Coated papers are available in many weights, and range from dull to very glossy in finish. They may be coated on one side (C1S) or on both sides (C2S). Because of their smoothness, high opacity, and high ink holdout, coated papers are excellent for both black-and-white and full-color halftone reproduction. High-gloss papers are not generally suitable for lengthy text applications, however, because their reflectivity makes reading difficult.

The clay or pigment coating may be applied on the papermaking machine (machine-coated), in a later process (off-machine-coated), or partly on and partly off the machine (conversion-coated). The paper may be finished by calendering, super-calendering, and/or embossing. Conversion-coated and off-machine-coated papers are usually more expensive and higher in quality than machine-coated papers. The most expensive papers are cast-coated, which is a special, off-machine process that produces a coating with very high gloss and unusually good ink receptivity.

Runnability and Printability. There are a number of paper characteristics that affect its runnability and printability. The importance of many of these characteristics depends upon the printing process employed.

Moisture Content. The relative humidity (RH) of the paper must be in balance with the pressroom RH. Higher pressroom RH will cause wavy edges, and lower pressroom RH will cause tight, or curled edges, thus resulting in wrinkles and/or misregister during printing.

Wavy edges   *Tight edges*

Pick Resistance. The surface of the paper must be strong enough to resist the pulling force of tacky ink. Since ink tackiness varies with printing processes, the degree of pick resistance depends upon the printing process employed. Offset paper, for example, must be very pick resistant.

Water Resistance. Because offset lithography uses water in the printing process, the pigments and coatings used in offset paper must be water resistant. Otherwise, they tend to pile on the offset blanket, thus necessitating frequent washups.

Paper/Ink Compatibility. In addition to the various consistencies of ink, there are also various ways in which they dry, such as by absorption, evaporation, or oxidation. If both of these ink characteristics are not compatible with the paper characteristics, serious printing problems can result, such as improper drying, chalking, or excessive ink holdout.

Paper/Printing Plate Compatibility. Letterpress and gravure require fairly smooth paper, while offset permits the use of both rough and smooth paper. In all three processes, halftones print best on smooth, coated paper.

Rotary embosser (Warren).   *Supercalender (Warren).*

Off-machine coater (Warren).

PAPER GRADES

Paper grade refers to the category or type of paper. In some categories, the quality of paper may also be indicated by an additional name or number. This section describes the most commonly used grades of printing papers. There are many other grades, however, such as kraft paper, blotting paper, duplicator paper, drawing paper, and boxboard. The basic size for each grade is shown in parentheses.

Bond (17″ x 22″). Many bond papers are further categorized as writing papers because they are specially formulated for writing, typewriting, and erasing, in addition to printing. Bond papers are commonly used for stationery and business forms, and are available in numerous weights, colors, and qualities. The better-quality papers have a rag content ranging from 25 to 100 percent. Ledger papers are similar to bond papers in all respects except that they are heavier, stiffer, and more durable.

Book (25″ x 38″). Book papers comprise the largest group of printing papers. In addition to being used for books, they are used for pamphlets, magazines, folders, book jackets, and posters. The various grades of book papers are described below.

Uncoated. Uncoated book papers range from rought to smooth in the following grades: antique, eggshell, machine finish (MF), English finish (EF), and super (SC). The antique and eggshell finishes are primarily intended for type and line illustration applications, while the smoother finishes are also suitable for medium-quality halftones, such as are used in magazines. Antique papers are available in two textures: wove and laid.

Coated. Coated finishes are exceptionally smooth, and range from dull to very glossy. Halftone printing quality depends on the coating method employed, and ranges from good to excellent (see Finish, page 28).

Text. Antique or eggshell finish papers are available in a wide variety of textures and colors, frequently with deckled edges. They are primarily intended for high-quality decorative applications in pamphlets, folders, brochures, announcements, and the like.

Offset. Offset papers are basically the same as conventional uncoated and coated book papers, but are treated so they are water-resistant and pick-resistant (see Runnability and Printability, page 29).

Cover (20″ x 26″). As the name suggests, cover papers are of cover weight, and are available in a wide variety of textures and colors, both coated and uncoated. Many cover papers match the textures and colors of text and coated book papers.

Bristol (Index: 25½″ x 30½″ — Mill or Printing: 22½″ x 35″). A heavy, stiff paper or board in antique, plate, and coated finishes and a variety of weights and colors. Applications include index cards, records, greeting cards, programs, menus, and tickets. Mill bristol is stiffer than index bristol.

Newsprint (24″ x 36″). Newsprint is the least expensive of all the printing papers. It lacks strength, has limited printing capabilities, and discolors and becomes brittle with age. For these reasons, its use is limited to newspapers, comic books, inexpensive paperbacks, and other low-quality applications.

Tag (24″ x 36″). A stiff, durable board in many weights and colors, including white and manila. It folds well, and can be stamped, printed, or written on. In addition to its use for tags and tickets, it is commonly used for menus, catalog inserts, folders, dividers, and so on.

ENVELOPES

Envelopes are stocked by paper merchants in many standard sizes, styles, and papers. In addition to the standard envelope papers — white wove, brown and gray kraft, and manila — there are many "millbrand" papers. These are printing papers from the various paper mills that have been converted to envelopes. If the paper merchant doesn't stock the envelope size, style, and/or millbrand desired, he can order it from an envelope company, or converter, who either has it in inventory or can quickly manufacture it.

Envelopes can be printed either before or after they are manufactured. Printing before manufacture is slightly more expensive, but for long runs and high-quality work is usually preferable because of better printing quality. For envelopes that are to be printed in flat sheets before cutting and folding, the converter will provide a layout and instructions for preparing the mechanical. Printing is sometimes more economical when done after die-cutting but before folding.

Standard sizes and styles of envelopes are cut with a high die, which is a solid, formed-steel die, shaped to cut one size and style. Special-size envelopes are cut with an adjustable die, which provides an almost limitless variety of sizes and styles. Special sizes are more expensive and take longer to make.

Inserting can be done by hand or by machine. For smooth hand inserting, the envelope should be approximately ¼″ larger, in both dimensions, than the enclosure. Extra clearance is required for thick enclosures. For machine inserting, it is necessary to follow the specifications for the particular equipment to be used. In both cases, a complete dummy of the mailing piece — the envelope plus all enclosures — must be made. This is not only necessary for practical purposes, such as inserting, postage costs, and postal requirements, but it enables the designer and client to assay its looks and feel. There are also many postal requirements that must be met. These involve the size and shape of the envelope, the size and location of the graphics, forwarding and return information, and the method of sealing. Information regarding these requirements can be obtained at a post office.

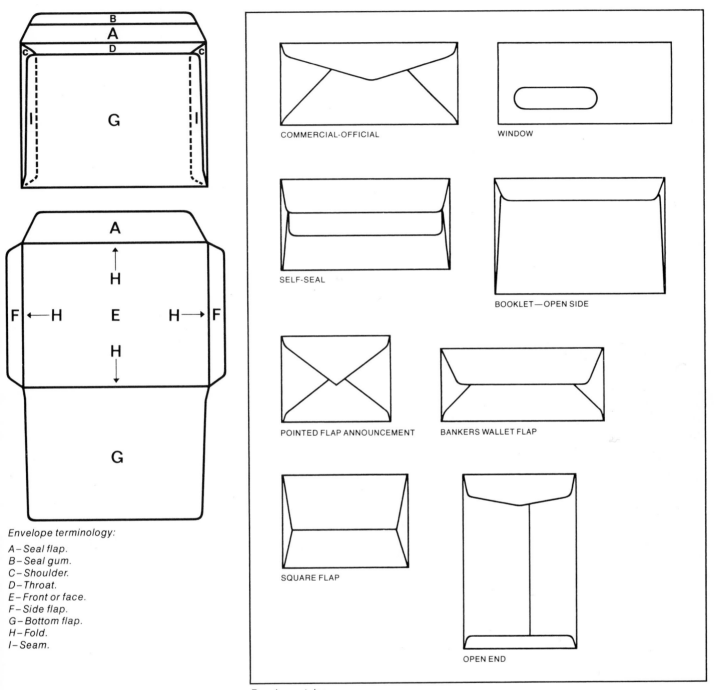

Envelope terminology:

A – Seal flap.
B – Seal gum.
C – Shoulder.
D – Throat.
E – Front or face.
F – Side flap.
G – Bottom flap.
H – Fold.
I – Seam.

COMMERCIAL-OFFICIAL

WINDOW

SELF-SEAL

BOOKLET—OPEN SIDE

POINTED FLAP ANNOUNCEMENT

BANKERS WALLET FLAP

SQUARE FLAP

OPEN END

Envelope styles.

Color Printing

FLAT COLOR PRINTING

In flat color printing, the printing plate for each color is made from black and white copy that has been separated according to the printing color designated on the mechanical. The printing colors are determined by the designer, and are specified on the mechanical either with color swatches or with standard printing ink formulas. The printer mixes the printing inks to match the specified colors.

The flat color printing plate can consist of line copy, halftones, and screen tints. The line copy will print in solid color, and the screened copy will print in tints of the same color. This provides an unlimited range of tones of that color. Since printing inks are quite transparent, both line and screened copy can be overprinted with other colors to achieve various color mixtures. For example, red overprinted with blue produces violet, yellow overprinted with red produces orange, etc. In a two-color job, therefore, a third color can be achieved by overprinting. At least 100 variations of the third color can be achieved by overprinting screen tints of various percentages.

Every printed color (not colors achieved by overprinting) requires a separate printing plate. Multicolor printing can be done with multiple passes through a one-color press, or with one pass through a multicolor press. Multicolor presses are usually either 2- or 4-color. No matter what kind of press is used, each additional color adds proportionately to the overall cost of the job. Any number of colors may be used in flat color printing, but for more than four colors it is usually preferable to use process color printing, which provides unlimited colors and tones with four basic colors (see Process Color Printing, page 40). It is important to understand that in printing terminology, black is counted as a color. A one-color job, therefore, means one printing plate and one run on the press, no matter what the color. It does not mean one color in addition to black.

Surprint	Dropout		Surprint	Dropout
10%			**60%**	
Surprint	Dropout		Surprint	Dropout
20%			**70%**	
Surprint	Dropout		Surprint	Dropout
30%			**80%**	
Surprint	Dropout		Surprint	Dropout
40%			**90%**	
Surprint	Dropout		Reverse	
50%			**100% (SOLID)**	

Screen tints from 10% to 100% (133-line screen). The legibility of surprint, dropout, and reverse type is influenced by the size and fineness of the type, the value contrast of the type with the screened background, the fineness of the screen, and the color of the ink (a 10% orange, for example, is lighter than a 10% black).

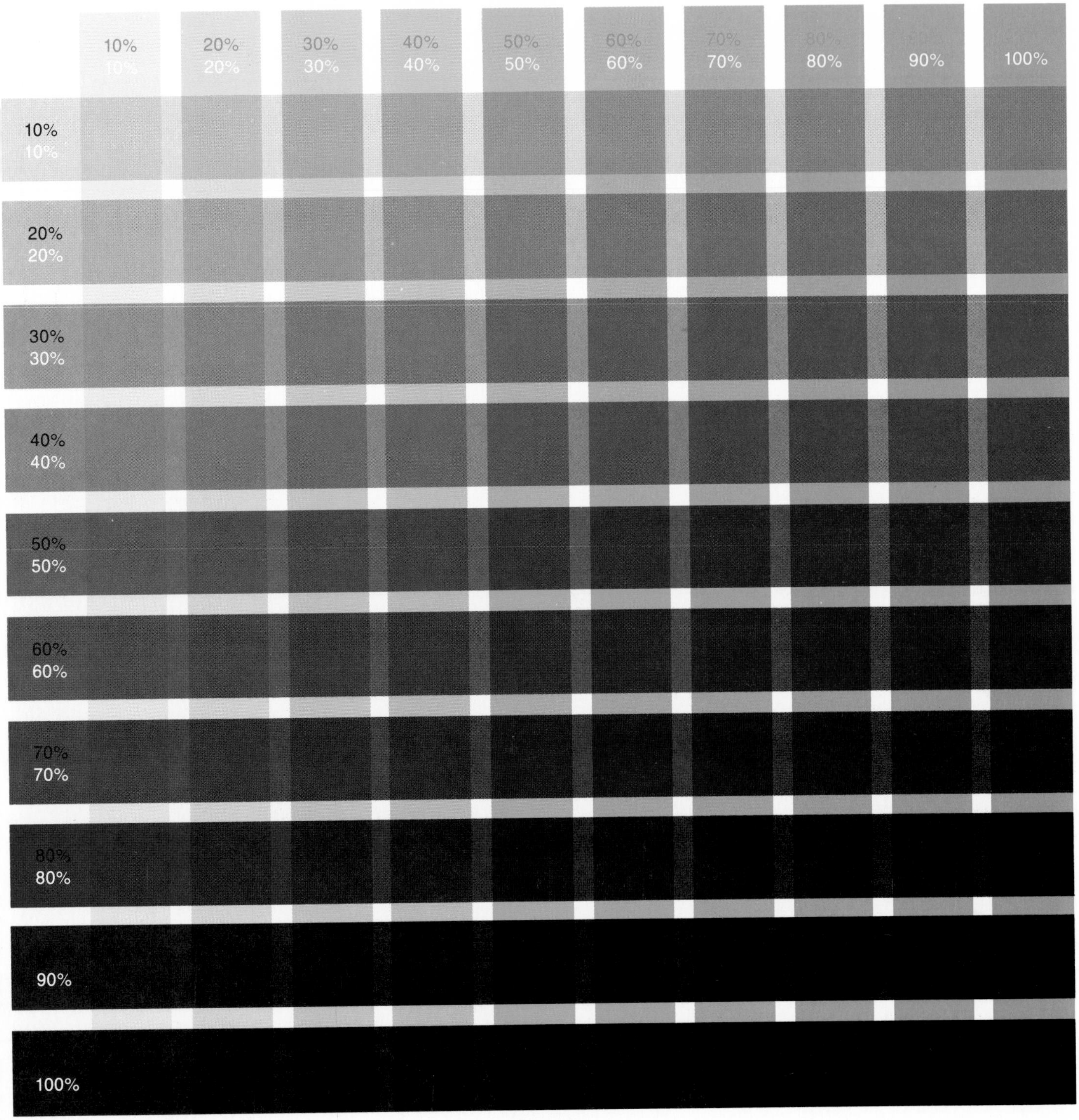

	10% 10%	20% 20%	30% 30%	40% 40%	50% 50%	60% 60%	70% 70%	80% 80%	90%	100%
10% 10%										
20% 20%										
30% 30%										
40% 40%										
50% 50%										
60% 60%										
70% 70%										
80% 80%										
90%										
100%										

This chart shows the effect of overprinting orange and black tints and solids.
Screens are also available in 5%, 15%, 25%, etc.

Duotones. A duotone is a halftone that has been printed in two colors, the purpose being to extend the range of tones of the conventional one-color halftone. To make a duotone, the printer shoots two halftone negatives from the original black and white continuous-tone copy, each at a different exposure and screen angle. One halftone accentuates the detail in the dark areas of the copy, and the other accentuates the details in the light areas. The dark-range halftone is printed in the darkest ink being used (usually black), and the light-range halftone is printed in a lighter ink, such as blue, green, or red. The light-range halftone can also be printed in gray or black ink rather than a color. If both plates are printed in black, it is called a double-black duotone. Double-black printing does not produce such subtle variations in light tones as gray/black printing, but it produces very rich dark tones.

A duotone requires two printing plates and two runs on the press, and is therefore two-color printing (even though both plate colors may be black). There is a method of combining both halftone negatives on one printing plate, thus eliminating a second press run. This is called a double-dot halftone. While it extends the range of tones, it is not as rich as two-impression printing.

The 2-color effect of a duotone can be achieved by printing a conventional black or dark colored halftone over a solid or screen tint background of another color. However, not only is the tonal range of the halftone not extended, but the colored background reduces contrast in the lighter areas. This method is less expensive than a duotone, and can be effective where color mood is more important than tonal contrast. It is called a fake duotone or flat-tint halftone.

Black halftone for duotone use.

100% orange halftone for duotone use.

Black and 30% orange duotone.

Black and 70% orange duotone.

Black and 100% orange duotone.

Flat-tint halftone (fake duotone).
Black halftone over 20% flat orange tint.

Specifying Flat Color. The simplest method of specifying a color is to attach a swatch of the desired color to the mechanical and let the printer match it by mixing basic ink colors. This is not a very accurate method, however, since it relies on the printer's color sense and color mixing ability, and it doesn't take the printing stock into account (a color printed on coated stock is brighter and richer than when printed on uncoated stock). Additionally, it is very difficult for the designer to accurately specify screen tint percentages from a swatch of solid color, since a dark color of a given percentage will have a darker tonal value than a light color of the same percentage.

For these reasons, almost all designers use a color matching system for specifying colors and screen tint percentages. The most popular is the Pantone Matching System, which is a standardized color system available to licensed manufacturers of ink and other color products. This system comprises 500 ink colors that can be matched from 10 basic inks. The designer selects the color from a book which contains 6 number-coded swatches of each of the 500 colors, printed on both coated and uncoated stock. The designer can specify the color by number, or he can tear out the swatch, which is perforated, and attach it to the mechanical. The printer matches the color by referring to a printer's edition of the book, which contains the ink mixing formula for every color.

Various other Pantone books and guides show screen tints and overprinting effects of both solid and screened colors. The Pantone Color/Tint Overlay Selector contains over 200 solid colors, 58 of which are also screened in various percentages. Each color is printed on a separate sheet of acetate, which makes it possible to judge the overprinting effect of different combinations of solid colors and/or color tints. Pantone colors are also available in various art materials, such as color-printed paper, solid and screen tint color film, and color markers. By using these materials for the layout or comp, and by specifying the same colors for printing, the designer is assured of accurate color reproduction.

Many paper manufacturers have color guides showing the effect of ink colors on their various printing papers. The colors are printed solid and in 10 percent screen tint gradations, and are overprinted with other colors to show all possible combinations of colors and screen tints. Some color guides are printed in flat color inks, and others are printed in process color inks. (Process color inks are described in the following section).

Proofs for flat color printing are made in the same way as proofs for process color printing (see page 38). Pre-press proofs of the Color-Key type are usually adequate for flat color printing.

Pantone Color/Tint Overlay Selector.

Pantone Color Specifier. Printer's Edition in front; Designer's Edition in rear.

PROCESS COLOR PRINTING

Process color printing, also known as four-color process printing, is used for reproducing full-color, continuous-tone copy such as color photographs, paintings, and full-color illustrations. It requires four printing plates: yellow, red, blue, and black. When overprinted in various tonal gradations, these three primary colors plus black accurately duplicate all colors in the original copy.

To reproduce all of the colors accurately, the ink pigments must be exceptionally pure, and the primary colors must be exactly equidistant in the color spectrum. These "balanced" primary colors are called process yellow, process magenta (or process red), and process cyan (or process blue). In theory, an equal mixture of these three primary colors will produce black. In application, however, because pigment colors are never entirely free of impurities, the black has a brownish tone. A separate black plate is therefore necessary to accurately reproduce neutral grays and blacks. (Full-color printing is sometimes done without a black plate, and the results can be quite good, especially in gravure printing. However, since a black plate is usually necessary for accompanying type, three-color process printing is not commonly employed.)

The full-color effect in process color printing is achieved by the optical mixture of the primary colors plus black. Each printing plate contains a halftone pattern of various-sized dots for one color. These dots are so small that when the four color plates are overprinted, the eyes optically mix the different colors of juxtaposed dots, thus producing a composite color sensation. (Some dots overprint other dots to create overprint mixtures, but the majority lie next to each other in a circular or rosette pattern. This pattern is achieved by using a different screen angle for each plate). The principle of optical color mixing, incidentally, was the basis of pointillist painting, as typified by the works of Georges Seurat.

The original copy for color process can be opaque, such as photographic color prints, paintings, and illustrations, or it can be transparent, such as color transparencies and color negatives. Transparent copy is usually preferable. Opaque copy is viewed by reflected light and is therefore called reflection copy, and transparent copy is viewed by transmitted light and is therefore called transmission copy. When rendering illustrations for

color process, colors should be darkened by using complementary colors rather than black. Black not only reduces color clarity, but creates difficulties in color separation and correction. Color transparencies as small as 35mm can be used for color process, but the larger formats produce better results. If a color transparency requires retouching, it may need to be converted into an opaque color print for this operation.

Electronic color scanner (Rutho-Graphic Magnascan 460).

Four-color process halftone (photo courtesy Four By Five, Inc.).

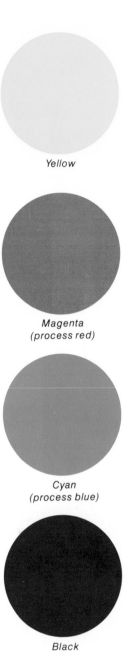

Yellow

Magenta
(process red)

Cyan
(process blue)

Black

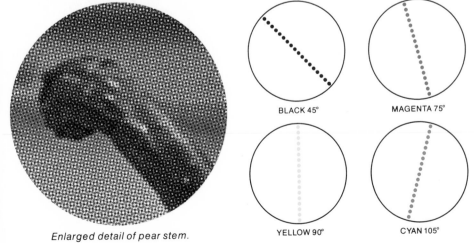

Enlarged detail of pear stem.

BLACK 45°

MAGENTA 75°

YELLOW 90°

CYAN 105°

Screen angles used to minimize moiré pattern.

Color Separation. To make process color printing plates, the original copy must be separated into the four process colors. This can be done either photographically or by electronic scanning, and involves the use of color filters which result in a black and white negative recording of each of the four colors. That is, the lighter or more transparent the film the stronger the color; the darker or more opaque the film, the weaker the color. When the negatives are converted to film positives or printing plates, the tones will be reversed so that they are right reading.

The yellow printer is made with a blue filter, the magenta printer is made with a green filter, and the cyan printer is made with a red filter. It is very difficult to separate the black from the other colors. Sometimes a yellow filter is used, and sometimes a split-filter method is used. In this method, the black printer negative is successively exposed through the red, green, and blue filters.

The negatives may be screened during the color separation operation (direct screening), or they may be photographed in continuous-tone, converted to continuous-tone film positives, and then screened (indirect screening). Direct screening is the simplest method, but indirect screening provides the opportunity to make color corrections on the continuous-tone negatives and/or positives before screening, and also permits re-sizing. (Re-sizing a screened image results in abnormal dot sizes.)

Color Correction. Because of color imbalances in the original copy, the inability of color filters to completely block unwanted colors, and the inability of black and white film to accurately record the exact ratios between color densities, color correction is an important aspect of process color separation. Color correcting can be done either photographically or electronically during the color separation operation, and further correcting can be done by masking or retouching the continuous-tone film negatives and/or positives. Screened positives may be color corrected to a certain extent by chemically reducing the size of the dots (dot etching).

Color Proofs. Proofs are used to check color accuracy before final reproduction. There are two types of proofs: pre-press and press. Pre-press proofs are made from the screened separations prior to platemaking. In one system (such as Color-Key), each separation is imaged, in its process color, on a sheet of acetate, and the four sheets are overlayed for viewing. In another system, all four separations are imaged on a single photopolymer sheet. Single-sheet proofs have greater color accuracy than four-sheet proofs.

BLUE FILTER

GREEN FILTER

YELLOW PROOF

MAGENTA PROOF

Color separations showing filters used.

YELLOW

YELLOW AND MAGENTA

Progressive proofs.

RED FILTER

MODIFIED FILTER

CYAN PROOF

BLACK PROOF

YELLOW, MAGENTA, AND CYAN

YELLOW, MAGENTA, CYAN, AND BLACK

Press proofs are made from the printing plates, usually on a four-color proofing press. The plates are printed individually, and then progressively overprinted with the other plates until all four have been combined. These are called progressive proofs, or progs, and are used by the printer as a color control guide.

Pre-press proofs are faster and less expensive to make than press proofs. Also, since they are made prior to the printing plates, further color correction of the film separations is easily accomplished. Even where press proofs are specified, pre-press proofs may also be made as a preliminary check on color accuracy.

When the client (designer, art director, etc.) checks proofs for size, imperfections, and color accuracy, it is important to view the proof under the same lighting conditions as used by the printer.

Pre-separated or Fake Color Process.
Full-color, continuous-tone illustrations can be economically reproduced by hand-separating the four process colors on acetate overlays, thus eliminating the need for photomechanical color separation and color correction. This can be done by the illustrator or by a printing industry specialist. The overlays are rendered in continuous tones of black and white, using a color guide that shows all possible overprinting combinations of process colors and tints. To make the printing plates, the printer merely photographs the overlays in halftone. Overlay separation is a very difficult technique, since the color percentages shown in the color guide must be converted to comparable gray values on the overlays. A gray scale with 10 percent gradations is necessary for this conversion.

Another illustrator's method of achieving full color by overlay separation is by using Bourges color film (see page 80). Since the overlays are rendered in color, overprinting combinations can be visually determined. The limitation to this technique is that the overlays must be rendered in flat colors and tints, not continuous tones. It is possible, however, to render the key (or illustration board) drawing in continuous tones of black and white.

USING PROCESS COLOR FOR FLAT COLOR PRINTING

Process color may also be used to reproduce black and white line copy in a full range of colors. This technique is commonly used in flat color printing when more than four colors are needed. Rather than using more than four mixed colors, which would require more printing plates and press runs, the four process colors are overprinted in various combinations and tints, thus making an unlimited range of colors possible. This same technique is also used for the line copy elements that accompany full-color, continuous-tone copy. For example, if the headline in a full-color ad is to be green, the green must be achieved by overprinting process yellow and process cyan. The methods of separating and specifying process colors and mixtures are described in the section on Multicolor Mechanicals (page 168).

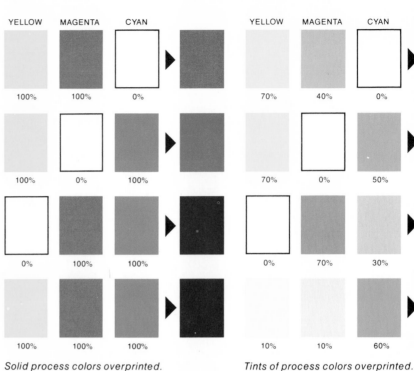

Solid process colors overprinted.   Tints of process colors overprinted.

Process color tints.

Process color used as flat color.
(Courtesy Hammermill Paper Company).

Tints used for illustration:

1. 100% C, 50% M.
2. 100% Y, 100% M.
3. 100% K (code for black).
4. 100% Y, 60% C.
5. 100% Y.
6. 100% Y, 50% M, 20% C.
7. 100% Y, 70% M.

Platemaking

This section describes photomechanical platemaking, which is the method used in most printing processes. It covers the various operations that are necessary to convert the designer's copy into a printing plate, including graphic arts photography, stripping, imposition, and platemaking. it does not cover the special techniques or operations that are necessary for multicolor printing. These are described in the section on Color Printing on page 32.

COPY

In the printing industry, copy refers to anything that is to be reproduced, which includes type, photographs, illustrations, etc. It can be divided into two categories: line and continuous-tone. Line copy is any image composed of solid black and white lines or shapes with no tonal gradations, such as type, and pen and ink drawings. Continuous-tone copy is any image composed of gradated tones of black and white or color, such as photographs, wash drawings, and paintings. The preparation of copy for reproduction is described in other sections of this book.

GRAPHIC ARTS PHOTOGRAPHY

The graphic arts camera, also called a process or copy camera, consists of an illuminated copyboard, lens, bellows, vacuum back, and bed. Usually, the vacuum back and control panel are built into the darkroom wall, which simplifies film loading and unloading. On many cameras, the copyboard can accommodate both reflection (opaque) and transmission (transparent) copy.

Graphic arts camera (Consolidated).

Line copy is photographed with high-contrast film, resulting in a negative in which the image is transparent and the non-image area is opaque. If a film positive is needed, it is made by placing the negative over a sheet of unexposed film in a printing frame and exposing it to light.

There are two methods of photographing continuous-tone copy. In one method, continuous-tone film is used, and the resulting negative is simply a tone reversal of the original copy. Continuous-tone negatives (and positives) are used for making gravure and collotype printing plates, and for color correction in four-color process work.

In the other method, the continuous-tone copy is photographed through a screen with high-contrast film. This screen, called a halftone screen, converts the tones into a pattern of various-sized black and white dots. When printed, these dots optically mix to simulate the effect of tonal gradations. The reason that continuous tones must be converted to dot patterns (or line copy) is that in every printing process except gravure and collotype, it is not possible to vary ink coverage. That is, all printing portions of the plate receive — and transfer to paper — the same amount of ink. Therefore, halftones are necessary to simulate continuous-tone gradations, and screen tints (page 32) are necessary to simulate flat tones.

 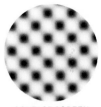

GLASS SCREEN   CONTACT SCREEN

Two types of screens used for making halftones. (Greatly enlarged).

Screens are available in 55, 65, 85, 100, 120, 133, and 150 lines per inch. The finer the screen, the more accurately it will simulate the original continuous-tone copy. The fineness of the screen is determined by the printing process and the quality of paper. For example, letterpress newspapers use 65- to 85-line screens, offset newspapers use 100- to 133-line screens, and magazines and commercial printers use 120- to 150-line screens. 150- to 300-line screens are also sometimes used in offset lithography and gravure.

65-line screen.

85-line screen.

100-line screen.

120-line screen.

133-line screen.

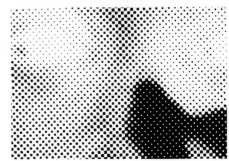
Detail of 85-line halftone.

Sometimes it is necessary to reproduce continuous-tone copy that has already been screened and printed. If the dots in the halftone reproduction are sharp, and if the reduction or enlargement is not excessive, the halftone may be shot as line copy. Otherwise, the halftone must be re-screened, using a special screen angle to avoid a moiré pattern. A moiré (pronounced mwah-ray') is a third pattern that occurs when two repetitive patterns are superposed. This can easily be demonstrated by superposing two pieces of shading film and moving them about.

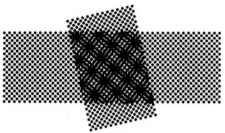

Moiré pattern.

TYPES OF HALFTONES
For the sake of brevity, the following descriptions refer specifically to photography. However, they apply to other forms of continuous-tone copy as well, such as illustrations and paintings. It is important to understand that there are no pure whites or blacks in halftones; white areas contain minute black dots, and black areas contain minute white dots. In a silhouette halftone, for example, even though the designer silhouettes a shape with white paint, the halftone negative will contain minute black dots in the silhouetted area. These must be removed by the printer, either by retouching or masking.

Square or Square-finish: a halftone that has "squared up" outer contours, just as in a normal photographic print. It can be either square or rectangular in shape. There are also round and oval halftones.

Silhouette or Outline: a halftone in which the background has been removed by retouching the original copy, and/or by retouching or masking the halftone negative. If part of the halftone is square and part is silhouetted, it is called a modified silhouette halftone.

Vignette: a halftone in which the image fades away to pure white. This is done by airbrushing the original copy, with further retouching or masking of the halftone negative.

Square halftone.

Silhouette or outline halftone.

Vignette halftone.

Dropout or highlight halftone. (Photo courtesy Dale Clark.) Also see page 146 for a dropout halftone of a pencil drawing.

Dropout or Highlight: a halftone in which the minute black dots in highlight areas have been eliminated, either by retouching the halftone negative or by a special exposure technique on the process camera.

For other methods of reproducing continuous-tone copy, see Duotones (page 34) and Veloxes and Line Conversions (page 144).

STRIPPING
Stripping is the process of assembling the various line, halftone, and screen tint negatives in position for platemaking. This is done on a light table, and requires a high degree of precision. The negatives are taped on to a sheet of yellow-orange masking paper called goldenrod, and windows are cut in the paper to permit the passage of light through the image areas of the negatives. The completed assemblage of negatives on the sheet of goldenrod is called the flat.

PLATEMAKING
Platemaking differs for each printing process, and the specific differences are described in the section on Printing Processes (page 18). In general, the stripped-up negatives (or positives) are placed over a printing plate that has a light-sensitive coating, and exposed to light in a vacuum frame. This hardens the coating in the exposed areas, making it insoluble in water or other solutions. The coating in the unexposed areas is dissolved, and the plate is then etched or otherwise processed according to the requirements of the printing process being used.

Vacuum frame (Nu-Arc Flip Top Platemaker).

IMPOSITION

Imposition, also called press layout, is the arranging of pages or printing units to fit the sheet of printing paper. In offset and gravure, this is done with film negatives and is part of the stripping operation, while in letterpress it is done by locking up the metal type and photoengravings in a chase.

There are two types of imposition: ganging-up and signature layout. In ganging-up, either a number of different jobs are printed on one sheet (such as a letterhead, memo, and invoice), or one job is printed in multiples. When printing multiples, multiple duplicate negatives can be assembled on a flat for exposure to the printing plate (gang negative), or one master negative can be exposed to the printing plate in a step and repeat, or photocomposing, machine.

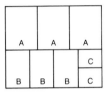 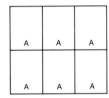

Left. Three jobs ganged up on one sheet.
Right. One job ganged 6-up.

In signature imposition, the pages must be arranged in such a way that when the sheet is folded and trimmed, the pages will be in correct sequence. To determine the correct press layout, a sheet of paper is folded into a signature of the desired number of pages, the pages are numbered, and the sheet is unfolded for use as a layout guide. The folding of signatures is described in Folding (page 44).

If two or more signatures will fit on one sheet, usually both the front and back of a signature are printed on the same side of the sheet. Thus, the sheet can be turned over and printed on the other side (backed up) with the same printing plate. If the layout is such that the sheet is turned over from left to right, using the same gripper edge, it is termed work and turn imposition. If the sheet is turned over from front to back, using the opposite gripper edge, it is termed work and tumble imposition. When a different plate is used for each side of the sheet, using the same gripper edge, it is termed sheetwise imposition.

Imposition is determined by the printer and binder, not the designer. Usually, the designer prepares his mechanical as a normal double-page spread, just as it will appear when printed and bound, and imposition is done during the stripping and/or platemaking operation.

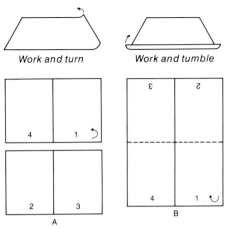

Work and turn   *Work and tumble*

A. Four page signature (folder).
One signature per sheet.
Sheetwise imposition.
B. Four page signature (folder).
Two signatures per sheet.
Work and tumble imposition.
Cut on dash line before folding.

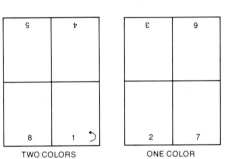

TWO COLORS   ONE COLOR

Eight page signature.
One signature per sheet.
One side printed two colors.
Sheetwise imposition.

Step-and-repeat machine (Ruth-O-Matic).

Sixteen page signature.
Two signatures per sheet.
Work and tumble imposition.
Cut on dash line before folding and trimming.

Bindery Operations

After paper is printed, one or more bindery operations usually follows. Bindery operations include trimming, folding, binding, and finishing. Finishing is a catch-all category for any additional operation, such as die-cutting, embossing, scoring, mounting, die-stamping, punching, etc. Some of the simpler bindery operations may be performed at the printing plant (such as trimming, folding, and pamphlet binding), but the more specialized operations are usually performed by a separate binding and/or finishing company. In certain types of high-speed, long-run work, the bindery operations may be "in-line" with the printing operation. For example, mass-circulation magazines are printed, folded, bound, and trimmed in one continuous, in-line operation.

The number and sequence of the bindery operations varies according to the job. With simple, single-sheet jobs, such as letterheads, posters, broadsides, and folders, the first—and in some cases the only — operation is trimming. If folding is necessary, it is done after trimming. With multi-paged jobs, such as pamphlets, magazines, and books, the printed sheet is folded into a signature, bound, and then trimmed. If other finishing operations are involved, they may fall between any one of the above operations. For example, die-cutting and embossing are usually done directly after printing.

TRIMMING

Trimming can be done on some folding and stitching machines, or it can be done on a guillotine-style paper cutter, which is capable of cutting hundreds of sheets at one time. Some paper cutters can be programmed to automatically shift to the correct spacing for each consecutive cut. This not only provides utmost accuracy, it greatly speeds up production.

FOLDING

Folding is usually done on an automatic folding machine that is capable of making multiple folds, both parallel and right-angle. Parallel folds are those that are parallel with each other, as in business letter folds. If the parallel folds are alternately reversed, an accordion fold results. Right-angle folds are those that are at right angles to a previous fold.

Some folding machines are equipped with attachments for scoring, slitting, trimming, perforating, and pasting. These operations can also be performed on other equipment, but are usually less expensive on the folding machine.

TYPES OF FOLDERS

There are two basic uses for folders. One is for single-sheet applications, such as circulars, flyers, broadsides, and posters. In this use, the fold or folds may be an inherent part of the design, or they may be simply a means of making a large, flat design compact enough for mailing. If the fold or folds are part of the design, the piece is called a direct mail folder. If they are not part of the design (as with broadsides and posters), the piece is simply described as folded for mailing. In both cases, trimming precedes folding.

The other use for folders is for making pamphlets, magazines, and books. In this use, each sheet is printed and folded in such a way that when it is later trimmed at the top, bottom, and right, one or more four-page folders, all in correct page sequence, results. The total number of pages that can be achieved from one printed sheet ranges from 4 to 64 in multiples of four, and is called a signature. The arrangement of pages on the sheet is called imposition, and is described on page 43. The methods of binding signatures are described in Binding Methods (page 46). Following is a description of the more common types of folders.

Automatic spacer cutter (Polar-Mohr Electromat 72).

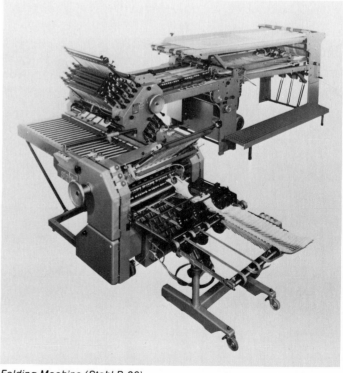

Folding Machine (Stahl B-20).

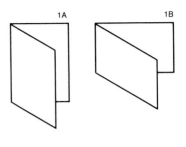

1. Four-page. One fold, in either the (A) long or (B) short dimension of the sheet. Used for greeting cards, direct mail pieces, etc.

2. Six-page. Two parallel folds, either (A) regular or (B) accordion. Used for business letters, direct mail pieces, self-mailers, etc.

3. Eight-page. Either (A) one parallel and one right-angle fold, (B) two parallel folds, or (C) three parallel accordion folds. (A) is called a French fold when the sheet is printed on one side and used as a four-page folder. Both (A) and (B) can be used as 8-page signatures.

4. Twelve-page. One parallel fold and two right-angle folds, either (A) regular or (B) accordion. (A) is used for 4-page letters (the two right-angle folds serve to reduce the letter to envelope size), and both (A) and (B) are used for folded broadsides and posters.

5. Sixteen-page. Either (A) one parallel and two right-angle folds, or (B) three parallel folds. (A) is used for folded broadsides and posters. (B) is used for schedules, and both (A) and (B) can be used for 16-page signatures.

The number of folds refers to the number of folding actions of the machine, not the number of folds in the folder. In (3B) for example, the machine makes two folds, resulting in three folds in the folder.

When planning folders, the designer, printer, and/or binder must take a number of factors into account, such as the number of pages that can be obtained from a standard-size sheet with minimum waste, the maximum sheet size of the press, and the capabilities of the folding machine. Other factors are the grain and weight of the paper. The grain of the paper must usually be parallel to the major folds (see page 28), and, if the weight of the paper is too heavy, it must be scored before folding (see page 48).

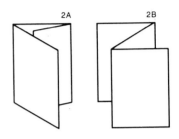

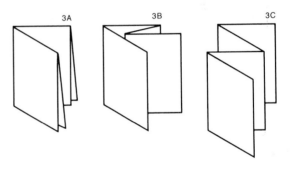

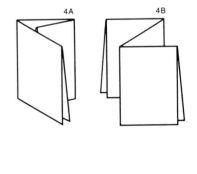

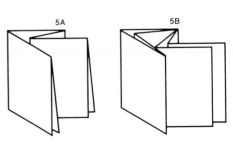

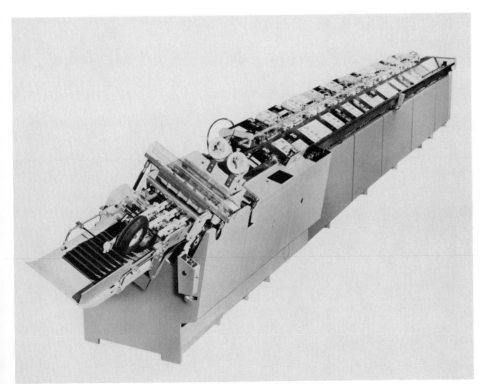

Macey Multibinder II collates, saddle-stitches, folds, and face-trims.

BINDING METHODS

After the sheets are folded into signatures, the signatures are gathered or collated in correct sequence for binding. Collating is usually done by machine, but small jobs may be done by hand.

Wire Stitching. There are two methods of wire stitching: saddle-stitching and side-stitching. Bother methods are used for pamphlet binding, which includes booklets, magazines, catalogs, etc., and the choice of method depends on the number and bulk of pages. Saddle-stitching is used for thin pamphlets, and side-stitching is used for thick pamphlets.

In saddle-stitching, the pamphlet is hung from its centerfold on a saddle and stapled through the backbone into the centerfold. This is the neatest, simplest, and most inexpensive method of binding, and permits the pages to open fully and lay fairly flat.

In side-stitching, the pamphlet is stapled from front to back about ¼" in from the backbone. A cover is glued on later to hide the raw backbone and staples. The inside, or gutter, margins must be increased in this method because the pages neither open fully nor lie flat. With the development of new adhesives, side-stitching is giving way to perfect binding.

Wire-stitched pamphlets are head, foot, and face trimmed after binding, either on a trimming attachment on the stitcher, or in a later operation on a guillotine-style paper cutter.

Collator (Maceymatic 401A).

Saddle stitcher (Consolidated Jetstream 225).

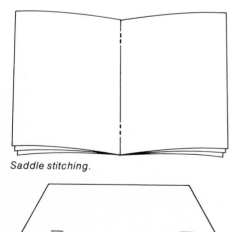

Saddle stitching.

Side stitching.

Mechanical Binding. In mechanical binding, the collated signatures are trimmed on all four sides, and the binding side is drilled or punched with a series of round or slotted holes. The covers, either hard or soft, are identically drilled or punched. A wire or plastic coil or similar mechanical binding device is then inserted through the holes.

The advantage to mechanical binding is that the pages lie perfectly flat, which is useful for textbooks, cookbooks, and other workbook applications. The inside, or gutter, margins must be increased in mechanical binding to provide space for the holes.

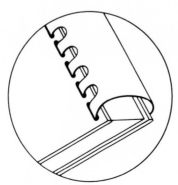

Plastic binding.

Spiral binding.

Edition Binding. Edition binding, also known as hardcover or casebound, is the oldest, most permanent, and most expensive method of bookbinding. In this method, the signatures are sewn together with thread, either through the backbone of each signature (Smyth-sewn), or through the entire book ⅛″ in from the binding edge (side-sewn). Heavy four-page endpapers are then pasted to the binding edge of the first and last signatures, and the book is trimmed on three sides. The spine is then glued, given either a rounded or flat contour, and a strip of gauze called super or crash is glued the length of the spine. The gauze is wider than the spine so it can later also be attached to the covers for reinforcement.

The covers are made from pieces of cardboard, called binding boards, that are covered with cloth or paper. They are either printed or stamped with the title of the book, the author, and the publisher. A casing-in machine applies paste to the endpapers and fits the book and cover in place. The completed books are then pressed for drying, and later wrapped with a printed dust jacket.

Sewn-signature books can also be given paper covers. In this case, the covers are applied before trimming. This method, however, is not classified as edition binding.

Perfect Binding. Perfect binding is primarily used for paperbacks, but may also be used for hardcover books. It is less expensive than sewing, and also less durable. In this method, the backs of the collated signatures are ground off, which exposes and roughens the edge of each page. A special, permanently flexible adhesive is applied to the spine, and covered with a strip of reinforcing material. With paperbacks, the cover is then attached and the book is trimmed. With hardcover books, endpapers are attached and the book is trimmed before the cover is added. This procedure is similar to edition binding.

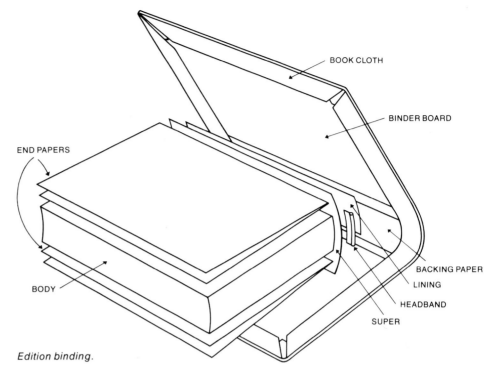

Edition binding.

This machine trims glued or perfect-bound booklets on three sides at speeds up to 12,000 per hour (Macey Feeder/Trimmer 563).

Types of book bindings:

1. Perfect binding—hard cover.
2. Mechanical binding—plastic.
3. Mechanical binding—concealed spiral.
4. Mechanical binding—spiral.
5. Sewn signature—soft cover.
6. Edition binding.
7. Perfect binding—soft cover.

FINISHING OPERATIONS

Die-cutting. Die-cutting is commonly used for direct mail pieces, greeting cards, point-of-purchase displays, and packages. The die is made by jig-sawing a shape in a piece of plywood. A strip of steel rule with a sharp cutting edge is then bent and wedged in the cut. Die-cutting is usually done on a platen letterpress. Flatbed cylinder presses are used for very large jobs, and rotary die-cutters are used for high-speed, long-run jobs. Sheets may be cut individually or in groups, depending upon their thickness. Perforations are made with a toothed die-cutting rule.

High or hollow die-cutting is used for labels and envelopes. These dies permit the cutting of many sheets at the same time, and are made of heavy steel that is bent to shape, welded, and then sharpened.

Scoring. Scoring is usually necessary to facilitate folding heavy paper and board. Scoring may be done on some folding machines, or it may be done on a platen or flatbed cylinder press much in the same way as die-cutting. In fact, scoring and die-cutting are frequently a combined operation. The steel rule used for scoring is round-faced, and is lower than the die-cutting rule so it creases but does not cut the paper (crease scoring). The thicker the paper, the wider the score must be. Also, very heavy board may require partial cutting to facilitate bending (cut scoring). This is done with a low knife rule.

Although an unscored fold works better when made parallel with the paper grain, a scored fold works better when made across the grain. At right angles to the grain, the scoring rule transforms the fibers into millions of hinges, whereas when parallel with the grain, it separates the fibers and weakens the fold.

When scoring a pamphlet cover, the scored ridge should be on the inside of the fold. Also, the thicker the pamphlet, the wider the score must be. The resulting W-shaped hinge accommodates the signature thickness much better.

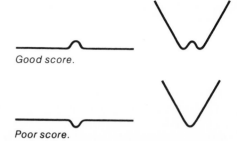

Good score.

Poor score.

Die-cut folder.

Die cutter and creaser (Consolidated BF-1270).

Embossing. Embossing is the molding of paper into a relief image. This is achieved by pressing the paper between a brass female die and a male bed or counter made of molding compound and shaped with an impression from the die. The relief image may be one or more levels of flat planes, or it may be modeled as with the figures on medallions and coins.

Light embossing is done without heat on a platen or cylinder press, and heavy embossing is done with heat on an arch press. Embossing may be done in register over a printed image, or it may be done on blank paper. When done on blank paper, it is called blind embossing.

Stamping. Stamping is the imprinting of casebound book covers. The stamping die is made from a mechanical provided by the designer. It may be used in conjunction with either ink or metallic foil. When used with metallic foil, the die must be heated. If no ink or foil is used in stamping, only the impression of the die is made. This is called blind stamping.

Laminating. Laminating is the application of transparent plastic, such as cellulose acetate, to paper or board with a special colorless, transparent adhesive. This serves as a protective coating, and is frequently used instead of varnishing for menus, book jackets, packages, displays, and signs.

Tipping. Tipping is the process of pasting endpapers or separately printed inserts into or onto a signature, usually before or during collating. If the tipping is done on the outside of the signature it is called a tip-on or outside tip and is done mechanically. If it is done on the inside of the signature it is called a tip-in and is done by hand.

Separately-printed inserts are frequently used where color printing is desired in a black-and-white book, magazine, etc. The insert may be either partial- or full-page size. If the insert is a 4-page or 8-page section, it may be placed inside or outside a signature and bound without tipping, either by sewing, stitching, or adhesive. This is called jacketing.

Portion of booklet with printed and blind embossing.

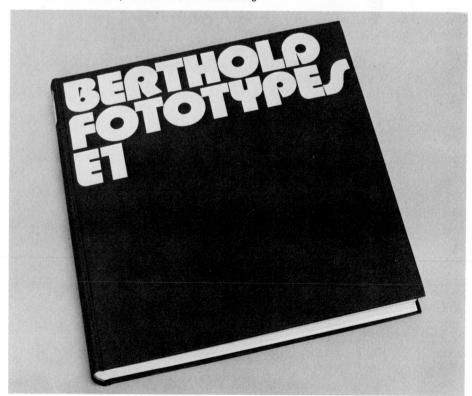

Book stamped with metallic foil.

Studio Equipment and Material

STUDIO FURNITURE

Drawing Table. A drawing board mounted on a wood or metal base. The board is adjustable in height and angle, and the most common sizes for graphic design work are 23" x 31" and 31" x 42". For work up to 24" wide, the 23" x 31" size is more convenient because the T-square can be operated with the left hand while the taboret remains within easy reach of the right hand. However, since artwork is sometimes wider than 24", and since reference books and materials must often be close at hand, most designers prefer the 31" x 42" size. This means, of course, that in order to reach the T-square and tools at the same time, the tools must be placed on the board (which is risky with such items as ink), or the taboret must be moved from the right to in front of the table.

For T-square accuracy, the drawing table top must have a metal edge. If it doesn't have a built-in metal edge, a clamp-on metal edge can be purchased. A metal edge is required only on the T-square side of the board. For right-handers, this would be the left side.

The drawing table top should be covered with heavy cardboard to protect it from cutting tools as well as to provide a resilient working surface. An ideal material for this is chipboard, which is identical to the backing on pads, and is available in 30" x 40" sheets. The chipboard should be fastened with thumbtacks so it can be periodically turned over or replaced.

A piece of absorbent cloth should be thumbtacked to the side or underside of the table top for wiping pens and brushes.

Drawing Board. This is a separate wooden board that may be used on any table or surface for drawing purposes. If a slant is desired, the board can be propped at the top edge with a block of wood. This arrangement is an economical and satisfactory alternative to a drawing table, the major drawback being that the board height is not adjustable, and the board slant is limited. Some designers prefer this arrangement since the surrounding flat table surface, if large enough, serves as a taboret as well as a convenient place for reference books and materials.

Most drawing boards have either wood cleats or metal edges at the ends to insure T-square accuracy. If not, a clamp-on metal edge can be attached to the T-square end.

Don't cut directly on a drawing board. Either protect it with a sheet of chipboard, or use the backing board from a discarded drawing paper pad for cutting.

Chairs and Stools. Most designers prefer to sit at normal chair height when working. Any chair will do, but a secretarial posture chair on casters is best. Some designers use a high stool, since the resulting raised height of the drawing table makes it possible to work either sitting or standing, which is often advantageous for very large work. Various types of stools are available, the best being a swivel drafting stool.

Taboret. A table or cabinet placed at the side of the drawing table for tools and materials. The top surface should be at least 15" x 20", and the height should be 24" to 28" for chair-sitting, and 30" to 36" for stool-sitting or standing. Ideally, the taboret should have a number of drawers and/or compartments for storage, leaving the top surface free for only those tools and materials currently in use.

Commercially made taborets are available, but since they are expensive as well as often less than satisfactory, many designers assemble their own out of found, purchased, or constructed elements. Various types of shallow drawer units are available from office supply companies. At least one of the drawers should be partitioned with wood or cardboard strips for pencils and pens. A plastic box with many small compartments is also useful for pen points and other small items. Hardware stores also stock small-parts cabinets, which can be placed in the taboret or on a nearby shelf or wall.

Since the taboret can be quite heavy when fully stocked, and since it may need to be frequently moved for best positioning, it should be mounted on casters if possible.

Drawing table lamp. A lamp with long, spring-balanced, adjustable arms that can be positioned anywhere over the drawing board. It should adjust easily, and should remain in position once adjusted. The Dazor and Luxo lamps are popular for graphic design work. They are available in fluorescent, fluorescent-incandescent, and incandescent models.

The fluorescent model, which contains two 15-watt tubes, lights the largest area and is coolest to work under. Good color balance can be achieved with a combination of daylight and cool-white tubes. A special advantage to this model is that it may be used as a light source for tracing. (See Tracing Box, page 51.)

Typical studio arrangement.

The fluorescent-incandescent model, which contains one 22-watt circline tube and one 60-watt bulb, is preferred by some designers because the incandescent bulb helps to mask the flicker inherent in fluorescent lighting. Good color balance can be achieved with a daylight fluorescent tube and a regular incandescent bulb.

The incandescent model is not commonly used in graphic design work. In addition to lighting too small an area, it is hot to work under. Also, color balance can only be achieved with a special lens or filter.

Flat Filing Cabinet. The ideal storage cabinet for large paper and board is a flat filing cabinet (also called a plan or blueprint file). Most cabinets contain five 2" high drawers, and can be stacked to any height. Since the standard size of most art paper and board is 20" x 30", the drawers should be somewhat larger than these dimensions. Most designers prefer a cabinet that holds 30" x 40" stock. Not only does this accommodate the occasional 30" x 40" sizes of paper and board, it doubles the 20" x 30" storage capacity of the cabinet without doubling the cost. A 30" x 40" cabinet costs only ¼ to ⅓ more than a 20" x 30" cabinet.

Since even secondhand flat filing cabinets are expensive, most beginners devise alternate means of storage, such as a closed cabinet with large, closely-spaced shelves, large manila envelopes, or large, flat corrugated boxes. Whatever the means, paper and board must be stored flat in a dust-free enclosure.

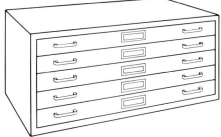
Flat filing cabinet.

Reference File. Every graphic designer saves all printed material that might have value for future reference. If the material is in book, booklet, or magazine form it is stored in a bookcase, but if it is in single sheet form it must be categorized and filed in folders. Categories and degrees of categorization depend on the interests of the designer and the amount of material involved. For example, one designer might make do with one folder for type specimens, while another might have a separate folder for each style of type.

The ideal cabinet for a reference file is a legal size metal office file. The legal size is desirable since many printed pieces are wider than 11", and folding would make them difficult to thumb through rapidly. An inexpensive alternative would be a fiber board transfer file, or just a corrugated carton of the proper width.

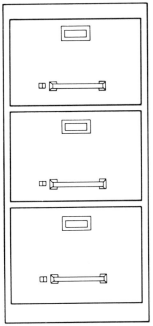
Legal file.

Tracing Box. A wood or metal box with a frosted glass or translucent plastic top and an interior light source (usually two or three fluorescent tubes). Its operation is simple; the artwork to be traced is placed on the lighted surface and a sheet of paper or board is placed over it for tracing. Since the light must pass through both materials, neither can be extremely opaque.

A tracing box is such a time-saver and convenience that every studio should have one. In addition to its use in tracing, it is also useful for sorting slides and examining transparencies and negatives. Commercial models are available, but many designers build their own. All that is needed is an old fluorescent lamp that has two or three 15-watt tubes, a 15" x 20" sheet of ³/₁₆" or ¼" translucent white plastic (available in plastic supply stores), and some very basic woodworking and electrical wiring ability.

A serviceable substitute for a tracing box is simply a plastic sheet propped against a fluorescent drawing table lamp that has been adjusted so it lies, tubes up, on the drawing table or a nearby surface. If the design of the lamp doesn't permit this arrangement, two stacks of books with a light in between will work, as will a drawer with a light inside. Translucent plastic is better than frosted glass because it is light in weight, unbreakable, and produces a brighter, more evenly lighted surface.

Tracing box.

Plastic sheet used for tracing.

PENCILS

Drawing Pencils. Graphite drawing pencils are available in 17 degrees of hardness, ranging from 6B (very soft) to 9H (very hard). Since the difference between consecutive degrees is slight, not every degree is needed. A good selection for graphic design work is 4B, 2B, HB, H, 3H, 5H, and 9H. This list may be modified for personal preference or special purposes, as long as the selection includes two or three degrees each of soft, medium, and hard pencils. For proper control, the pencil must rest against the large knuckle of the first finger. When it becomes too short to reach this point, it should either be discarded or fitted with an inexpensive pencil lengthener.

In place of the wood-encased drawing pencil, some designers prefer a mechanical lead holder that uses refill lead, which is available in most degrees of hardness. Although the initial expense is higher than for a wood-encased pencil, it is ultimately more economical in both time and money, at least for the most commonly used degrees of hardness. This is because it eliminates the cutting away of wood, and permits full use of the lead.

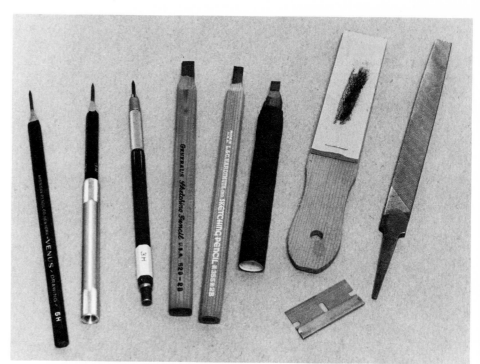

Left to right: drawing pencil; drawing pencil with metal lengthener; mechanical lead holder; General's sketching pencil; Koh-I-Noor sketching pencil; sketching pencil with handmade lengthener; sand pad; razor blade; flat bastard file.

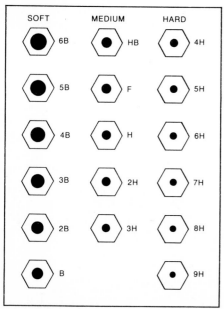

Drawing pencil chart.

SOFT	MEDIUM	HARD
6B	HB	4H
5B	F	5H
4B	H	6H
3B	2H	7H
2B	3H	8H
B		9H

Layout and Sketching Pencils. These are large, soft, intense black graphite pencils that are commonly used for rough layouts and sketches.

Flat Sketching Pencils. Large, rectangular-lead graphite pencils are available in 2B, 4B, and 6B degrees of hardness. There are two sizes: the larger General's Sketching Pencil and the smaller Koh-I-Noor Sketching Pencil. While they may be used for general layout sketching, they are primarily used for lettering layouts.

When a flat sketching pencil becomes too short for comfortable use, it can be lengthened by rolling a piece of 2-ply bristol board tightly around it, followed by wrapping with tape. Finally, wrap a separate piece of tape at the junction of the bristol board and the pencil, exposing 1″ to 1½″ of the pencil tip. As the pencil wears, the tip can be further exposed by removing and re-taping only the junction wrapping.

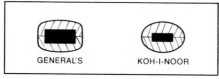

GENERAL'S   KOH-I-NOOR

Cross-section of flat sketching pencils.

Carbon and Charcoal Pencils. Available in soft, medium, and hard degrees, carbon and charcoal pencils produce a flat, intense black that closely resembles the qualities of black printing ink. This is as compared to graphite, which produces a shiny gray-black. For this reason, carbon and charcoal pencils are commonly used in layout and comp lettering to quickly and accurately achieve a printed effect. Being brittle and powdery, however, they are not easy to use. They resemble pastels in appearance, qualities, and technique of application, and, in fact, are often used for details in black and white pastel layout sketches. (See Layout Techniques, page 118).

Colored Pencils. Two types of colored pencils are commonly used in graphic design work. A thin, hard pencil, such as Eagle Verithin, is used for line work or wherever a sharp point is desirable. A thick, waxy pencil, such as Prismacolor, is used for large areas or wherever a thick coverage and intense color is desirable. The Prismacolor type of pencil can be sharply pointed, but wears rapidly because of its high wax content.

China Marking Pencils. This soft wax pencil is available in many colors. As the name implies, it will write on all glossy surfaces, and is commonly used to mark photographs for cropping. It can be removed from photographs and other non-porous surfaces with a facial tissue moistened with rubber cement thinner.

Lithographic Crayons and Pencils. Black wax crayons and pencils that come in many degrees of hardness for drawing on lithographic stones or plates. Graphic designers use lithographic pencils for marking glossy surfaces, as well as for creating halftone effects in line art through the use of a stippled drawing board such as Ross or Coquille board.

Pencil Sharpening Tools and Techniques. Most designers sharpen pencils by first cutting away the wood with an industrial razor blade and then pointing the lead on a sandpaper pad or file. Not only is this necessary for unusually shaped pencils that do not fit into a mechanical sharpener, it permits a variety of point shapes.

In order to avoid personal injury or damaged lead, a specific technique must be used with the razor blade. For right-handers, the razor blade is held between the thumb and forefinger of the right hand, and the pencil is held in the fist of the left hand, with about one inch of pencil protruding beyond the thumb. The right thumb and forefinger guide the blade in a

scooping movement, and the left thumb applies pressure to the blade. Since the left thumb can flex only about ½", there is no danger of the blade slipping out of control, as would be the case if the cutting pressure were to be applied by the right thumb and forefinger. Avoid nicking the lead, since even a slight nick may cause the lead to break during use. For most pencils, about ½" to ⅝" of lead should be exposed, but if the lead is very soft or very thin, less exposure may be desirable. As a general rule, expose as much lead as possible without unduly weakening the lead. This enables the lead to be pointed the maximum number of times before further wood cutting is necessary.

When pointing the lead on the sand-paper pad, a needle point is obtained by twirling the pencil as it is moved back and forth on the pad. A long point is usually used on hard pencils, and a short point is usually used on soft pencils. A chisel point is made by sanding the lead on opposite sides. The width of the chisel should be adjusted by sanding the side edges parallel to each other. Do not make a screwdriver shape, since the width of the chisel would widen each time the point is resharpened.

Very large pencils, such as flat sketching pencils, will quickly clog a sandpaper pad. If they are frequently used, therefore, as they would be in lettering, it is best to sharpen them on a machinist's file. A 6" or 8" flat bastard file is best, since it has a coarse cross-cut that is self-

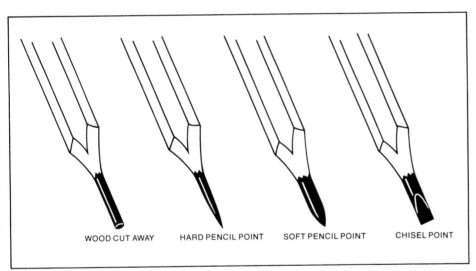

WOOD CUT AWAY   HARD PENCIL POINT   SOFT PENCIL POINT   CHISEL POINT

Pencil sharpening chart.

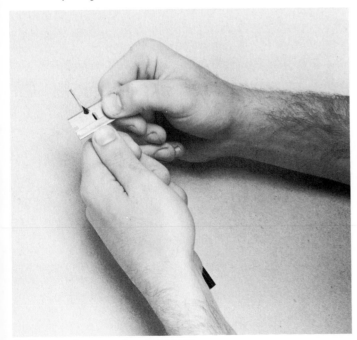

Cutting wood away on drawing pencil.

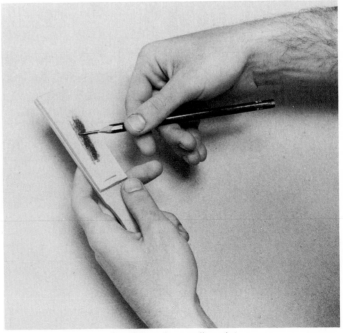

Twirling pencil on sand pad to make needle point.

cleaning. Avoid the finer, diagonal-cut mill file; although it looks like it might do a smoother job, it will quickly clog up and become useless. Some art supply stores stock flat bastard files. If not, they can be purchased in a hardware store.

While a mechanical pencil sharpener is not used for most types of pencils in graphic design work, it is useful for rapidly sharpening layout and other pencils where the point made by the pencil sharpener proves adequate. It is also useful for colored pencils, which cannot be easily sharpened with a razor blade and sandpaper pad. If a regular pencil sharpener isn't available for sharpening colored pencils, a small hand sharpener is a satisfactory substitute.

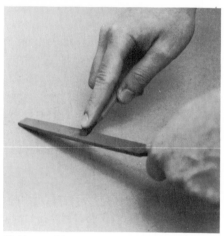

Making a chisel point with a flat bastard file.

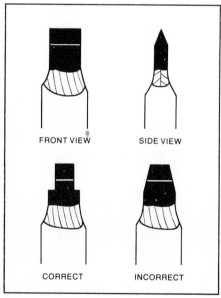

Sharpening the flat sketching pencil.

PENS

Split-nib Drawing Pens. The design of the split-nib drawing pen has remained virtually unchanged for over 100 years. Available in many degrees of fineness and flexibility, the popular brands are Gillott's, Brandauer, Hunt, and Esterbrook. The split-nib pen is commonly used for line illustrations, as well as for lettering and other graphic design applications. In addition to being very inexpensive and easily used and cleaned, its greatest feature is the variety of lines produced by merely changing the pressure on the pen and/or the direction of the stroke. Popular pens for lettering and graphic design applications are the Gillott #170, which has a medium-fine point, and the Gillott #290, which has a super-fine point.

Speedball Pens. This is the brand name for a dip-type pen with round, square, oval, or chisel-shaped nibs. Each nib style is available in a number of sizes. The round "B" style and the chisel-shaped "C" style are commonly used for finished lettering, comp lettering, and general graphic design work.

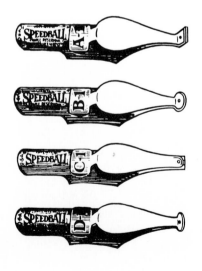

Penholders. Both split-nib drawing pens and Speedball type pens require a penholder. The best penholders are similar in thickness and weight to a drawing pencil. The Hardtmuth #116½ penholder is ideal for split-nib drawing pens, and the Hardtmuth #03½ penholder is ideal for heavier pens, such as Speedball, because it employs a lever-clamp to hold and release the pen, thus eliminating the problem of wobbly or frozen pen points.

Ruling Pens. An adjustable-thickness pen for ruling lines. (See Drawing Instruments — Ruling Pens, page 62).

Scriber Lettering Pens. This inexpensive tube-feed pen has interchangeable points in many sizes. Not a fountain pen, it is filled with an ink dropper and must be cleaned after use (which is easy because of its simple mechanism). Although specifically designed for use with drafting lettering guides, it is excellent for use with curves and templates. While the tube-feed technical fountain pen is better for constant use, the scriber lettering pen is better for occasional use since it is cheaper and doesn't require continuing maintenance once it has been cleaned. A popular brand is the Wrico Standard Lettering Pen.

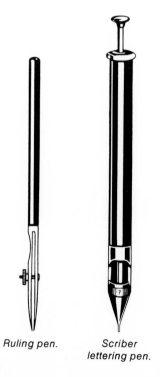

Ruling pen.   Scriber lettering pen.

Technical Fountain Pens. These self-feeding pens use waterproof drawing ink, either in cartridge or bulk form. There are two basic types of technical fountain pens, the tube-feed pen such as the Rapidograph and the Pelikan Technos, and the combination tube-feed and nib-feed pen such as the Pelikan Graphos.

The tube-feed pen has interchangeable tubular points of many sizes through which the ink flows. An internal wire, which is weighted so it easily moves up and down with a shake of the hand, insures against ink clogging. Tube-feed pens are used for ruling, freehand drawing, and lettering. Because the line width remains constant in any direction, and because the ink does not come in contact with the outside of the tube, tube-feed pens are ideal for use with curves, templates, and lettering guides. Special compasses and compass attachments are available for use with most brands of tube-feed pens.

The Pelikan Graphos pen has an assortment of tubular points that perform as described above, as well as an assortment of nib points in various sizes and shapes for ruling, lettering, and freehand drawing. Many of the nib points are similar to Speedball pens.

While the technical fountain pen is superior to the ruling pen for many line-ruling purposes, it does have drawbacks. As compared to the ruling pen, it is more expensive, it requires constant use and care to work properly, it provides only limited widths of lines, and it cannot be used with designers color and other liquid color mediums. Therefore, unless there is a specific and continuing need for a technical fountain pen, a good-quality ruling pen will better serve the needs of the beginning designer.

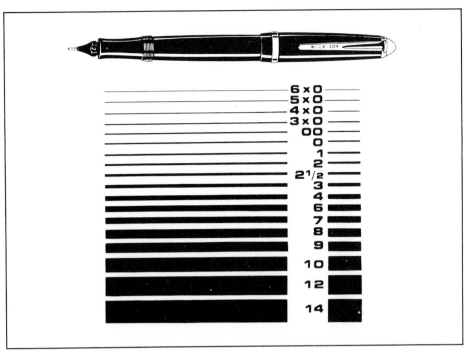

Koh-I-Noor No. 3060 Rapidograph pen and line width chart.

Pelikan Graphos pen.

Pelikan Graphos nib styles.

Pelikan Graphos Master Set.

BRUSHES

Watercolor Brushes. Pointed brushes come in 14 or more sizes ranging from #000 up to #14. The watercolor brush is the most commonly used brush in the graphic design studio, and only the very best quality should be purchased. The best brushes are made of red sable, and the most popular brands are Winsor & Newton Series 7 and Grumbacher No. 197. The most commonly used sizes are #1, #3, and #5 or #6. Larger sizes are occasionally needed, but since they are used so infrequently, they don't have to be of first quality. A large, flat brush, commonly called a single-stroke brush, is useful for covering large areas without streaking.

The #1 watercolor brush is used for very fine rendering and retouching. Some designers prefer the smaller #0, #00, and #000 sizes, but they don't hold much paint and dry out rapidly. The #3 brush is used for general rendering and retouching (such as white retouching in lettering). The #5 or #6 brush is used for general rendering where larger areas are involved, but is not commonly used for retouching. Since white retouching requires the utmost from a brush, reserve the best #1 and #3 brushes for this purpose. Never use white retouching brushes with color. Even with thorough washing, some color will remain inside the ferrule and seep out during subsequent white retouching. To get the most out of brushes, many designers use them first for white retouching. After they have become the least bit worn, they are then used for general designers color work, and finally for ink. Ink quickly ruins brushes because it can't be washed out after it has dried. It hardens around the hairs, which then break off when the brush is flexed.

Most new brushes need to be "broken in" before they work perfectly. The reason for this is that a few extraneous hairs extend beyond the true point of the brush, and until they are worn off, they make the brush difficult to use. They dry out rapidly, and when wet they spring about. To avoid the break-in period, many designers trim off the extraneous hairs. The procedure for this is to wet and point the brush in the mouth, twirl the point on a piece of white paper until the true point of the brush can be determined, and then trim it with a very sharp blade. Very good eyesight or a magnifying glass is necessary for this operation, since even the slightest miscalculation will result in a chisel-tip brush.

Paint should never be permitted to dry in brushes. Also, after a brush has been used, it should be thoroughly rinsed in water and pointed in the mouth. Saliva, being slightly sticky, keeps the brush pointed after it has dried. Washing with mild soap and lukewarm water after every use is recommended for infrequently used brushes, but brushes in daily use usually need only an occasional thorough washing. Store brushes points up in a jar, or points down in a spiral wire brush holder. Infrequently used brushes should be stored in a flat, airtight container so moths can't attack them. In any case, never permit brushes to rest on their hairs.

Trimming a brush.

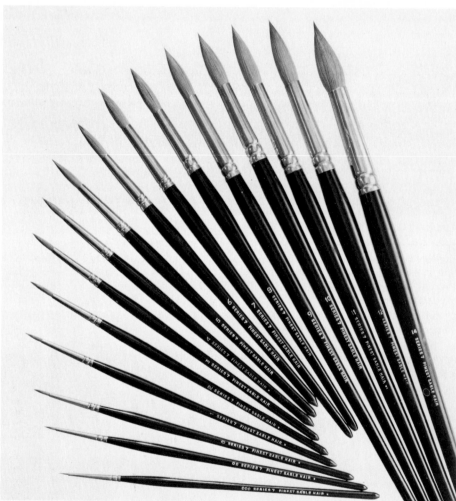

Winsor & Newton Series 7 watercolor brushes.

Lettering Brushes. Chisel-tip brushes in many sizes from ⅛" to 1" in width. Red sable and sabeline brushes are generally used in graphic design for comp lettering, but ox hair, white bristle, and camel hair brushes are also available in many styles and sizes for sign painting. Wide lettering brushes are useful for covering large background areas without streaking. Very small chisel-tip brushes can be made from watercolor brushes by trimming the point with a blade.

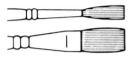

Stencil Brushes. These round, stiff, white or black bristle brushes have flat tips. Available in many sizes, stencil brushes are used with stencil paper or frisket paper masks for applying ink, dye, pastel, charcoal, and other mediums to artwork. In addition to solid tones, stencil brushes are capable of producing various effects, such as stippling, striations, and airbrush-like continuous-tone modeling.

Dusting Brush. An 8" long, soft bristle brush with a handle. It is used for removing eraser crumbs and other particles from artwork and the drawing board. The brush not only rapidly cleans surfaces, it avoids smudging or embedding dirt in the artwork, which could happen if the hand or fingers were used. It should occasionally be washed with mild soap and lukewarm water, and then shaped by placing it between thick folds of newspaper until dry.

ERASERS

Pencil Eraser. A soft, rubber eraser for pencil lines. Popular brands are Pink Pearl, Ruby, and Rub Kleen.

Kneaded Eraser. A soft, pliable eraser that can be molded into any point or shape. It is used for pencil erasing as well as for removing pastel and charcoal. It can also be used for lightening pencil lines or areas by tamping instead of rubbing. During use it should be frequently kneaded to bring a fresh portion of eraser to the surface.

Gum Eraser. This is a large, soft, crumbly eraser that will not harm even the most delicate surface. A popular brand is Artgum. It is the only eraser that should be used directly over an inked area such as lettering. (Both pencil and kneaded erasers, surprisingly, can remove enough ink to result in streaking or mottling.) If the gum eraser is rubbed on a cheese grater, the resulting fine crumbs can be rubbed over a pencil drawing to remove dirt and smudges without substantially lightening the pencil lines.

Rubber Ink Eraser. A hard rubber eraser that contains an abrasive. This eraser should be used with great caution, since it will seriously damage the paper surface, thus making further inking impossible.

Ink Erasing with a Razor Blade. The most successful method of ink erasing is with an industrial razor blade. Use a new blade, since an extremely sharp edge is required. Hold the blade upright between the thumb and forefinger, and scrape its whole edge, not just one corner, over the ink (which must be thoroughly dry). This process cannot be rushed; excess pressure, or the use of the corner of the blade, will gouge the surface of the paper. Scrape from various directions, and replace the blade as soon as it becomes the least bit dull. The blade will powder off the paper fibers as well as the ink, thereby producing a surface which is even smoother than the original. (This presupposes, of course, a good-quality paper or board. Cheap paper or board will not stand up to any method of ink erasing.) If ink must be removed from an area where the blade cannot be held flat without damaging adjacent artwork, the blade may be tilted slightly so only one corner touches the surface. Keep the tilting to a minimum, however, and use extremely light pressure.

Erasing Shield. A thin, flexible metal shield with various shaped slots permits accurate erasing without damaging adjacent artwork. A scrap of bond paper also makes a good erasing shield when cleaning up a pencil or pastel layout with a kneaded eraser.

Erasing shield.

Ink erasing with a razor blade.

T-SQUARES, TRIANGLES, RULERS, AND SCALES

T-square. This is a T-shaped device comprised of a long, thin blade attached at 90° to a short, thick head. It is available in wood, wood with a plastic-edged blade, aluminum, and steel. Blade lengths are 18″, 24″, 30″, 36″, 42″ and 48″. While the steel T-square is the most expensive, it is indispensable for graphic design work. In addition to being just about indestructible in regard to head/blade alignment, it has a beveled undercut to the blade that minimizes the possibility of ink run-under. Also, since the graphic designer uses the T-square as much for cutting as he does for ruling, only a steel blade could withstand such use.

A 24″ or 30″ steel T-square is most popular for general studio use. It is long enough for the majority of ruling and cutting operations, but not so long that it is unwieldy. A long, inexpensive wood T-square is handy for the occasional longer jobs. Used only occasionally, it will serve well. Do not use a wood, plastic, or aluminum T-square for cutting, however, since blade damage would most likely result.

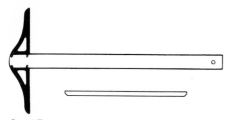

Steel T-square with cross-section of blade.

Triangles. Standard triangles are 45° and 30°/60°. They are made of transparent plastic and are available in a variety of sizes from 6″ to 18″. In normal use, triangles are placed against the upper edge of the T-square blade. In addition to producing 30°, 45°, 60°, and 90° angles when used individually, they may be combined to produce 15° and 75° angles. Since triangles are primarily used for drawing vertical lines, their right-angle length is important. While most designers eventually accumulate a large variety of lengths, a basic selection would be an 8″ 45° triangle for smaller work, and a 12″ 30°/60° triangle for larger work.

Plastic triangles should never be used for cutting, since they can so easily be damaged. If it is desirable to make verti-

cal cuts on artwork attached to the drawing board, as is often the case in paste-up work, metal and metal-edged plastic triangles are available. The metal-edged plastic triangle is preferable, since the all-metal triangle is expensive, heavy, and hides underlying guidelines.

The adjustable triangle is a very desirable studio tool. Adjustable to any angle, it combines the function of a protractor and a ruling guide. It is especially useful in lettering and similar graphic work.

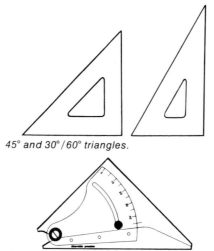

45° and 30°/60° triangles.

Adjustable triangle.

Protractor. This inexpensive circular or semi-circular flat plastic device measures angles other than those obtainable with standard triangles.

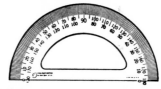

Protractor.

Rulers and Scales. As explained in Ruling, page 86, measuring tools should never be used for ruling. Therefore, while we refer to the common measuring tool of the studio as a ruler, we really mean a scale. However, the term "scale" can mean more than one thing. In one context, it can refer to any direct measuring tool, such as an inch/foot ruler, and in another, it can refer to a measuring tool that enlarges or reduces distances by proportional ratio. For that reason, we have come to refer to direct measuring tools as rulers (even though they are never used for ruling), and reducing or enlarging measuring tools as scales.

Rulers. While any school-grade ruler may be used in graphic design work, it will eventually prove to be inadequate. The ideal tool for general direct-measuring purposes in the professional studio is a 24″ stainless steel flat ruler with inch, pica, and agate scales. In addition to being very accurate, and long enough to span most work, its pica and agate measurements make it very useful for typographic design work. Even though it is steel, it should not be used for ruling or cutting, since this might damage the engraved markings.

Some brands of steel rulers, such as the Gaebel Printers Comparative Scale, also have a point scale. While a point scale is not a necessity in typographic design work, it can be very useful.

Architects Scale Rule. A 12″ triangular wood or plastic rule that includes direct inch measurements as well as scales divided $3/32″$, $1/8″$, $3/16″$, $1/4″$, $3/8″$, 1″, $11/2″$, and 3″ to the foot. While this rule is specifically designed for the scaling of architectural drawings, it can be used for any scaling operation in graphic design, as well as for general use as a very accurate and conveniently sized inch ruler.

Architects scale rule.

Engineers Scale Rule. A 12″ triangular wood or plastic rule similar to the architects rule in function except that all divisions are in decimal parts to the inch. This eliminates the need to convert decimal answers of mathematical division to fractions of inches. The engineers scale is especially useful for map drawing, since land distances are measured in feet and tenths of feet (for example, 51.6′).

Circular Proportional Scale. An inexpensive plastic device for determining proportional enlargements and reductions. This scale is described in the section on Enlarging and Reducing (page 85).

Note: All tools described in this section should be cleaned occasionally with soap and water and then dried immediately to avoid rust or warpage. Wood and plastic tools in particular tend to pick up dirt, which either obliterates their markings or is later transferred to the artwork.

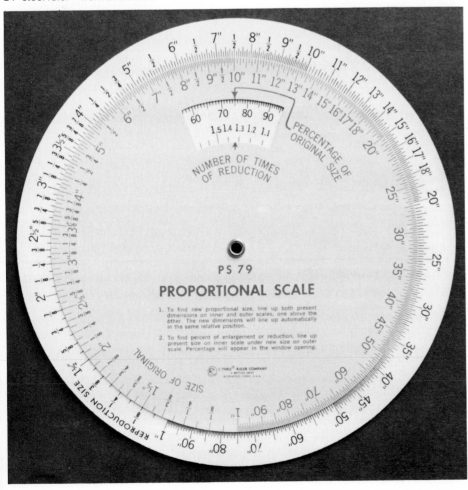

24" steel ruler—front and back.

CURVES, TEMPLATES, AND GUIDES

Irregular or French Curves. Transparent plastic templates are geometrically designed to cover a wide variety of irregular curve conformations. They may be purchased individually, or in sets ranging from 3 to 12 templates. A set of 3 templates in small, medium, and large sizes is usually adequate for most graphic design applications.

The use of irregular curves is described in the section on Ruling (page 87).

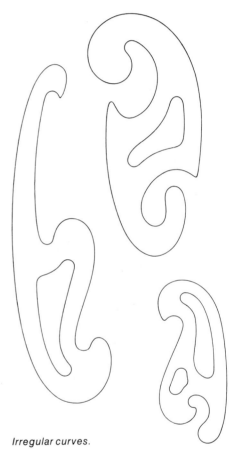

Irregular curves.

Adjustable or Flexible Curve. This is a strip of flexible material that can be adjusted to any desired curve. Available in lengths from 12" to 24", it is best suited for large, simple curves.

Flexible curve.

Circular proportional scale.

Ellipse Guides. In isometric, dimetric, trimetric, and perspective illustrations, circles become ellipses. Although ellipses may be geometrically plotted and then ruled with irregular curves, the process is so difficult and time-consuming that ellipse guides are used whenever possible. There are two types of ellipse guides: the isometric series and the angle series. The isometric series are used only for isometric drawings and the angle of foreshortening is 35°–16'. The angle series are used for dimetric, trimetric, and perspective drawings, and the ellipses are foreshortened by angles of from 15° to 60°.

The angle series, which are very useful in graphic design and illustration, are available in sets of small, medium, and large ellipses. The size of an ellipse refers to its major axis and is indicated in inches. The minor axis is controlled by the angle of foreshortening or projection. Complete sets have 10 or more projections in increments of 5 degrees, but a set

with 4 projections (15°, 30°, 45°, 60°) is usually adequate for most graphic design and illustration work.

In addition to the normal use of ellipse guides in pictorial drawing, they are also frequently used in graphic design to make decorative shapes.

Lettering Guides. A strip of transparent plastic that is perforated with a complete alphabet, numerals, and punctuation marks. Many sizes and styles of lettering are available. For inking with lettering guides, a tube-feed pen is necessary. Lettering guides are primarily used in technical drawing, and have very little, if any, use in graphic design.

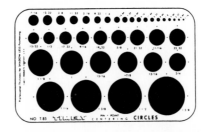

Miscellaneous Templates. A great variety of templates are used in architectural and engineering drafting. Some of these, such as circle and square templates, can be useful in the graphic design studio.

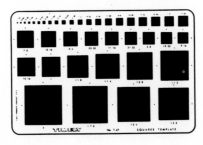

DRAWING INSTRUMENTS

Drawing (or drafting) instruments consist of compasses, dividers, and ruling pens. They are available in a variety of sizes and designs, and may be purchased individually or in sets. A set is preferable, since it usually contains a good selection of instruments as well as extra pen and pencil points, needles, leads, and an extension bar and a screwdriver.

For reasons of economy, the beginner usually makes do with an inexpensive ruling pen and a giant bow compass with interchangeable pen, pencil, and divider points. As soon as possible, however, a complete set of instruments should be purchased. A good-quality set is recommended, but an economy set is acceptable as long as it contains two or more compasses and two dividers, in large and small sizes. Although such an economy set is less accurate and durable than a good set, its variety of instruments and size ranges makes it far superior to a giant bow compass.

Following is a description of the drawing instruments commonly used in the graphic design studio. Most are included in good-quality sets, but if not, they may be purchased individually.

Compasses. Most sets contain one 6″ regular compass with pen and pencil points, and two spring bow compasses, one for pencil and one for ink. The spring bow compasses are used for small circles up to 1½″ in radius, and the regular compass is used for larger circles up to 6″ in radius. The extension bar can be used with the regular compass to make circles up to 11″ in radius. Separate spring bow pen and pencil compasses are necessary because interchangeable points are not suitable for small compasses. (An exception to this is the drop compass, described in the next paragraph.)

Expensive sets also contain a drop, or rotating, compass for very small circles up to ¼″ in radius. The drop compass, which has interchangeable points for pen and pencil, is so far superior to the spring bow compass for making very small circles that it is recommended as an individual purchase if it is not included in the set. The drop compass is comprised of two major parts: the central pivot shaft and the rotating drawing assembly. The index finger is placed on top of the pivot shaft, and the thumb and second finger grasp the knurled part of the drawing assembly. The point of the vertically-held pivot shaft is positioned on the paper, and

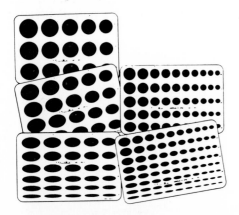

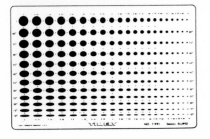

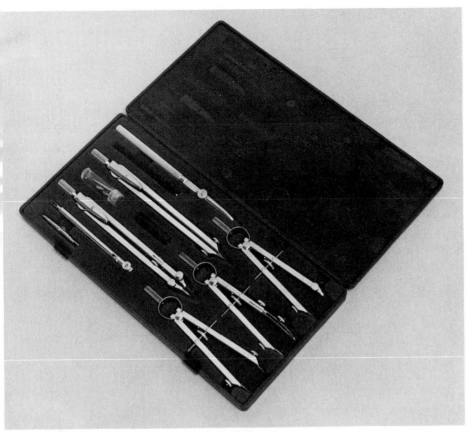

Medium-priced drawing instrument set (Keuffel & Esser).

Using the Compass. Grasp the knurled top of the compass with the thumb and forefinger of the right hand, and the drawing leg with the left hand. Position the pivot point at the center of the desired circle, and, without touching the drawing point to the paper, adjust the drawing leg to the desired radius with the left hand. To draw the circle, rotate the compass clockwise with the right thumb and forefinger, tipping the drawing point slightly forward in the direction of rotation. When using the pen point, lower the point to the paper after it is in motion, and raise it after it overlaps the beginning of the stroke, and while it is still in motion. Don't start or stop with the pen point on the paper, and maintain a smooth, steady movement. The pen point, incidentally, is identical to the ruling pen in filling and operation (see page 62).

When large circles are drawn with the regular compass, the legs of the compass must be "broken" so the points are perpendicular to the drawing surface. This is particularly important with the pen point, since both nibs must make contact with the paper.

On mechanicals and other finished line copy, the pivot hole made by the compass can be filled in with retouch white. On comps and presentations, where it is desirable to eliminate the pivot hole entirely, a small piece of cardboard should be taped or rubber-cemented over the center of the circle to be drawn or cut. After the circle is drawn or cut, the cardboard is removed, and there will be no pivot hole in the artwork.

Drop compass.

the drawing assembly is lowered to the paper and rotated. The drawing assembly is then raised, and finally the entire instrument is removed.

Circles larger than 11″ in radius require the use of a beam compass. Such large sizes, however, are not commonly encountered in the graphic design studio.

Beam compass.

The spring bow compass may be fitted with a tiny blade for cutting circles in thin materials. The regular friction-joint compass cannot be used for circle cutting because the pressure necessary for cutting would spread the legs. For larger circles, therefore, a cutting blade may be fitted to an all-purpose giant bow compass, or a compass made especially for cutting may be purchased (see Cutting Tools, page 64).

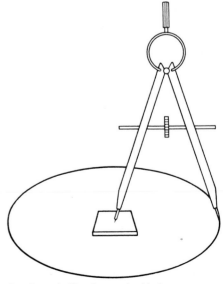

Cardboard affixed over pivot hole.

Using a drop compass.

Dividers. The divider is used for dividing distances into equal parts as well as for transferring measurements from one location to another. For these purposes, it is more accurate and much easier to use than a ruler. Since dividers are probably the most frequently used drawing instruments in the graphic design studio, only sets which contain both the 6″ regular divider and the spring bow divider are acceptable. Because the friction-joint regular divider can be adjusted so rapidly, it is used for small as well as large measurements. For utmost accuracy in small measurements, however, the spring bow divider should be used. In addition to being more precise in adjustment, the setting cannot be accidentally changed.

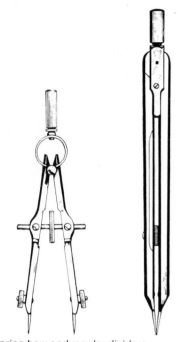

Spring bow and regular dividers.

Ruling Pens. In graphic design, the ruling pen is used so frequently, and the work is so precise, that only the very best quality ruling pen will do. Since the ruling pen in low- and medium-priced drawing instruments sets is most likely of low or medium quality, it should be replaced with one of the highest quality. A high-quality pen not only produces lines of the highest precision, it is highly resistant to wear and corrosion. In the long run, therefore, it is the most economical choice.

A ruling pen with either jackknife or cross-joint blades is very desirable. Both of these pens permit the blades to be opened for cleaning without changing the line thickness setting. Also desirable is an adjusting screw with numbered graduations for setting the line thickness. If more than one line thickness is used on a drawing, the pen can be adjusted back and forth by merely dialing the right number. This not only provides the greatest precision, it eliminates the need for thickness testing on scrap paper each time the setting is changed.

A large border, or detail, pen is available for drawing very long or very heavy lines. This pen is primarily used in drafting, however, and has little use in graphic design.

A railroad ruling pen is available for ruling double lines. This pen is also useful for ruling very heavy lines: the outlines of the heavy line are ruled with the railroad ruling pen, and then filled in with a Speedball pen, drawing pen, or brush.

Using the Ruling Pen. The ruling pen is always used with a ruling guide, never freehand. Ink, dye, designers color, retouch color, and other similar mediums can be used in the ruling pen. When using designers or retouch color, the consistency must be slightly thinner than for brush use. Never fill the ruling pen by dipping. For ink, use the dropper incorporated in the cap, and for other mediums, wipe a loaded brush along the side of one nib. When filling the pen, hold the pen vertically in the left hand and the ink dropper or brush in the right. Steady the hands by pressing the small fingers of both hands together. Fill the pen with ¼″ to ⅜″ of ink or other medium. More than this will cause the pen to flow too rapidly. Use a facial tissue to wipe off any medium that may have gotten on the outside of the nibs.

Fill the ruling pen immediately before use, and if it is laid down for more than seconds during use, clean and refill it. Fresh ink can be cleaned out by merely wiping the sides of the nibs with an absorbent wiping rag or facial tissue. With a thicker medium such as designers color, the nibs should be swished in water before wiping. At the completion of a job, and periodically during the job, the nibs should be opened and thoroughly cleaned inside and out. A small bottle of household ammonia is useful for removing dried ink. Never scrape off dried ink with a blade, as this would obviously damage the pen.

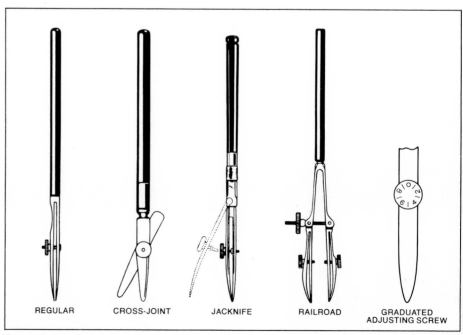

REGULAR   CROSS-JOINT   JACKNIFE   RAILROAD   GRADUATED ADJUSTING SCREW

Types of ruling pens.

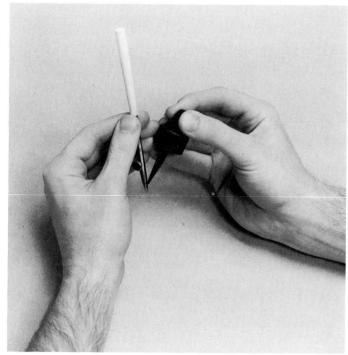

Filling the ruling pen.

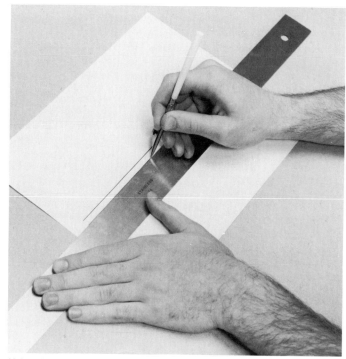

Using the ruling pen.

When ruling, hold the pen vertically, in side view, so that both nibs touch the paper, and tip the pen forward in the direction of the stroke. About 60° from the paper is the usual slant for straight lines. The nibs of the pen must be parallel to the line being ruled, and the adjusting screw must face away from the hand and ruling edge. It is adjusted by the thumb and first or second finger of the same hand holding the pen.

When ruling curved lines with an irregular curve or other template, the pen should be tipped forward only slightly. About 75° to 85° from the paper is the usual slant. The nibs of the pen must be parallel to the line being ruled, which means that the pen must be rotated during the drawing of the curve. Since the adjusting screw must face away from the hand, only a limited amount of rotation is possible without repositioning the artwork. For example, when ruling with the outside edge of an irregular curve, only the upper edge should be used.

Before ruling, adjust the width of the line by testing the pen on a scrap of the same paper that is to be ruled, since different paper may produce a line of different width. Always use the ruling guide for testing line width; a freehand test is seldom accurate. The maximum width of a ruling pen line is $1/32''$ to $3/64''$. If the line must be wider, build it up with more than one stroke. Very heavy lines can be outlined and later filled in with a Speedball

pen, drawing pen, or brush. Make the lines heavy enough for easy filling in. (A railroad ruling pen, as described previously, can also be used for outlining heavy lines.)

To insure an even weight line from beginning to end, the pen movement must be steady throughout; a slow-moving pen makes a thicker line than a fast-moving pen. Also, don't press the nibs tightly against the T-square or other ruling guide, since this will reduce the width of the line. When ruling more than one line of the same weight, make sure that all working conditions remain the same, such as the position of the pen, the movement of the pen, the type and amount of ink or other medium in the pen, and the type of paper.

Maintenance of Drawing Instruments.
Regular compasses and dividers have friction joints which occasionally need adjustment with the screwdriver provided in the set. The tension should be adjusted so the legs move smoothly and easily, but no so easily that they will not hold a "setting" in normal operation. Do not use oil on joints, since friction is necessary for proper tension.

The nibs of the ruling pen will eventually become so worn that they cease to produce good lines. If a ruling pen no longer works well, examine its nibs under a magnifying glass; a worn nib will reveal a flat, bright spot at the ruling point. Ruling pens can be resharpened, but only

good-quality pens are worth the effort or money. Most designers return worn ruling pens to an art supply dealer for resharpening, but some prefer to do it themselves with a hard Arkansas oil stone made expressly for sharpening small instruments.

To resharpen a ruling pen, first close the nibs to see if they are equal in length. If not, run the vertically-held pen over the stone in an oscillating motion until they are equal. Then open the nibs and sharpen each on the outside with a rolling motion. In addition to preserving their convexity, it is important to return them to their original elliptical shape. If too much of the pen contacts the paper it will not feed at all. Continue sharpening until the flat, bright spots have disappeared, but do not make the nibs so sharp that they cut into the paper. Never sharpen the nibs on the inside, since this will ruin the pen.

Compass pen points are sharpened in the same way as ruling pens. Sharpening is rarely required, however, because they are used so infrequently.

Compass pencil points should be sharpened on the outside with a sandpaper pad. The angle of the cut should be as steep as possible.

Compass pencil point.

CUTTING TOOLS

Industrial Razor Blades. Single-edge, heavy-gauge blades made expressly for slicing and cutting operations. By far the most important cutting tool in the graphic design studio, they are used for cutting paper and board as well as for cutting away the wood of pencils prior to sharpening on the sandpaper pad. The reason for their popularity is that they are very sharp, very inexpensive, and require no holder. When a blade dulls, it can immediately be replaced with no lost time and no concern for cost.(Discarded blades should be put into a closed container so they will not be a hazard to rubbish handlers.)

Mat Knife. This is a heavy-duty knife with a fist-sized handle and replaceable blades. Refill blades are stored in the handle. As its name suggests, the mat knife is used for cutting mats and other thick materials where heavy pressure is desirable. Since even heavy materials can be cut with many light passes of the razor blade, some designers use the mat knife only for particularly difficult cutting jobs. The reason for this is that paper and board dull cutting blades very quickly, and frequent mat knife blade replacement is a nuisance.

#1 X-acto Knife. This pencil-sized aluminum handle can be fitted with various styles of blades for small, precision work. The #11 blade, which has a long, steep angle, is used for tiny cutting operations where the razor blade proves too unwieldy. The #16 blade, which has a short, low angle, is used for curve cutting, and is very similar to a frisket knife in looks and operation. Other blade styles are available, but they are not commonly used in graphic design work.

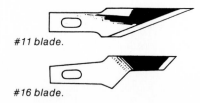

#11 blade.

#16 blade.

Frisket Knife. A tiny, low-angled blade in a pencil-sized handle. Especially designed for cutting friskets, it may also be used for film and light stencil cutting. Some models have replaceable blades, and some models swivel for better curve cutting.

Frisket knife.

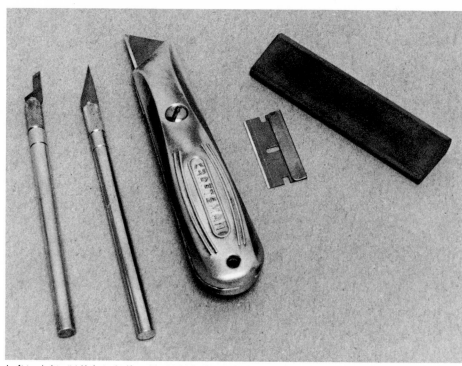

Left to right: #1 X-Acto knife with #16 blade; #1 X-Acto knife with #11 blade; mat knife; industrial razor blade; slip stone for sharpening blades.

Circle Cutters. A bow compass cutter is available for small circles, and beam compass cutters are available for both small and large circles. Tiny cutting blades may also be purchased for use in pen and pencil bow compasses. (See Drawing Instruments — Compasses, page 61.)

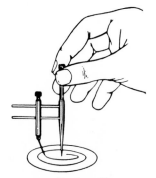

Beam compass cutter (small).

Beam compass cutter (large).

Scissors. Irregular shapes in thin, unmounted material are best cut with scissors. (A frisket knife is used when the material is mounted.) Scissors 6″ to 9″ in length are the best size for graphic design work, and high quality is important. In addition to being keen and smooth operating, they must be durable enough to withstand paper cutting, which is much harder on scissors than fabric cutting.

Very tiny scissors, called silhouette scissors, are useful for intricate work. These are available at stores that specialize in cutlery.

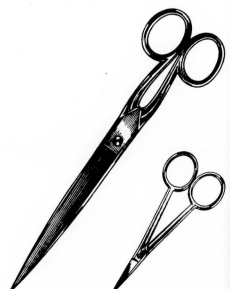

Paper shears.   *Silhouette scissors.*

Paper Cutters. A paper cutter that is large enough and accurate enough for graphic design work is both too space-consuming and too costly for the amount of use it would receive in a one-man studio. If much photographic work is done, however, a small paper cutter is useful for trimming prints.

Paper cutter.

Sharpening Cutting Tools. The key to successful cutting is a sharp cutting tool. Although the purpose of replaceable-blade tools is to eliminate the need for sharpening, their shortcoming is that blades don't usually get replaced until they are inordinately dull. In order to insure an always-perfect edge, therefore, even replaceable blades should be sharpened frequently on a small slip stone. If done frequently enough, just a few strokes on the stone will return the blade to perfect condition. A side benefit of this practice, of course, is the greatly reduced need to buy blades. While razor blades are generally regarded as too flimsy, too inexpensive, and too easily replaced to warrant sharpening, even they can be successfully sharpened a few times.

In addition to a slip stone or India oil stone for general blade sharpening, a hard Arkansas oil stone is needed for drawing instruments and other very delicate tools. (See Drawing Instruments, page 63.) All sharpening stones should be lubricated with a light oil to prevent glazing with metal particles.

MAGNIFYING AND REDUCING GLASSES

Magnifying Glasses. Three types of magnifiers are available: hand-held, headband, and stand-held. The hand-held magnifier is least desirable because it encumbers a hand and is difficult to keep properly focused. The headband magnifier is binocular, and is good for extended periods of use. Some people find it objectionable because it encumbers the head, and must be removed or adjusted to switch to normal vision. Most popular is the stand-held magnifier, which leaves both hands free and remains in exact focus. Some models are illuminated. For bargains in magnifiers, check mail order catalogs of hardware and electronics firms.

In addition to a 2- or 3-power magnifying glass for general work, a 5-power linen tester is useful for examining halftone dots, retouching velox prints, and so on.

Many people believe that an unusually steady hand is necessary for very fine work. This is not true. Anyone with reasonably good ability (plus good tools and techniques) can perform very fine work, providing it can be seen properly. The problem is, even people with normal vision cannot see very fine details without the aid of a magnifier.

Reducing Glasses. A hand-held square or round lens, with or without a handle, that reduces the image seen through it. A reducing glass is very helpful in judging figure-ground patterns, as in lettering. By using a reducing glass, the designer is able to view artwork as if it were ten or more feet away without getting up from the drawing table, and without the blurriness that often occurs in long-distance viewing. The reducing glass is also useful for judging how a piece of art will look when reduced for reproduction.

Clockwise from top: stand magnifier, linen tester, reducing glass.

AIR BRUSH

A small, pencil-shaped spray gun that is operated by compressed air. A great variety of models is available for specialized purposes in sign and display work, fine arts, and graphic design, illustration, and photo retouching. For graphic design, illustration, and photo retouching, the Thayer and Chandler Model A, Paasche Model V, and Wold Models A-1 and A-2 are most popular. These are "double-action" air brushes, which means that air volume is controlled by a downward movement of the finger lever, and color volume is controlled by a backward movement of the same lever. This double-action feature is essential for fine control of lines and tones.

A source of compressed air is needed for an air brush. A lightweight, portable air compressor made expressly for air brush use is available, but any air compressor will work if it can be regulated to between 25 and 35 pounds, and if it is fitted with a filter to remove water, oil, and dirt from the air. All compressors are noisy, and should be located in a closet or soundproofed compartment if possible.

An inexpensive and noiseless source of compressed air is a tank of carbonic gas (CO_2), which can be rented from any

Thayer & Chandler
Model A air brush.

Portable air compressor.

Gauge and regulator for carbonic gas tank.

concern that services soda fountains. (Carbonic gas is used to make carbonated water.) An air gauge and regulator must be purchased for attachment to the rented tank. Carbonic gas is commonly used by studios located in office buildings where the noise of a compressor would be objectionable. A tank of gas lasts for many months with average use. Although inexpensive, its disadvantage is that the tank must be periodically returned for refilling. Also, because there is no way to measure the amount of gas in the tank, it always runs dry in the middle of a job. Large users of carbonic gas avoid this problem by keeping a spare tank on hand.

Ink, dye, water color, designers color, and retouch color can be used in an airbrush. Designers color and retouch color must be thinner than for regular brushing, and waterproof black ink may need to be diluted slightly with household ammonia. The air brush is a very delicate instrument and must be carefully cleaned after every use. Household ammonia is used to remove waterproof ink, and laundry bleach is used to remove dye. Flush the air brush thoroughly with water after using these cleaning agents.

Using an Air Brush. The technique of using an air brush is not complicated, but it takes a good amount of practice to become proficient. The air brush is held like a pencil, using the lower joint of the index finger, not the tip, to operate the lever. The tip of the thumb is positioned to limit the backward movement of the finger. As mentioned previously, air volume is controlled by a downward movement of the lever, and color volume is controlled by a backward movement of the lever. At the beginning of a stroke, the lever is moved downward to start the air and then backward to start the color. At the end of a stroke, the lever is moved forward to stop

the color and then upward to stop the air. Throughout this process, the air brush must be kept in constant and steady motion to avoid uneven deposits of color, particularly at the beginnings and endings of strokes, where they tend to get heavy. With practice, these "stroking" movements occur almost simultaneously, and are entirely automatic. The width of the stroke is controlled by the distance of the air brush from the surface.

Although the unique function of an air brush is to apply gradated tones, it is equally useful for applying flat tones, particularly on large areas where a regular brush would most likely cause streaking. Frisket paper masks are commonly used in airbrushing to protect surrounding areas from overspray.

When ruling straight lines with the air brush, use the same technique that is used for ruling straight lines with a regular brush (see page 88).

Using an air brush.
Note hose wrapped around wrist.

METAL FASTENERS

Pushpins. Available with aluminum heads, or clear or colored plastic heads, with ⅜″, ½″, or ⅝″ points. The ½″ aluminum head pin is most popular for general studio use. Pushpins are used for pinning work on bulletin boards as well as on drawing boards. Their advantage over thumbtacks is that they are easily grasped for insertion or removal. On the drawing board, they are used for fastening rigid materials such as illustration, bristol, and mat board. Only two pins at the upper corners of the work are usually required. For thinner materials that might shift or tear through pins, drafting tape at all four corners is recommended. Drafting tape or thumbtacks are also recommended if the protruding heads of the pushpins seriously interfere with the operation of the T-square and triangle. In mechanical work, where the paste-up surface is rigid board, and where frequent fastening and removal may be necessary, pushpins usually provide the greatest speed and accuracy.

Thumbtacks. Nickeled steel solid head thumbtacks with ½″ heads and ½″ points are the most popular for general studio use. Since they are difficult to remove, especially when fully inserted, they are usually used only for applications where the protruding heads of pushpins would be objectionable, such as for attaching chipboard to the drawing board as a protective covering.

Map Pins. These pins with plastic ball heads come in three sizes and many colors. Used primarily to locate points on maps, charts, and graphs, they are also used for attaching work in exhibits and displays where thumbtacks, pushpins, or staples would be objectionable.

Staples. A sturdy desk stapler will find much use in the graphic design studio. In addition to stapling papers together, it can be used to tack materials to bulletin boards or other fairly soft backing surfaces. For harder backing surfaces or thicker materials, the use of a compression stapler may be necessary.

TAPES

Drafting Tape. This tan, crepe-paper tape is primarily used for holding work on the drawing board. It has a mild, pressure-sensitive adhesive, and can be easily removed without damaging the surface to which it is applied. It is also commonly used for hinging overlays. Masking tape is similar to drafting tape, except that it has a slightly stronger adhesive.

Cellophane Tape. A shiny, transparent, pressure-sensitive tape for general studio use. It has a strong adhesive and cannot be removed from most materials without damaging them. Scotch Tape, the brand name of the 3M Company, has become the generic name for all brands of cellophane tape.

Magic Transparent Tape. The 3M Company brand name for a translucent matte finish acetate film tape that becomes clear and almost invisible upon application. Also, the matte finish accepts pencil, pen, ink, paint, etc. It is more permanent than cellophane tape and is used for mending, holding, and splicing. Since its invention, it has come to replace cellophane tape for most studio purposes.

Correction or White Tape. A smooth, white paper tape that is primarily used for making corrections on mechanicals. It has a mild, pressure-sensitive adhesive identical to that of drafting tape. It is also used for labeling and hinging acetate overlays, as well as for other purposes where a smooth white tape is preferable to drafting tape.

Photographic Tape. A black, fully opaque crepe-paper tape that is used for masking, assembling negative photostats, hinging black storyboard masks, and so on. It has a mild, pressure-sensitive adhesive identical to that of drafting tape.

Two-sided Tape. Various types of two-sided tape are available, but the best type for general studio use is the "Dubl-Stik" brand. This is a pressure-sensitive two-sided adhesive on a waxed-paper carrier tape. The tape is cut to length, applied, and rubbed down. The waxed-paper carrier tape is then removed and the two surfaces adhered. The carrier tape is easy to remove (as opposed to other brands) because one edge is free of adhesive.

The adhesive on two-sided tape is quite strong, thus making it useful for applications where rubber cement would fail, such as with package dummies.

Cloth Tape. A strong, waterproof, pressure-sensitive cloth tape in many widths and colors. It is used for binding, hinging, splicing, and repairing materials where strength, durability, and looks are important. The most popular brand is Mystik Tape.

Printed Tape. Low-tack, adhesive-backed acetate tape printed in a great variety of colors, patterns, screens, and lines. Many of these tapes are useful in preparing finished art for reproduction. Register mark tape is particularly useful because it is quicker to apply and more accurate than pen-ruled register marks.

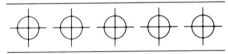

Register mark tape.

Note: Rubber cement thinner will aid in the removal of most types of pressure-sensitive tapes. This is useful when the tape has been position for a long time.

Tape dispensers for 1″ and 3″ core rolls.

ADHESIVES

Rubber Cement.

Rubber cement is the most commonly used paper adhesive in the graphic design studio. It will not penetrate, stain, wrinkle, or shrink paper, and excess cement can easily be removed. Additionally, dried cement can be dissolved with rubber cement thinner, thus permitting the re-positioning or removal of previously cemented elements.

The major drawback to rubber cement is that it is not a permanent adhesive. Being rubber, it eventually deteriorates through oxidation, the rate of deterioration depending upon the method of application as well as the later exposure to light and heat. Under poor conditions, rubber cement could fail in a few weeks, and under good conditions it could last for many years. Since most graphic design work, such as layouts, comps, and mechanicals, need only last for a limited period, however, the limited life of rubber cement is not usually a problem.

Another drawback to rubber cement is that it is not very strong. It is entirely adequate for cementing flat materials, but it will not hold on materials where stress is involved, such as with package dummies, severely warped photographs, etc.

If the foregoing description of rubber cement suggests that it is not well suited for a particular application, investigate the other adhesives described later in this section.

Since rubber cement is so frequently used in graphic design work, proper rubber cementing equipment and procedures are extremely important to even the beginner. Following is a description of the equipment and procedures essential to successful rubber cementing.

Rubber Cement Dispenser. The most popular dispenser is a pint-sized glass or plastic bottle with a brush whose handle slides up and down through the cover, thus permitting the brush to be adjusted so that it is immersed in about one inch of the cement. (A quart metal dispenser with a cone-shaped top is popular for large work and/or continuous use, but it is not usually practical for the one-man studio.) A can of rubber cement is needed for filling the dispenser, and a can of rubber cement thinner is needed to maintain proper consistency of the cement. Both are available in pint, quart, and gallon cans, with the quart size being the most suitable for the beginner.

Rubber cementing equipment.

Fresh rubber cement poured directly from a sealed can is usually the right consistency for most purposes. However, through exposure to air in the frequently-opened dispenser, the cement rapidly thickens. It is therefore necessary to dilute the cement every so often with rubber cement thinner. How often depends upon how long the dispenser is open, and how tightly it is sealed between openings. Do not thin the cement excessively; while thin cement flows nicely, it will hold for only a short period of time.

Rubber Cement Thinner Dispenser. As mentioned earlier, previously cemented work may be removed by applying rubber cement thinner. Since the thinner must be applied generously, the best applicator is an oil can. A sealable spout model (such as the Valvespout dispenser sold in art supply stores) is desirable, because rubber cement thinner evaporates rapidly. If a regular oil can is used, the spout can be sealed with a homemade device, such as a piece of pencil eraser. A plastic bottle with a small-opening, sealable dispenser top also makes a serviceable dispenser.

Rubber Cement Pickup. Dried rubber cement can be removed by merely rubbing with the finger. This is a slow process, however, and there is the risk that dirt, oil, or moisture on the finger will stain the paper. A better method is to accumulate a ball of dried cement from cemented surfaces and the mouth of the cement dispenser. When this ball is rubbed over dried cemented surfaces, it will pick up the dried cement. The best rubber cement pickup is a square of crepe latex sold in art supply stores. It can be cut into various shapes, such as a pointed shape for corners and crevices, or a wide, flat shape for rapid removal of cement on large surfaces. A folded piece of drafting tape is also useful for removing dried cement from very tiny crevices.

Dry Bonding. The strongest and most permanent rubber cement bond is achieved by coating both surfaces thoroughly and evenly and permitting them to dry before adhering. This method is particularly recommended for large surfaces, especially when the material being cemented is thin, flexible, or easily wrinkled, such as tracing, visualizer, or bond paper. Because the surfaces will bond upon contact, accurate positioning is difficult. Fairly rigid material can often be dropped into place, but thin, flexible material, or very accurate positioning, requires the use of a slip sheet. The slip sheet must be larger than the cemented area, and transparent enough to see underlying positioning marks or lines. Tracing or visualizer paper is ideal. The slip sheet is placed upon the cemented mounting surface so it covers all but a narrow band of cement along the top edge. It will not adhere to the cemented surface, since dried rubber cement adheres only to itself. The material to be mounted is then placed upon the slip sheet and positioned. The two surfaces are pressed together along the narrow band of exposed cement, and the slip sheet is slowly pulled out, using the edge of the hand or plastic triangle to smooth and bond the surfaces as each inch or two of cemented area is exposed. A center-to-edge hand movement will minimize the possibility of bubbles and wrinkles. If a bubble occurs, it can usually be eliminated by puncturing with a pushpin and pressing to expel the air. If a wrinkle occurs, it is usually necessary to separate the cemented pieces, either partly or entirely, by squirting rubber cement thinner between them as they are being pulled apart. After the thinner has evaporated, the pieces can usually be re-adhered without applying more rubber cement. If the application of more rubber cement is necessary, the two pieces should be separated completely, the dried rubber cement thoroughly removed, and the entire procedure re-performed. After the materials have been smoothly bonded, the slip sheet is placed over the bonded surface for protection, and the surface thoroughly burnished with the edge of a plastic triangle. This insures maximum adhesion.

For very large surfaces or easily wrinkled material, it is desirable to use two slip sheets. The slip sheets are overlapped about one inch at the center of the mounting surface, and the piece to be mounted is then positioned. Holding one end of the piece to be mounted, the slip sheet is

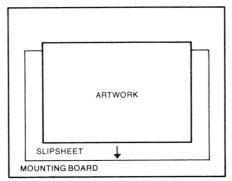

Single slip sheet.

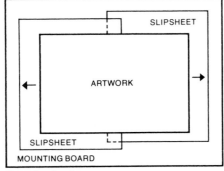

Two slip sheets.

removed at the other end, using the technique described earlier. The second slip sheet is then removed in the same way, and the entire cemented area is burnished. This method of working from center to edge minimizes the possibility of bubbles and wrinkles.

Whenever thin or somewhat transparent material is cemented, it is important that the cemented surfaces be entirely free of smudges, dirt particles, and cement lumps, since they would be visible after bonding.

Dry/Wet Bonding. In this method, the piece to be mounted is coated with cement and permitted to dry. The mounting surface is then cemented, and the piece to be mounted is placed upon it and positioned while the cement is still wet. The cement will begin to take hold within a minute or two, but full adhesion will not occur for ten or fifteen minutes. During this period, therefore, care must be taken to not disturb the cemented piece.

This method is fast and simple, and the resulting bond is very good. It is recommended for small to medium-sized pieces that require very accurate positioning, such as the elements of a mechanical. It cannot easily be used for large work, however, since the cement will begin to dry before the mounting surface can be completely coated and the piece to be mounted can be positioned. If that hap-

pens, let the mounting surface dry completely and then use a slip sheet.

Tweezers may be used to pick up and position small paste-up elements. Another method is to pick up the piece to be positioned with a light jab of the point of a razor blade, frisket knife, or divider. The resulting tiny jab marks are not objectionable as long as they do not damage the graphic work. Since a razor blade, knife, or divider is usually in hand anyway, this second method saves time by reducing the number of tools that need to be handled.

Wet Bonding. Wet bonding is simply the method of cementing one surface only and adhering while still wet. This is not a commonly used method because the resulting bond is so poor. It possibly has some value in temporary work, but should never be used otherwise.

Removing Cemented Work. Previously cemented work is easily removed by using a rubber cement thinner dispenser to squirt a little rubber cement thinner on one corner of the piece to be removed. This will soften the cement enough to permit the corner to be lifted with a fingernail, razor blade, or knife blade. Then, more thinner is squirted between the pieces as they are slowly pulled apart. Recently cemented work will come apart readily, but older work will require proportionately larger amounts of thinner to soften the cement. Hold the work at a slant so the excess thinner will run off. Don't worry about it staining or damaging anything; it quickly evaporates without leaving a trace.

Because the rubber cement thinner softens but does not wash away the rubber cement, it is often possible to re-adhere removed pieces without re-coating with cement. If re-coating is necessary, it is sometimes desirable to remove the old cement, particularly with thin or transparent materials, where underlying dirt or lumps would be visible after mounting.

Removing Excess Cement. Because rubber cement is usually non-staining and easily removed, it is normally applied to a larger area of the mounting surface than will be covered by the piece to be mounted. After the piece is mounted and the cement has dried, the excess cement is removed with a rubber cement pickup. If the dry/wet bonding method was used, excess cement should not be removed for at least one half hour after bonding, since the pressure of the pickup might disturb the alignment of the mounted piece. As mentioned earlier, a square of crepe rubber purchased at an art supply store makes the best pickup. It can be cut into various shapes, and its firm, sharp edges enable it to reach into corners and crevices.

Rubber Cement Stains. Excess rubber cement can be removed from most materials without leaving a stain. There are a few exceptions, however, such as certain types of mat board, and certain color-coated papers such as Color-Aid. The only solution to staining is to coat the entire surface with rubber cement and remove when dry. Hopefully, this will stain the entire surface equally, thus masking the problem. If mottling still persists, a spray coat of matte fixative might be tried.

If a material is known beforehand to be stainable by rubber cement, rubber cement should be applied only to those areas that will later be covered.

One-coat Rubber Cement.
A specially prepared rubber cement that is applied only to the material being mounted. Since it remains tacky indefinitely, mounted work can easily be removed or re-positioned, but the bond is not so strong as with regular rubber cement. Also, excess cement is difficult to remove.

While one-coat rubber cement has advantages for certain applications, it does not replace regular rubber cement for general studio use. It is therefore not recommended unless there is a specific and continuing application that warrants its use.

Wax Coater.
This electrically operated device applies a hot coat of pressure-sensitive wax to the back of material to be mounted. Only one surface needs to be coated, and mounted material can be removed and re-positioned without solvent. For simple, extensive paste-ups such as books, this device is more efficient than rubber cement. It is not practical, however, for general graphic design work. Very small pieces are difficult to handle, and very large pieces will not fit in the machine. Additionally, when material is re-positioned, some wax remains on the mounting board, where it is extremely difficult, if not impossible, to remove.

Spray Adhesive.
This one-coat, pressure-sensitive adhesive comes in a spray can. It provides temporary or permanent bonds depending on the method of application, and can be applied to paper, foil, plastic, and styrofoam. It is particularly useful for permanent bonds when only one surface can be coated, which rules out the use of rubber cement. For very strong, permanent bonds, spray the material to be mounted several times, letting each coat dry.

Spray adhesive can be used for paste-ups, and for mounting thin materials such as tracing paper and glassine type proofs. The adhesive will not transfer to the mounting surface, and mounted material can be picked up and re-positioned

Wax coater.

easily. With most brands, the bond becomes permanent with time. To avoid spraying surrounding surfaces, center the material to be sprayed on a large sheet of newspaper.

White Glue.

A strong, white, water-based, synthetic resin glue that becomes waterproof, permanent, and transparent when dry. It is used for paper, wood, leather, and other porous and semi-porous materials. It may be applied in a bead directly from the squeeze bottle, or, for large, flat surfaces, it may be applied with a flat acrylic brush. For better brushing consistency, it may be diluted to a certain extent with water. Since white glue is water-based, it will affect the dimensional stability of most thin, porous materials, such as paper. A good solution to this problem is to first seal the surface with a diluted coat of glue. After that has dried, the adhering coat can be applied with no fear of subsequent bubbling or buckling of the material. Clamping or pressing may be necessary with some materials.

Diluted white glue also makes a good protective coating, but it should not be applied to water-soluble materials such as designers color. Popular brands are Sobo and Elmer's Glue-All.

Airplane Cement.

A very strong, very fast drying adhesive for all materials including china and glass. It is waterproof and transparent when dry. Since it dries so fast, it cannot easily be used for cementing large surfaces. A popular brand is Duco.

Dry Mounting.

A heat-bonding process that involves the use of thermosetting adhesive tissue and a heating device. The heating device can be a household iron, a hand dry-mounting iron, or a dry-mounting press. Used primarily for mounting photographic prints, this process is also ideal for any flat material of any size that requires a strong, permanent bond. Since the dry-mounting press works much better than hand-held devices, its use is strongly recommended.

The procedure for dry mounting is to first "tack" the dry-mounting tissue on the back of the piece to be mounted with a hand iron. The tissue, which is available in sheets and rolls, should extend beyond the edges of the piece to be mounted. If more than one sheet is used, they should

Dry mounting press.

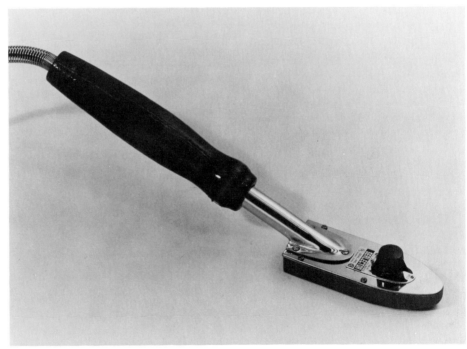

Tacking iron.

be butted, not overlapped. The tissue is then trimmed, with a razor blade and steel T-square, so that it is about $1/32''$ less than the dimensions of the piece to be mounted. This avoids the possibility of the oozing of adhesive when heat is applied. The piece to be mounted is then positioned on the mounting surface and tacked, and the entire assembly is heat pressed, either in the dry-mounting press or with

a hand iron. Surfaces larger than the dry-mounting press may be bonded in sections.

A dry-mounting cloth is available for backing maps, charts, and prints, and a polyester film is available for laminating.

DRAWING INKS

India Ink. Waterproof black ink is best for general drawing purposes. Higgins Waterproof India Ink is popular for fine line work with pens and drawing instruments because it is thin, free flowing, and won't clog fine pens. Because of its thinness, however, it doesn't cover large areas well. For heavy lines or large-area work with brushes or Speedball pens, Higgins Black Magic Ink is preferable. In fact, not only does it cover large areas well with one coat, it is excellent for fine line work, and can be used on plastic film and tracing cloth as well as paper. Pelikan Drawing Ink is also a good fine line ink, and covers large areas with fairly good density. Higgins Non-Waterproof India Ink is specifically intended for wash drawings. It should not be used where white retouching is involved, since the white retouch paint would pick up the ink and turn gray.

When India ink stands for an extended period of time, its pigment may settle. A few shakes of the bottle will usually correct the problem, but stirring may also be necessary. India ink will also thicken through evaporation, which makes it difficult to use for fine line work. If this happens, add a few drops of household ammonia and shake well. Household ammonia, incidentally, makes a good pen cleaner, and many designers keep a small bottle of it on their taboret for rinsing pens during and after use. It eventually loses its potency through exposure to air, and should be replaced as soon as the pungent smell disappears.

Never apply ink over designers or retouch colors because the ink will cause the paint to flake off. The only exception to this is in lettering and similar retouching, where the area and amount of ink involved is very small. Even there, flaking can be a problem, but most designers prefer to contend with this rather than having the retouch white turn gray, which usually happens when it is applied over a water-soluble black.

Colored Ink. Waterproof, translucent (except white) colors are available for drawing, transparent washes, and air brush use. Most colors are not very permanent and will fade in time. Colored ink is mainly used for illustration and does not find much general use in the graphic design studio. An exception to this is red and blue ink, which are used in mechanicals.

Acetate Ink. This non-waterproof ink comes in black, white, and transparent and opaque colors, and will adhere to any plastic surface without spreading or crawling. It can be applied by pen or brush and removed with a water-moistened cloth or swab. Being heavily pigmented, it requires stirring and shaking before and during use, and is difficult to apply evenly. Also, it remains slightly gummy when dry. Acetate ink may be used on color separation overlays (only black and transparent red are needed), but because of its gumminess, most designers prefer to use masking ink, which is described later. Opaque acetate ink may also be used for comps and finished art purposes, but again because of its gumminess, most designers prefer to use designers color on prepared acetate. (Regular acetate may be used if a plasticizing agent [page 74] is added to color.)

Masking Ink. A non-waterproof acetate ink that is made especially for color separation overlays and masking. It has all the properties of regular acetate ink except that it is not gummy when dry. It is available in transparent red and opaque matte black. A popular brand is Grumbacher Patent Red and Patent Black (the black is also called Ink Concentrate). A red opaque masking ink (Grumbacher Speed-o-paque) is available for use on film negatives.

Engrossing Ink. This is waterproof carbon black ink for calligraphic purposes. Being very thin and free flowing, it produces extremely fine lines as well as subtle gradations in tone. While these tonal gradations are esthetically desirable in calligraphy, they not only can't be reproduced by line plate, but they may even cause platemaking difficulties. Therefore, if the calligraphy is to be reproduced, it is usually better to use regular fine line India ink.

Higgins pen cleaner with retrieving tray.

COLOR MEDIUMS

Designers Colors. These opaque water colors are also referred to as gouache or tempera. Available in tubes in a large selection of colors, designers colors are the most commonly used color medium in graphic design work. Winsor & Newton, Grumbacher, Pelikan, and Shiva Nu-Tempera are popular brands. Shiva Nu-Tempera is formulated to adhere to plastics and other glossy surfaces, but because of this feature it remains slightly gummy when dry.

Most brands of designers colors are available in introductory sets of basic colors plus black and white. Other colors can be added as there is a particular need for them. Color charts for every brand are available from the dealer or manufacturer.

When properly thinned with water, designers colors can be applied by brush, ruling pen, or air brush. The most popular tray for thinning and mixing designers colors is a circular aluminum watercolor palette with 6 or more wells. Being very inexpensive, most designers keep a number on hand so that colors mixed for a specific job can be saved for possible later corrections. For larger amounts of color, a plastic egg tray makes a good palette. For adding water to designers colors, an eyedropper or a rubber ear syringe (available in drugstores) is useful.

Designers colors are also available in pan form in sets of 12 or 24 colors. Such a set is handy when small amounts of many colors are needed, as in making small color sketches or correcting previous work.

To avoid the hardening of designers color in the tube, always replace the cap immediately after squeezing out color. If the cap is not immediately replaced, color will harden on the threads and make later re-sealing difficult. If designers color thickens in the tube, water can be injected with a plastic medical syringe of the type used for shots and inoculations. This is a disposable syringe that the doctor uses once and then discards after breaking off the needle. Most doctors are happy to give away discarded syringes so long as they know it's for a worthy cause. If a tube of designers color is completely hardened, remove the cap and immerse the tube in water for a few days. This will usually soften it enough to then permit an injection of water with a syringe.

Introductory set of designers colors.

Many designers and illustrators store designers colors in a humidified container. An easily made humidifier is an airtight plastic container with some kind of absorbent material at the botton. The absorbent material must be dampened occasionally with water to insure a constant high humidity. If the dampness makes paper labels fall off, tape them back on with cellophane tape, which is water resistant.

Poster Colors. Ready-to-use opaque watercolors that come in jars. Of lower quality than tube designers colors, poster colors are largely used for sign writing and other studio purposes where the superior qualities of designers colors are not necessary.

Poster colors will harden in the jar if the screw cover is not sealed perfectly. A good way to insure an airtight seal is to store the jars upside down.

Retouch Colors. These opaque watercolors are for retouching photographs as well as for general studio purposes. Available in tubes and pans, a complete set contains 5 or 6 values of both warm and cool grays, plus white, matte black, and glossy black. Also available is a set of neutral grays, which can be used on average warm or cool tone prints. If the print is decidedly warm or cool in tone, then warm or cool grays must be used. Do not combine warm, cool, or neutral grays on one print. Even though the values may appear the same to the eye, warm grays will photograph darker than cool grays. While extensive photo retouching requires an air brush and specialized training, most graphic designers are able to do minor retouching. For minor retouching, a set of pan colors is best. For further information, see Retouching the Photograph, page 151.

Retouch white is also commonly used for making corrections on drawings, mechanicals, and lettering. For delicate retouching, zinc white is the best pigment because it is free-flowing and smooth-spreading. For covering large areas in one coat, titanium white (also called permanent white) is the best pigment because it is more opaque than zinc white. It does not work well for delicate retouching, however, because it is too viscous. Zinc white is used in most brands of photo retouch colors, whereas titanium white is used in most brands of designers colors. Both zinc white and permanent (titanium) white are available in Winsor & Newton designers colors.

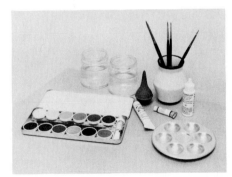

Pan and tube retouch colors on taboret.

Clockwise from top left: water jars; ear syringe; watercolor brushes; plasticizing agent; tubes of designers colors; aluminum palette.

Bleed-proof White. This opaque white watercolor covers dyes, color markers, and designers colors without bleeding. Since most dye and marker colors, as well as a few designers colors, will bleed through normal white, bleed-proof white is indispensable in graphic design work.

Plasticizing Agent. This viscous liquid is added to opaque watercolors to make them adhere to plastics and other glossy surfaces without crawling, chipping, or peeling. Popular brands are Non-Crawl, Flex-Opaque, and Cel-Grip. This agent should be used very sparingly, since too much will result in pin-hole bubbles and gumminess in the dried pigment. If a commercial preparation is not available, soap can be used in an emergency.

Cartoon Colors. These opaque, waterproof, matte colors will adhere to acetate, glass, foil, and most plastic surfaces. While used primarily for film animation, their unusual properties make them useful for other applications as well.

Watercolors. Transparent watercolors are available in tubes and pans. Watercolors are primarily a fine art and illustration medium, and are not commonly used in the graphic design studio. An exception to this is lampblack watercolor, which is preferred by many designers as a retouch black for lettering and other fine applications.

Liquid Watercolors and Dyes. The difference between watercolor and dye is that watercolor is a colored pigment that is deposited on the surface of the paper, whereas dye is a non-pigmented coloring agent that stains the paper or material. Commercially prepared liquid watercolors, such as Dr. Ph. Martin's Transparent Water Color, Dr. Ph. Martin's Concentrated Water Color, and Luma Brilliant Concentrated Water Color are actually aniline dyes, not watercolors. The term "liquid watercolor" is therefore a misnomer.

Dyes are very transparent and intensely brilliant. They can be mixed, diluted to lighter tints with water, and can be applied by brush, pen, ruling pen, and air

brush. They are commonly used for layouts, renderings, and illustrations, and because of their high transparency are ideal for coloring black and white photostats and photographs. They are also used for retouching color photographs, but must be used in conjunction with opaque retouch color if details are to be altered.

Because dye stains the surface to which it is applied, corrections are extremely difficult. Laundry bleach will remove dye, and for most colors it should be diluted with water. Apply the bleach with a cotton swab (never a brush), and when the color is removed, immediately remove the bleach by thoroughly washing the area with cotton swabs dipped in water. If the bleach is not removed, it will ultimately damage the surface. Brushes that have been used in dye should be cleaned with soap and water, never bleach.

Dyes will usually bleed through designers colors applied over them. A special bleed-proof white is made to overcome this problem, but it doesn't work with all dyes. If the dye bleeds through even bleed-proof white, try spraying the surface with a few light coats of matte fixative. Don't soak the surface with fixative, as this will cause the dye to spread.

Transparent color dye is also available in spray cans. Made by Magic Marker, the colors match their marker colors.

Pastels. Pigment, chalk, and binder that is pressed into stick or pencil form. Primarily a fine art and illustration medium, pastels are also used for layouts. For layout work, half-hard pastels, such as Nupastel or Carb-Othello, are preferred to soft and semi-soft pastels because they are less dusty and hold a point well. Since pastel colors become muddy and dull when mixed on the paper, it is desirable to have an assortment of at least 24 colors. In addition to a set of pastel sticks, a set of pastel pencils is useful for details. Carb-Othello makes a combination set of sticks and pencils. For black and white layouts, a set of gray pastels is available. Carbon or charcoal pencils can be used with them for details and lettering. A sandpaper pad can be used for sharpening pastels to various point shapes.

Although color markers are the most popular layout medium, pastels are much less expensive and work better for some applications. They are excellent for simulating photography and for large areas of color. They may also be used in conjunction with designers color, ink, and other mediums.

Fingers, paper stomps, facial tissues, and cotton wads can be used for blending pastels. Paper stomps are made of blotter-like paper rolled into stick form and pointed. They are available in large and small sizes. Fingers, paper stomps, and facial tissues are equally good for large-area blending, but paper stomps are better for small areas and tight corners. Cotton wads not only blend, they remove pastels. They are therefore used only when an area must be lightened, and/or lightened and blended. A kneaded eraser is useful for removing (not blending) pastels. Depending upon whether it is rubbed or tamped, it will remove pastels either entirely or partially.

Because pastels are so chalky, they must be sprayed with a fixative to avoid smudging. Pastel fixative is available in liquid form for use with a mouth-type atomizer, and also in spray cans. The spray-can fixative is most popular in graphic design work, and can be used for pastel, charcoal, and pencil drawings. It is clear, waterproof, dries to a matte finish, and can be worked over with pastel as well as other mediums. It is referred to as "workable matte fixative". One light coat provides adequate protection, but two or more light coats are necessary for maximum protection. Before spraying with fixative, blow hard on the layout to remove any pastel dust that may have settled. This is particularly important in areas that are to remain white; pastel dust often becomes visible only after spraying, and then, of course, it can't easily be removed. Excess dust and smudges may be removed by tamping and/ or rubbing with a kneaded eraser. Scraps of bond paper can be used as erasing shields to protect rendered areas.

The procedure for rendering a layout in pastels is to start with the large areas and work progressively toward the small areas and details. It is also desirable, whenever possible, to work from light tones to dark tones. As each area is completed it should be fixed. This will prevent smudging as well as permitting colors to be superposed without mixing with underlying colors. White or light-toned lettering and type indications can be applied to a dark pastel background with designers color. If the color crawls because of the fixative, dull the surface with a kneaded eraser, or use a plasticizing agent in the color. (See Plasticizing Agent, page 74.)

Bond paper masks are used to produce sharp, clean edges with pastels. Scraps of bond paper with straight edges are most commonly used for straight-edged shapes, but masks may also be cut for specific shapes. Stroke away from the edge of the mask so that pastel dust doesn't seep under. Adhesive-backed frisket paper may also be used for masking, but only over well-fixed areas. Since frisket paper can be cut to shape only after it is applied, care must be taken to avoid cutting through the layout paper.

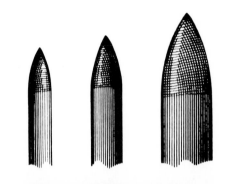

Paper stomps.

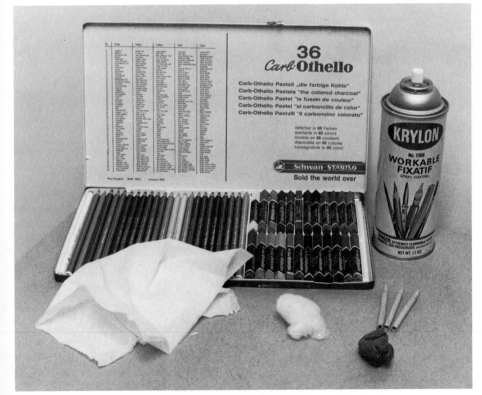

Set of pastel sticks and pencils with facial tissue, cotton wad, kneaded eraser, paper stomps, and fixative.

Color Markers. Markers are spirit-based or water-based dye in a tube or bottle with an attached applicator nib made of felt or synthetic fiber. In most brands, at least two nib sizes are available: the broad felt nib and the pointed felt or synthetic fiber nib. A superfine pointed synthetic fiber nib pen is also available in some brands. Although color markers may be purchased individually, it is advisable to purchase a basic assortment of colors in both broad and pointed nibs. Other colors can be added later as they are needed. Ask your art supply dealer for a color chart of the manufacturer so you will know the full range of colors available. Color markers are also available in sets of grays for black and white layout work.

Spirit-based dye is used in most brands of markers. It is waterproof, intense, and blends with little or no streaking. Colors can be mixed while still wet or by superpositioning when dry. Spirit-based dye will bleed through most layout papers. When working on a layout pad, therefore, always use a preliminary sketch or scrap paper under the top sheet to prevent damage to succeeding sheets in the pad. A piece of acetate cut to the size of the pad also makes a good, reusable barrier sheet. Layout pads designed especially for color markers are available. The paper is bleedproof, and is particularly receptive to color markers.

Watercolor markers are available in some brands. While they do not bleed through paper, they also do not blend as well as spirit-based markers. Being non-waterproof, however, colors can later be

Introductory set of markers.

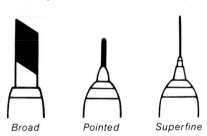

Broad   Pointed   Superfine

blended with a wet brush or swab. Watercolor markers are popular in the superfine nib style, but for broad coverage, spirit-based markers are preferred.

Color markers have largely replaced pastels and other mediums in layout work. In addition to being quick and clean, the colors accurately simulate printing ink colors. As with any other medium, however, much practice and experimentation is necessary to achieve a good layout technique. Many illustrators, incidentally, are so adept with color markers that they use them for finished art. On the other hand, while designers use color markers for layouts, they seldom use them for tightly-rendered comps and presentations. In addition to being less precise than other mediums, little or no reworking or retouching is possible, and they can't easily be combined with other mediums. As with liquid dyes, color markers will bleed through designers colors applied over them. See page 73 for the methods of overcoming this problem.

When indicating photographs or continuous-tone illustrations with color markers, first block in the main areas with light tones, then use medium tones to more firmly indicate the pictorial elements, and finally add the deepest tones. Details can later be indicated with pointed-nib markers. This method of working from light to dark tones, and from broad to detailed indication, makes it easier to correct mistakes and to control shapes. Colors can be blended while still wet, or, when dry, they can be blended with a brush or cotton swab dipped in water for watercolor markers, or rubber cement thinner for spirit-based markers. Rubber cement thinner will completely remove spirit-based dyes from non-absorbent materials, such as glossy photostats, acetate, and plastic triangles. Watercolor dyes can be completely removed from acetate and plastic, but leave a stain on glossy photostats.

For covering very large surfaces, Magic Marker makes a spray dye that matches their marker colors.

ABSORBENT COTTON

An indispensable tool in the graphic design studio, absorbent cotton can be purchased in drugstores in roll, puff, and swab form. A roll is handiest, since it can be used to make both wads and swabs. High-quality surgical cotton is necessary, because inferior qualities contain coarse fibers, lint, and other impurities that might scratch, cause smears, or leave residue.

Cotton wads are used to apply inks and dyes, to apply and/or blend pastel and charcoal, and to clean photostats and photographs. When cleaning a print prior to retouching, a cotton wad wetted with print conditioner or saliva is used. When cleaning a photostat or photograph of rubber cement specks and other particles after it has been pasted up, a cotton wad wetted with rubber cement thinner is used. The rubber cement thinner won't harm retouching.

Cotton swabs may be purchased, but most designers prefer to make their own because the size and shape of the swab can be modified to fit the job. A re-usable swab stick is made by pointing the end of an old brush with a razor blade. When a small piece of cotton is twirled on to the point, the exposed wood fibers grab the cotton fibers, thus holding the cotton in any desired shape.

Cotton swabs are used for the same purposes as cotton wads, except they are better suited for small areas. When wetted with saliva, they are very useful in photostat and photograph retouching for wiping off retouch color and ink. This is easily done without damage to the print.

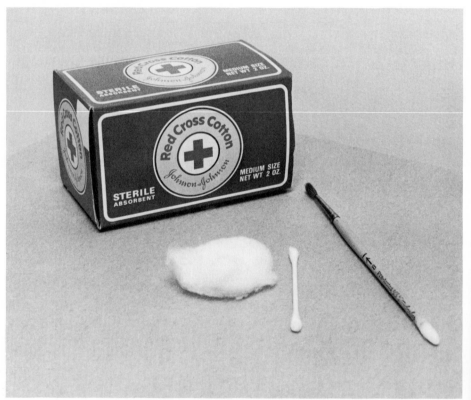

Foreground left to right: cotton wad; purchased cotton swab; handmade cotton swab.

FIXATIVES AND SPRAY COATINGS

Fixative. A thin, transparent, colorless liquid that is used to prevent dusting or smudging of graphite, charcoal, and pastel drawings and layouts. It dries to a matte finish, and the sprayed surface may be worked over in all mediums. Erasable artwork remains erasable after spraying. Fixative may also be used as a light, protective coating for other types of artwork; it doesn't alter the finish of most surfaces, and there is little if any darkening of tones. (It is always wise, of course, to make a test before spraying.) Most water-repellent surfaces become receptive to water-based color when sprayed with fixative. It is good insurance, however, to also add a plasticizing agent to the color. Fixative is available in spray cans and bottles. A mouth-type atomizer is used for spraying bottled fixative.

Acrylic Spray Coating. A transparent, colorless spray coating for paper, metal, glass, plastic, etc. It seals out dirt, water, and fumes, will not discolor, and is weatherproof. Spraying darkens matte colors, and sprayed surfaces cannot be worked over with most mediums. (A plasticizing agent, as described on page 74, will enable designer and retouch color to adhere to sprayed surfaces.)

Acrylic spray coating is available in both glossy and matte finishes. Some brands are made especially for protecting dry transfer lettering, but most general purpose products seem to be reasonably comparable for this purpose.

Dulling Spray. This is a quick-drying, easily removed spray which eliminates highlights on shiny surfaces. In photography, it serves to simplify lighting and minimize retouching.

STUDIO PAPERS AND BOARDS

Studio papers and boards are designed specifically for the preparation and presentation of artwork. This is as compared to printing papers and boards, which are designed specifically for printing and related processes of commercial reproduction. Studio papers and boards are available for so many specialized purposes in art and design that it is necessary to limit this section to only those papers and boards that are commonly used in the graphic design studio. A complete listing and description of specialized papers and boards can be found in an art supply catalog.

Tracing paper. This is a smooth, highly transparent paper that is used for all tracing purposes. It is available in various weights in rolls and pads. The heavier weights are usually referred to as tracing vellum, and are often used for ink drawings and finished lettering. Vellum is also sometimes used for color separation overlays, but it should not be used for tight register work, since it is not as dimensionally stable as acetate. A lightweight paper in 14″ x 17″ and 19″ x 24″ pads is most commonly used in graphic design work.

Layout and Visualizing Paper. This is a white, translucent paper with a slight tooth that responds well to pencil, crayon, pastel, and color markers. Available in pads in 13, 16, and 20 lb. weights. Thirteen pound paper is usually used for rough layouts, and sixteen and twenty pound paper is usually used for finished layouts. The 14″ x 17″ and 19″ x 24″ pad sizes are most commonly used in graphic design work.

Bond Paper. This is a white, opaque paper with a fine tooth that is used for finished layouts as well as finished art in most mediums. Available in pads in medium to heavy weights. The heavier weights are usually referred to as ledger bond. The 14″ x 17″ and 19″ x 24″ pad sizes are most commonly used in graphic design work.

Using Paper in Pads. Layouts and other forms of artwork are usually made directly on the pad of paper. This has a number of advantages: the pad provides a resilient working surface; previous sketches may be placed under the top sheet for tracing; and drafting tape is not needed to hold the paper in position. To keep the cover of the pad from getting in the way of the T-square, the black tape holding the cover should be pulled away from the glued-gauze binding that holds the paper in position. This will enable the cover to be folded flat under the pad. The black tape only holds the cover to the backing board; pulling it away from the gauze binding will not release the paper. Do not remove the cover entirely, since it serves to keep the paper clean between jobs.

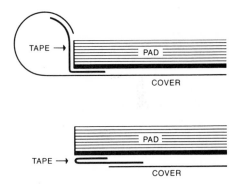

Illustration Board. White drawing paper laminated to stiff backing board. Surfaces range from smooth to very rough, and quality varies with the rag content of the face paper and the type and thickess of the backing board. Single-thick illustration board is about $1/16''$ in thickness, and double-thick illustration board is slightly less than $1/8''$ in thickness. Most brands are available in 20″ x 30″ and 30″ x 40″ sizes. Medium and rough surface board is used for all mediums, while smooth surface board is usually used only for pen and ink, air brush, and paste-up work. Illustration board is always used when large areas are to be heavily covered with a water-based medium, such as ink, designers color, or watercolor. This is because thinner paper and board will buckle when the medium is applied. (Thinner paper and board will work if it is first firmly rubber cemented to a stiff backing board.) If the artwork rendered on illustration board must later be incorporated into a paste-up or other artwork, the face paper can be stripped from the backing board by pulling one corner loose and then diagonally rolling off the face paper onto a large-diameter mailing tube. Fine sandpaper is then used on the reverse side of the face paper to remove unwanted backing board residue as well as to "feather" edges so that shadows will be minimized when the face paper is cemented onto another surface.

Bristol Board. This white drawing paper comes in various thicknesses. The thickness is achieved by laminating sheets of paper together into as many as five plies. Two finishes are available: plate (smooth) and kid (medium). The quality of bristol board depends upon its rag content. A high rag content (as least 50 percent) is necessary for pen and ink work such as lettering, since ink erasing cannot be performed on cheaper board. Available in 23″ x 29″ and 30″ x 40″ sheets as well as pads, the 23″ x 29″ sheet is most popular for graphic design work.

Almost any medium will work on bristol board, but its main use is for pen and ink. The kid finish is preferred over the plate finish for pen and ink because its slight "tooth" makes the ink flow more smoothly from most pens. Contrary to what one might expect, it produces better fine lines than the plate finish. Also, ink erasures and retouching are much less obvious than on plate finish.

Two-ply bristol is most commonly used for pen and ink work. It is thick enough to withstand average handling and erasing, and yet thin enough to see through on a tracing box.

Mat Board. This single-thick board is colored on one side and usually white on the other, with a white interior. Available in smooth, pebbled, and linen finishes in 30″ x 40″ sheets, mat board is used for matting and mounting artwork. For graphic design work, only white, gray, or black mats should be used. Colored mats interact with the colors of the artwork, thus making it impossible to envision the artwork as it will be seen after reproduction, when it doesn't have a mat. The only way to select the proper value mat is to lay the artwork on white, black, and various gray mat boards and make a visual judgment. This means, of course, that it is necessary to have a variety of mat boards on hand in the studio.

Stippled Drawing Board. A deeply textured white board that is available in many stipple patterns. By using a dense black pencil or crayon, or a sparsely-loaded brush (drybrush), a variety of tones can be obtained. Since these tones are actually composed of tiny black and white shapes, the drawing can be reproduced as line copy. Solid blacks can be made with ink, and highlights can be made by scratching, or with white paint. Ross and Coquille board are popular brands.

Invisible-tone Drawing Board. This is white, 3-ply bristol board on which are printed two invisible shading screens, one light and one dark. Many patterns are available. Special chemicals (supplied with the board) are applied by pen or brush to develop the tones. The resulting toned drawing can be reproduced as line art.

Scratchboard. This is a white board coated with clay or whiting. India ink is applied to the board and then scratched away with a special scratchboard knife or needle, thus exposing the white coating. Scratchboard illustrations are very sharp and brilliant, and reproduce particularly well in newspapers.

Mounting Board. An inexpensive board, white-faced on both sides, for mounting photographs and artwork. It is available in various weights in sheets from 22″ x 28″ to 40″ x 60″. Since the face paper is inferior to drawing paper, it is not suitable for rendering artwork. It can be used, however, for show card work.

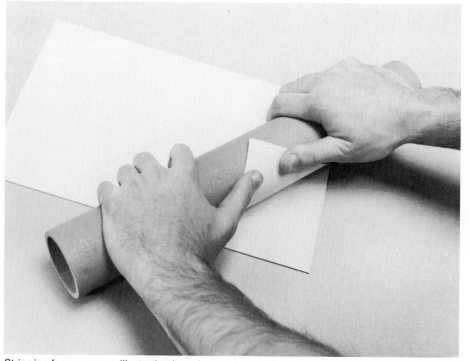

Stripping face paper on illustration board.

Chipboard (Newsboard). A heavy, gray board that is identical to the backing board in pads of paper. It is available in two weights in 30″ x 40″ sheets. It is used for mounting, and also makes an excellent working surface for the drawing board.

Foam Core Board. This is a ³⁄₁₆″ thick board with a foam center and faced on both sides with white paper. It is very light, very stiff, and resists warping, but at the same time is very easy to cut. It is available in 30″ x 40″ and 40″ x 60″ sheets, and is used for mounting, cut-outs, and other display purposes.

Poster (Show Card) Board. A smooth, matte finish board that is similar in weight to single-thick mat board. It is available in many colors (one side only) in 28″ x 44″ sheets, and is used for posters, signs, and show cards. It is not commonly used in graphic design work. Railroad board is similar to poster board, but it is thinner, colored on both sides, and measures 22″ x 28″.

Text and Cover Papers. These printing papers are used in graphic design for making comps and dummies, and for flapping artwork. They are available at art supply stores in 20″ x 26″ sheets in many textures, colors, and weights. Cover papers are heavier than text papers. Smooth, black cover paper (and also black bristol) is commonly used for making negative paste-ups of photostats.

Printing Papers. Printing papers (which include the text and cover papers listed above) are available in hundreds of weights, colors, and textures. They are sometimes used for making comps and dummies, and may be acquired in single sheets from paper merchants or printers. Some paper companies, such as Champion, have kits containing large sheets of many of their printing papers, which are available at low cost to designers.

Construction Paper. An inexpensive, soft, medium-weight paper that is available in white, black, and limited colors. The paper is inferior and the colors eventually fade. There is little if any use for this paper in graphic design work.

Color-coated Papers. Thin, white paper that has been coated on one side with ink or paint. Color-Aid and Color-Vu papers are medium priced and available in 18″ x 24″ sheets in more than 200 colors. Cello-tak opaque papers are also medium priced, and are available in 20″ x 26″ sheets in 229 standard printing ink colors, with or without low-tack adhesive backing. Aurora papers are less expensive, and are available in basic colors in 18″ x 24″ sheets and 36″ wide rolls. Pantone papers are the most expensive, and are available in 20″ x 26″ sheets in 500 colors that can be accurately matched in printing inks through the use of the Pantone Matching System. Color-coated papers are also available in many colors in 80″ and 107″ wide rolls. Although this very wide paper can be used for graphic design purposes, its major use is for photographic backgrounds.

Rubber cement may stain color-coated papers, particularly dark colors. Test a scrap of the paper to be cemented, and if it stains, apply cement only to the mounting area, not beyond. Erasing will shine and darken color-coated papers. The only guidelines that should be used, therefore, are those that will be covered by paint or paper.

Flint paper is an ink-coated (not paint-coated) glossy finish paper that is used for package dummies and other graphic design applications. It is available in basic colors in 20″ x 26″ sheets.

Swatch books may be purchased for Color-Aid, Color-Vu, Cello-tak, and Pantone papers. For brands of color-coated papers in basic colors, color charts are usually available at no charge.

Frisket Paper. This thin, transparent paper or film comes in sheets and rolls and is used for masking artwork prior to applying a color medium by brush, air brush, stipple brush, or sponge. It may also be used with pastels if previously applied pastel has been sprayed with matte fixative. Frisket paper is available with and without wax adhesive backing. The adhesive-backed paper is only mildly tacky, and can be removed without damage to the artwork and without leaving

adhesive residue. If any residue remains, it can be removed with a rubber cement pickup or rubber cement thinner on a cotton wad or swab. Non-adhesive frisket paper must be coated with rubber cement before use. Since this is not easy to do properly, most designers use adhesive-backed paper.

Frisket paper is applied in the same way as color film. Cut a larger piece than required from the sheet, but do not cut through the protective backing paper. Peel off the frisket paper (using a knife to lift a corner) and apply to the artwork. Press firmly on the artwork, cut to the desired shape with a very sharp frisket knife (don't cut into the artwork), and remove the surplus paper. Do not burnish the frisket paper as firmly as for color film, since this would make it difficult to remove later. If the frisket paper cannot be removed easily, the wax adhesive can be softened with rubber cement thinner.

A liquid frisket is available in bottles for application by brush, pen, or ruling pen. It is difficult to use since it becomes waterproof when dry, but it is very handy for small areas or intricate shapes that can't easily be cut from frisket paper. It can be used in conjunction with frisket paper, either to add details or to correct mistakes in cutting. Use an old brush for applying liquid frisket because it damages the bristles.

If a non-adhering frisket or mask is needed, use bond or stencil paper. Stencil paper is a heavy, easily-cut paper that withstands moisture and rough handling.

Transfer Paper. This is a thin paper in sheets or rolls that is coated with graphite or colors. It is used as an interlay to transfer drawings from tracing, layout, or bond paper to bristol or illustration board with a hard, sharp pencil. Carbon transfer paper is available in black, white, and basic colors, but it produces greasy lines that cannot be erased or covered with paint. Graphite transfer paper and Saral Transfer Paper (a brand of transfer paper available in graphite, white, and basic colors) produce grease-free lines that can be erased easily.

Some designers make their own graphite transfer paper by using a broad-lead pencil and a sandpaper pad or machinist's file to cover a sheet of tracing paper with powdered graphite, then smoothing and adhering the graphite with a wad of cotton saturated with rubber cement thinner.

ACETATE AND FILMS

Acetate. Non-flammable cellulose acetate comes in sheets, rolls, and pads. It is available in many thicknesses, but the 3 mil and 5 mil (.003″ and .005″) thicknesses are most commonly used for overlays and other graphic design purposes. Three surfaces are available: clear, matte (or frosted), and prepared (or pre-fixed). The only mediums that will not crawl, chip, or peel on clear acetate are acetate paints and inks. Opaque watercolors may also be used if a plasticizing agent such as Flex-Opaque has been added to the paint. Matte acetate will accept any medium, and is therefore commonly used for color separation overlays. Prepared acetate is clear acetate that has been specially prepared to accept any medium. It is used for color separation overlays, as well as for any application where the frosted surface of matte acetate is objectionable. Since the surface of prepared acetate is slightly gummy, always use a scrap of paper under the drawing hand to avoid damaging it. Even though frosted and prepared acetate will accept any medium, heavy paint may chip off because of the flexibility of the acetate. Therefore, it is wise to use a plasticizing agent when applying paint to any type of acetate.

A very thin, clear acetate (often called cellophane) is available in rolls for protecting artwork. It comes in several weights, the #150 weight being most popular. If the artwork is on stiff board, the acetate is wrapped around it and stretched tightly on the back, using small pieces of tape approximately every inch to adhere it to the board. If it is not possible to wrap the artwork, attach the acetate behind the opening of the mat, pulling it tight and taping it in the same way as for wrapping. Thin acetate is much better than thick acetate for protecting artwork. In addition to being much less expensive, it can be stretched tightly, thus eliminating the wavy reflections that make thicker acetate so difficult to see through.

A trick for stretching very thin acetate as tight as a drum is to lay the acetate on dampened newspaper or blotting paper when wrapping the artwork. When the moisture later evaporates, the acetate will shrink. Do not stretch the acetate too tightly when it has been dampened or it will either bend the artwork or burst when it shrinks.

Color Film. Transparent color printed on acetate film that is backed with low-tack adhesive. Available in various-sized sheets in hundreds of colors, color film is primarily used for comps and presentations, although black and ruby red (which is transparent, yet photographs as opaque are also used for mechanicals. Matte and glossy surfaces are available in color film, and the matte surface is receptive to all mediums. Colors can be removed by scraping, erasing, or solvent. Rubbing alcohol works with most brands, but some may require a special solvent. A special cutting needle and burnisher are desirable for cutting and burnishing color film.

In using color film, cut a piece larger than required from the sheet, but do not cut through the protective backing paper. Peel off the film (using a knife to lift a corner) and apply to the artwork. Press firmly on the artwork, cut to the desired shape with a frisket knife or cutting needle, and remove the surplus film. Finally, place a sheet of paper over the film for protection, and burnish evenly and smoothly. Be careful not to scratch the film. Since the film is transparent, two overlapping colors will produce a third color. If a third color is not wanted, the two films must be very carefully butted. The technique for butting and insetting is described on page 92.

When applying full sheets, separate about 1″ of film from the backing sheet, fold the backing sheet at that point, and attach the exposed edge of film to the artwork. Hold the edge of the attached film firmly, and slowly pull off the backing sheet, progressively smoothing and adhering the film. The artwork should be firmly attached to the drawing board so that both hands will be free for pulling and smoothing.

Bourges (brand) color film can be used in the same way as other brands, but it can also be used to produce multicolor illustrations by means of color-separated overlays. The film is available in standard printing ink colors and tints, with and without adhesive backing. The color coating can be removed by stylus or by solvent. When the overlays are placed over one another, the illustrator can see exactly what the colors will look like when overprinted in reproduction. (See Process Color Printing, page 39.)

Bourges also make Solotone, which is a translucent film for lightening or darkening the backgrounds of photographs. The film coating is removable, and is available in numerous values of gray and white.

Shading Film. Screen tints printed on acetate film that is backed with low-tack adhesive. Shading film, which is identical in manufacture and application to color film, is primarily used for applying screen tints to finished art for reproduction, and is therefore only available in black and white. An exception to this is the Pantone Screen/Dot Tint Shading Film, which is available in many colors and is used with Pantone Solid Color Overlay Film on comps and dummies to accurately simulate color effects in printing.

Screen tints applied during the plate-making process are generally superior to screen tints applied to the artwork with shading film because they are sharper, and are available in finer screens. For many applications, however, shading film is not only adequate in regard to sharpness and fineness, it is less expensive, and permits re-working by the designer.

Alphabet, Symbol, and Pattern Film. Low-tack, adhesive-backed acetate film identical to color and shading film in manufacture and application. Available in black and white in a great variety of typefaces, symbols, and patterns, these films are primarily used for finished art for reproduction. Adhesive-backed film is often preferred to dry transfer film for lettering on finished art because the letters can be adjusted for perfect alignment and spacing before they are fully adhered by burnishing. The surrounding pieces of film, however, make this product unsatisfactory for comps, dummies, and presentations.

Dry Transfer Film. This is acetate film backed with typeface alphabets, symbols, or patterns that can be transferred to another surface by rubbing with a ballpoint pen or similar stylus tool. All dry transfer products are available in black and white, and some typefaces are also available in basic colors.

Custom-made dry transfer line art can be made in the studio with the 3M I.N.T. system. I.N.T. sheets are available in many colors, and are processed in normal room light (see Super Comps, page 111).

Shading film being applied to a line drawing (Formatt).

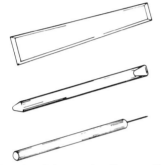

Zipatone burnishers and cutting needle.

A few of the hundreds of screen tints and patterns available in shading and pattern film (Zipatone).

Letter being cut and lifted from a sheet of alphabet film (Formatt).

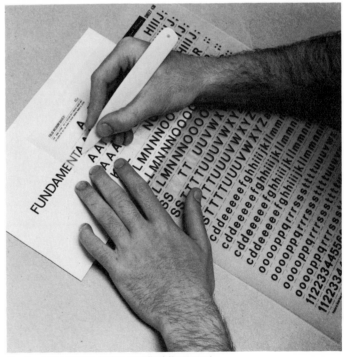

Dry transfer letters being applied (Letraset).

Basic Studio Techniques

ENLARGING AND REDUCING

Diagonal-line Scaling. A simple, fairly accurate method for scaling the outside dimensions of photographs and artwork. Tape a piece of tracing paper over the photograph or artwork, draw a rectangle at the outside dimensions of the area to be enlarged or reduced (using a T-square, triangle, and sharp pencil), and draw a line through diagonal corners of the rectangle. Measuring from either diagonal corner, then, any new size rectangle whose horizontal and vertical lines intersect on this diagonal line will be in exact proportion to the original rectangle.

Arithmetical Scaling. The equation for proportion is "a is to b as c is to d," which is written "a:b::c:d." Both dimensions of the original rectangle a/b are known, and only the c dimension of the new rectangle c/d is known. To find the unknown dimension d, the solution is performed in the following manner:

$$a:b::c:d$$
$$ad = bc$$
$$d = \frac{bc}{a}$$

For example, if rectangle a/b is 4"/8", and rectangle c/d is 2"/?, the equation would be solved thus:

$$4:8::2:d$$
$$4d = 16$$
$$d = \frac{16}{4}$$
$$d = 4$$

By always using d as the unknown number, only this one formula needs to be remembered. If the height of the new rectangle is unknown, then a/c should represent width and b/d should represent height. If the width of the new rectangle is unknown, then a/c should represent height, and b/d should represent width.

Grid Scaling. If the details of a photograph or artwork must be rendered in larger or smaller scale, the best methods are by camera lucida, Lacey-Luci projector, or photostat (these methods are described later in this section). A fairly satisfactory alternative to these methods is the grid scaling method. In fact, for very large reductions or enlargements, grid scaling might even be preferable, since the other methods are limited in amount of reduction or enlargement. The procedure for grid scaling is to first determine the outside dimensions of the photograph or artwork by using the diagonal-line scaling method as described previously, and then draw a grid on the tracing paper overlay covering the original copy, and a similarly-proportioned grid on the resized drawing. With such a proportionately scaled grid, it is then easy to convert details from one size to another.

To make proportionately scaled grids without measuring, draw a diagonal line opposite to the one that already exists, and then draw horizontal and vertical lines at their intersection, thus dividing the box into 4 equal boxes. Repeat this process in each of the 4 boxes, thus dividing the box into 16 equal boxes. A 16-box grid is usually adequate, but it may be further divided by the same process if desired.

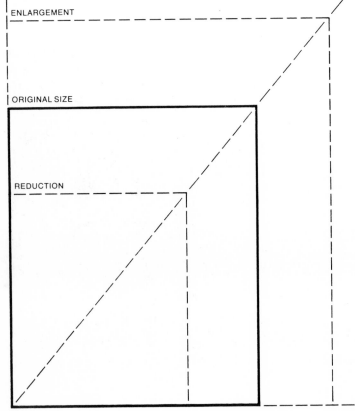

ENLARGEMENT

ORIGINAL SIZE

REDUCTION

Diagonal-line scaling

16-box grid.

Pantograph. This is an inexpensive wood or metal device comprised of four crisscrossed arms, a tracing point, a pencil point, and an attaching bracket. The bracket is attached to the drawing board and the arms are adjusted to the desired setting of enlargement or reduction. As the tracing point is guided over the original copy, the pencil point draws the same shapes in larger or smaller proportion on the drawing paper. The hand holds the pencil point, guiding the tracing point by remote control.

The pantograph is awkward to use, takes time to assemble and disassemble, and is limited to predetermined settings of enlargement and reduction. For these reasons, the pantograph is not commonly used by graphic designers. If a camera lucida or other art projector is not available, most designers use the grid method for rough scaling, and photostats for accurate scaling.

Camera Lucida. This is an optical device comprised of a prismatic viewer, a long, adjustable arm, and a clamp. The original copy is taped or pinned to a wall or vertical surface, and the drawing paper is placed on a small table in front of the original copy. The camera lucida is clamped onto the side of the table top and adjusted so when looking down through the prism, both the original copy and the drawing paper can be seen. The eyes combine these two views, and it appears that the original copy is projected on to the drawing paper. By maintaining this double view, the "projected" image can be traced on to the drawing paper. The image can be enlarged or reduced by adjusting the distances between the original copy, the prism, and the drawing paper. A set of lenses is provided for sharp focusing at various distances. In addition to copying graphic work, the camera lucida can be used to copy 3-dimensional objects and views, such as packages, furniture, interiors, and landscapes.

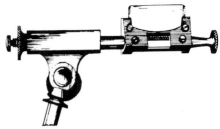
Camera lucida prismatic viewer.

The camera lucida is compact, portable, and reasonably accurate once the ability to see two views simultaneously has been mastered. A good-quality camera lucida is expensive, but not nearly as expensive as an art projector of the Lacey-Luci type. It is therefore commonly used by small studios that need an enlarging/reducing device, but can't afford a very expensive one.

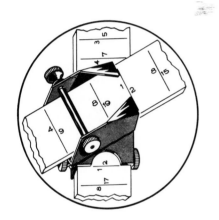

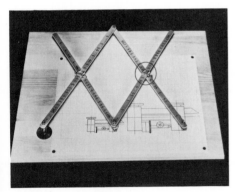
Pantograph with detail of adjusting device (Anco).

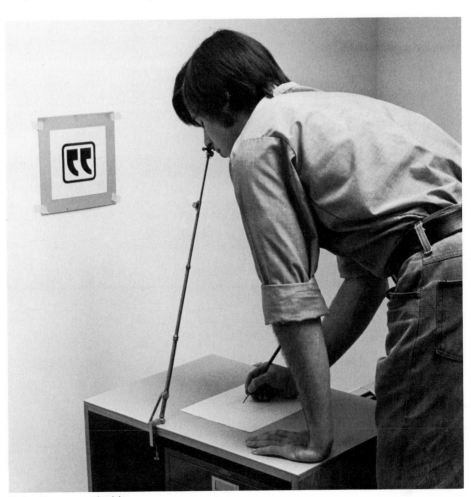
Using the camera lucida.

Lacey-Luci Projector. This brand of art projector has become the generic name for all art projectors of the same type. The Lacey-Luci is comprised of an illuminated copy board that holds the original copy, and a lens and bellows that projects the image of the original copy through the rear of a ground-glass drawing surface. Since the projected image must penetrate the drawing paper, only tracing or other fairly transparent paper can be used. Two knobs or cranks control the size and focus of the projected image.

Another type of Lacey-Luci is the direct projector. Rather than projecting the image through the back of a ground-glass drawing surface, it projects directly on to the front of the drawing paper or board. This is a popular model with illustrators, since it permits work to be copied directly on to illustration board. It is generally larger than rear projection models, however, and the hand and pencil must be kept out of the way of the projected light rays.

The Lacey-Luci can be used to project opaque copy, transparencies, and 3-dimensional objects. Some models can also be used to make photographic prints and photostats.

The Lacey-Luci is the fastest, most accurate, and easiest-to-use device for enlarging and reducing. Even the cheapest model, however, costs many hundreds of dollars, and it is therefore usually too expensive for the one-man studio.

Goodkin Model A projector.

Opaque Projector. A device for projecting opaque copy on to a screen or wall. Depending on the model, copy from 4″ to 10″ square can be projected at one time, and larger copy can be projected in sections. The opaque projector is good for giant blowups, but it is not practical for general graphic design work because it doesn't reduce, and because it must be used in a darkened room. If there is only an occasional need for a giant blowup, it is often possible to photograph the copy on to a slide and project it with a regular slide projector.

Photostats. If the work to be enlarged or reduced is intricate, or if great accuracy is desirable, a photostat is preferable to a Lacey-Luci or camera lucida drawing. For example, since finished lettering, symbols, and illustrations are almost always rendered larger than reproduction size, it is often advantageous to work from an enlarged photostat of the comp or layout. This is particularly the case with a very well-rendered comp, which can be converted into finished art with less effort if no loss of accuracy occurs during the enlarging process.

When a photostat is used merely as a method for enlarging or reducing, and not as finished art in itself, a matte print is preferred. Not only is it cheaper than a glossy print, it holds tonal gradations better. Only a negative print is usually required, since the original copy can be used to match tones and/or "color." (See the section on Photostats, page 138.)

Proportional Divider. A proportioning instrument that is comprised of two metal bars with points on both ends, a knurled adjusting screw, and a ratio scale. When the adjusting screw is set at the desired ratio of enlargement/reduction, any measurement taken at one end of the divider is proportionately enlarged or reduced at the other end. The proportional divider is very useful for scaling measurements, but has little or no value for scaling and drawing non-mechanical shapes. Since it is a fairly expensive instrument, and since it can only be used for measuring, it is not commonly employed in graphic design work.

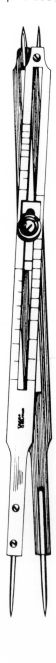

Circular Proportional Scale. This is an inexpensive plastic device comprised of two rotating disks, one smaller than the other. On the smaller disk is a scale for the measurements of the original copy, and on the larger disk is a scale for the measurements of the enlarged or reduced reproduction. The smaller disk also contains a window that shows the enlargement or reduction by percentage ratio, and the number of times of reduction.

The use of the proportional scale is simple. If a photograph is to be reduced in width from 8″ to 6″, align 8″ on the "original" scale with 6″ on the "reproduction" scale. This setting is then used to convert all other measurements in the same ratio. For example, if the original photograph is 10″ in height, the reproduction will be 7½″ in height.

The percentage scale is used to make settings on platemaking and photostat cameras. Given the above reduction of 8″ to 6″, the camera operator would set the proportional scale as described previously, and then refer to the percentage scale for the proper camera setting, which in this case is 75 percent (6″ is 75 percent of 8″). To save money, designers often make use of the percentage scale for ordering photostats, as well as for scaling photographs and artwork for halftone plates. If a number of pieces are found, by percentage, to be the same or very close in ratio of enlargement or reduction, if is often possible to adjust their sizes so that they can all be shot at the same ratio. For example, ratios of 73, 74, 75, 76, and 77 percent might all be shot at 75 percent. In the case of photostats, all same-ratio pieces must be taped on to one sheet and marked by percentage so one print can be made. In the case of photographs and artwork for halftone plates, same-ratio pieces should be individually marked by percentage and then grouped together with a notation to the platemaker that they are all "same-focus."

Architects and Engineers Scale Rules. These rules are described in the section on T-squares, triangles, rulers, and scales, page 58. The architects scale rule is used for architectural drawings as well as for exhibit and display drawings. The engineers scale rule is primarily used for map drawings, but it is also used wherever it is desirable to work in decimal parts to the inch rather than fractions of an inch.

Scaleograph. The brand name for a scaling and cropping device. Since this device is used primarily for scaling and cropping photographs and other forms of continuous-tone copy, it is described in that chapter on page 150.

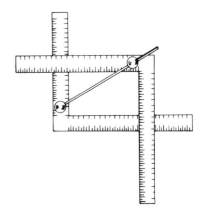

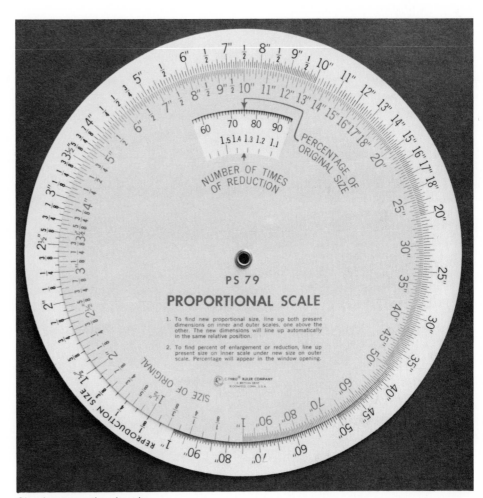

Circular proportional scale.

RULING

The everyday ruler with which we are all familiar combines the functions of ruling and measuring. In graphic design work, however, the measuring tool is not usually used as a straightedge for ruling. This is because the graduated lines would eventually become indistinct by the constant rubbing of pens and pencils, thus reducing the measuring accuracy of the tool. Also, since the graduated lines on a good-quality ruler or scale are incised, they create a serrated edge that will not produce a perfect line. For straight-line ruling, a T-square and/or triangle should always be used. Properly employed, they provide the greatest accuracy and speed.

Using the T-square. The various types of T-squares are described on page 58. As used by a right-handed person, the head of the T-square is hooked firmly over the left edge of the drawing board with the left hand, and the top edge of the T-square blade is used as a guide to horizontally align the artwork on the drawing board. The artwork is then fastened to the drawing board with tape or pins. As the T-square head is subsequently moved up or down along the edge of the drawing board, the blade will always be in exact horizontal alignment on the artwork. (This presupposes, of course, that the head is firmly hooked on the edge of the drawing board, and that the edge of the drawing board is perfectly straight.)

After the blade is positioned, it is usually necessary to move the left hand to the center of the blade so it will not shift when ruling pressure is applied. Hold the blade with the right hand during this movement to avoid shifting the T-square. Then, with the head firmly hooked on the edge of the drawing board, and the blade firmly held by the left hand, the line is ruled with the right hand. This may sound like a slow, complicated procedure, but with practice it becomes both rapid and automatic. Do not avoid learning it, since it is the primary operation at the drawing board.

Using the Triangle. The various types of triangles are described on page 58. The triangle is used for ruling vertical lines as well as other angles. Do not attempt to rule vertical lines by placing the T-square head at the top or bottom of the drawing board. While individual sides of the drawing board may be straight, they are seldom in square with each other. And even when they check out to be square, they will remain so only until the next change in humidity.

Vertical lines are ruled by setting the base of a triangle along the top edge of the T-square blade. For right-handers, the 90° angle of the triangle should be to the left. This permits the pen or pencil to run more naturally along the raised edge of the triangle, thus producing a better line. Also, when using a pen it minimizes the possibility of ink running under the triangle. Both the T-square blade and the triangle are held in alignment with the left hand, some fingers holding the blade and some holding the triangle. By moving only the triangle-holding fingers, the triangle may be shifted back or forth for exact positioning.

When ruling angles other than 90°, the desired angle of the triangle may not be on the left. If it is not, shift the body and hands so the ruling instrument runs naturally along the raised edge of the triangle.

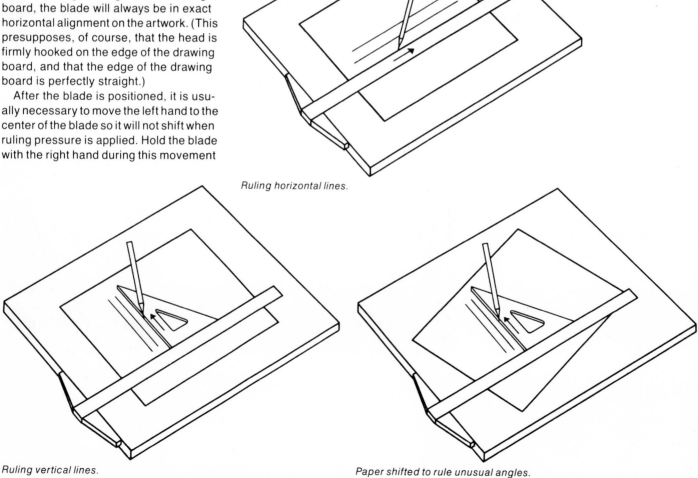

Ruling horizontal lines.

Ruling vertical lines.

Paper shifted to rule unusual angles.

As described on page 58, the standard triangles are 45° and 30°/60°, and can be combined to also make 15° and 75° angles. An adjustable triangle or protractor is necessary for other angles. When an unusual angle is to be repeated in a drawing, and an adjustable triangle is not available, first determine the angle by protractor or other means, and then reposition the artwork on the drawing board, lining up the angle with the normally-positioned T-square and triangle. By sliding the triangle along the T-square blade, the angle can be repeated. This is a commonly used technique for ruling italic guidelines in lettering. If it is not possible or desirable to reposition the artwork, then merely slant the T-square. Not being hooked to the edge of the drawing board, however, it must be held very firmly to avoid slippage.

Using Irregular Curves. As described on page 59, irregular curves are used to draw mechancial curves other than circles or arcs of circles. When used in technical drawing, the shape of the curve is usually first geometrically plotted with a succession of points, and the curve templates are then used to connect the points. When used in graphic design, the shape of the curve is usually first lightly sketched freehand, and the curve templates are then used as a ruling guide for the pencil and/or pen.

Since curve templates seldom conform entirely to the curve being drawn, various segments of the templates must usually be combined. When drawing symmetrical

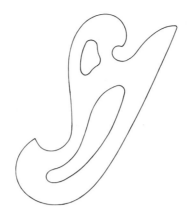

shapes, such as ellipses, the same segment of the template must be employed on all similar curves. Also, segments employed in the pencil drawing must also be employed in the ink drawing. To do this, mark the template segment with a china (wax) marker or a pointed color marker. The wax or dye can later be removed with a facial tissue moistened with rubber cement thinner. Pencil can also be used if the template is first rubbed with a hard eraser.

When combining segments of curves, the template should match the curve being drawn for some distance beyond both ends of the segment actually employed. This insures against abrupt changes in curvature where the segments join.

Irregular curves are difficult to use, and there is frequently some retouching necessary where segments join. This is still easier, however, than attempting to draw such shapes entirely freehand.

General Ruling Procedure. Always rule horizontal lines from left to right, and vertical lines from bottom to top. (Left-handers should reverse the horizontal procedure but not the vertical procedure.) Hold the ruling instrument vertically in side view, and tip it forward in the direction of the stroke. About 60° from the paper is the usual slant for straight lines, and about 75° to 85° is the usual slant for curved lines. (The only exception to this is the tube-feed pen, which must be vertical in both elevations.) Grasp the instrument lightly, with the tips of the thumb and forefinger about 1½″ from the point, and the tip of the second finger about ¾″ from the point. One or both of the small fingers should ride lightly along the ruling guide. Never grasp the instrument too tightly or too close to the point, and never press the instrument too firmly against the ruling guide. Any of these actions will result in uneven or crooked lines.

Pencil Ruling. When drawing accurate guidelines and construction lines on tracing or layout paper, a 4H, 5H, or 6H pencil is usually used. It maintains a sharp point, and is light enough to not interfere visually with the subsequent drawing. Such a hard pencil should not be used directly on finished art, however, because it can too easily score the drawing surface. For finished art on bristol or illustration board, therefore, guidelines and construction lines should be drawn with nothing harder than a 2H or 3H pencil.

Pen Ruling. Various types of pens can be used for ruling. The choice depends on the medium, the paper surface, the ruling guide, and the quality of line desired. Following is a list of the most commonly used pens and their applications. They are fully described in the section on Studio Equipment and Material. The page on which they are described is indicated in parentheses.

Ruling Pen (page 62). The ruling pen can be used with ink, dye, designers color, retouch color, and other similar liquid mediums. Also, it can be adjusted to any line width. For these reasons, it is the most commonly used pen for ruling lines. The only disadvantage to the ruling pen is that it is difficult to use with templates.

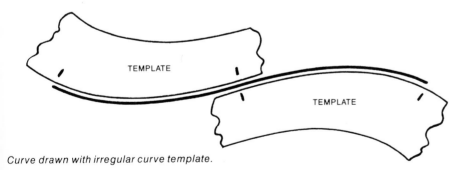

TEMPLATE

TEMPLATE

Curve drawn with irregular curve template.

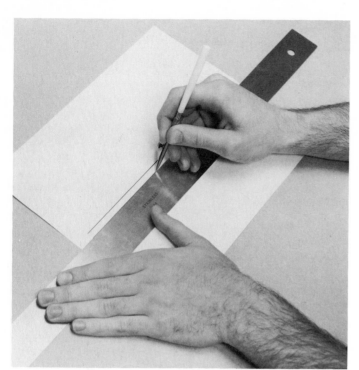

Ruling with a ruling pen and T-square.

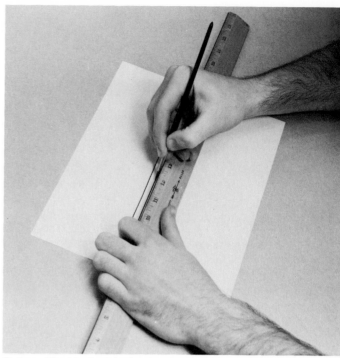

Ruling with a brush and ruler.

Tube-feed Pens (page 55). Most technical fountain pens and all scriber lettering pens are of tube-feed design. Only ink can be used in these pens, and line widths are limited to the point sizes available. Since the line width of a tube-feed pen remains constant in every direction, it is ideal for use with irregular curves, ellipses, and other templates.

Drawing Pens (page 54). Whatever drawing pen was employed for the freehand portions of an illustration or lettering design should also be employed for the ruled portions. Every type of pen has a distinctive line quality, and it is important that this quality be consistent throughout the drawing. Only a steel T-square should be used for ruling with drawing pens. The beveled undercut of the blade insures against ink run-under, and the perfectly smooth edge of the blade insures against pen snagging, which is a particular problem with very flexible split-nib pens. To rule vertical and slanted lines, therefore, the artwork must be turned so that they line up with the normally-positioned T-square.

Brush Ruling. Brush ruling is desirable for brush-rendered illustrations, as well as for glossy photographs and other surfaces that are not receptive to pen ruling. It is particularly useful when silhouetting straight shapes on a photograph. The ruling guide must be stiff and narrow, such as a sturdy wood ruler. The ruler is grasped in the left hand so the fingers are on the back, and the palm and thumb are on the front. When the ruler is positioned, the fingers rest on the drawing surface, holding the ruling edge about ¾″ above the surface. The thumb and heel of the hand rest on the lower front edge of the ruler as well as on the drawing surface.

The brush is grasped in the right hand so the tips of the index finger and thumb are about 2″ above the point, and the tip of the second finger is about 1″ above the point. The ferrule of the brush is placed against the ruling edge, and the nails of the second, third, and fourth fingers ride along the front of the ruler. There are many variations to this technique, and whichever provides the maximum control should be employed.

When ruling the line, use a steady, smooth motion and an even pressure. The width of the line is adjusted by the distance that the brush extends beyond the fingers, and the pressure of the fingers on the ruler.

Ruling Lines with Ink and other Liquid Mediums. If the medium tends to run under the ruling guide even when the pen is positioned correctly, raise the guide above the surface of the paper with a piece of blotter or cardboard. Some designers permanently tape a strip of bristol board to the underside of frequently-used triangles. (The blade of the steel T-square is beveled on its underside to avoid run-under.)

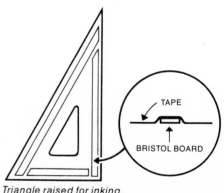

Triangle raised for inking.

If the line must be wider than the maximum width line of the pen, build it up with more than one stroke. Very heavy lines can be outlined and later filled in with a Speedball pen, drawing pen, or brush. Make the outlines heavy enough for easy filling-in.

Heavy line outlined and then filled in.

Because the line widths of most types of pens are affected by the speed of movement, always rule with a steady motion, avoiding slow starts and stops. Also, start ruling as soon as the pen touches the paper, and lift the pen as soon as the line is completed.

Intersecting Lines. When ruling intersecting lines, all previous lines must be dry. Otherwise, the intersection will be blobby. Ink tends to bleed into intersecting lines, even when the previously drawn lines are dry. This is obviously no problem when all lines are black, but it is a problem when some lines are in color, such as red and blue lines on a mechanical. To avoid the problem, rule the black lines first, the red lines next, and the blue lines last. If the red or blue bleeds into the black, then, it will not be visible. And if the blue bleeds into the red, it may darken the red but it won't affect reproduction.

When lines end at an intersection, as with a box shape, it is very difficult to make the lines end exactly at the corner. Also, because the pen movement may be slower near the intersection, the lines may get wider. The solution to this problem is to rule the lines beyond the intersection and later trim them off with retouch white and a brush. This technique should be used for mechanicals and other finished art for reproduction. It is not usually used for comps, however, because the retouching would be more objectionable than imperfect corners.

Lines rules beyond intersection.

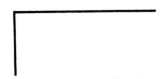

Intersection trimmed with white paint.

Dash Lines. On comps, a dash line is made by simply drawing a series of dashes with the pen. Such a line, however, is not accurate enough for finished art; the dashes are uneven in length, and their ends are not sharp. For finished art, the dash line is made by first drawing a continuous line of the desired weight, and then breaking it into dashes with retouch white and a brush.

The length of the dashes are ticked off lightly in pencil, using a ruler or divider for measuring. When determining the distance between tick marks, keep in mind that this distance includes the length of the dash as well as the width of the line break. Start the tick marks from both ends of the line, and if they don't coincide at the center, adjust the distances in the central area by eye. Slightly different lengths of dashes at the center of the line are usually not noticeable.

The width of the line breaks are judged by eye, and should be fairly consistent throughout the line. If adjustment is necessary, it is better to adjust the length of the dash rather than the width of the line break. When forming a corner with dashes, the corner dashes should join, and should be equal in length to nearby dashes.

Some designers break a line into dashes entirely by eye, but this is a procedure that requires a good amount of experience.

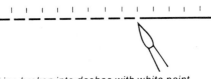

Dashes ruled with pen.

Line broken into dashes with white paint.

Corner formed with dashes.

Rounded Corners. Rounded corners can be made with an ink compass, or with a circle template and a tube-feed pen, such as a Rapidograph. A compass is preferable when the straight lines are to be ruled with a ruling pen, and a circle template is preferable when the straight lines are to be ruled with a tube-feed pen.

Draw the entire shape carefully in pencil. If a compass is being used, bisect the corners with a light pencil line (for right-angle or 90° corners, use a 45° triangle), so the pivot point of the compass can be accurately positioned.

In the final rendering in ink or other medium, rule the corners first. Then rule the straight lines, connecting the straight lines to the curved lines even if it is necessary to deviate slightly from the pencil drawing. A slight deviation will usually not be noticeable. A noticeable deviation, of course, means that the shape must be entirely re-drawn. This is still easier, however, than attempting to correct a misaligned junction.

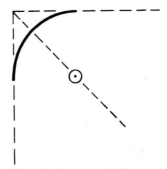

Rounded corner ruled first.

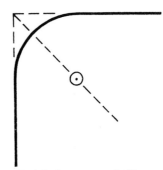

Straight lines connected to rounded corner.

DIVIDING DISTANCES INTO EQUAL PARTS

If a distance can easily be divided into equal parts with a ruler, then that is usually the simplest method to use. For example, if a distance of 8½" is divided into 4 equal parts, each part would measure 2⅛". This is not difficult to calculate or to measure, since all measurements coincide with ruler divisions. If a distance and/or its divisions do not coincide with ruler divisions, then it is necessary to use one of the following methods.

Divider Method. As described on page 62, the divider is used for dividing distances into equal parts, as well as for transferring measurements from one location to another. Dividing is done by trial and error. The divider is adjusted by eye to the approximate width of one division, and then "walked" across the total distance by lifting and pivoting one leg at a time. The knurled top is grasped between the thumb and forefinger, and the pivot movements should alternate from clockwise to counterclockwise so that the thumb and forefinger do not have to be periodically re-positioned. Hold the divider very lightly, and don't puncture the paper surface.

After the entire distance has been stepped off, the difference between the last divider point and the total distance is used as a guide for adjusting the divider for the next trial run. For example, if the last divider point falls short of the total distance, and if there are five divisions involved, expand the divider, by eye, to one fifth of the distance. Continue making trial runs and adjustments until the divisions are perfect, and then mark the divisions with a hard, sharp pencil.

If the divisions are even in number, first divide the total distance in half. If the divisions within the half distance are also even in number, then divide them in half, and so forth. For example, when dividing a distance into eight equal parts, divide it first into halves, then quarters, and then eights. Dividing a distance into halves, and halves again, is easier than dividing it all at once into quarters, eighths, etc.

Diagonal Ruler Method. When dividing a horizontal line into equal parts, first draw a vertical guide line at the right end of the horizontal line. Then place the 0" mark of a ruler at the left end of the horizontal line, and pivot the ruler so that the desired number of ruler divisions align with the vertical guide line. For example, if a 5" horizontal line is to be divided into six equal parts, align the 6" mark on the ruler with the vertical guide line. Similarly, if a 2½" horizontal line is to be divided into six equal parts, align the 3" mark on the ruler with the vertical guide line. In other words, use any ruler measurement that can be divided equally into the desired number of parts, and that extends from the left end of the horizontal line to some point on the right vertical line.

After the ruler has been positioned, mark the division points with tick marks, and extend the marks to the horizontal line, using a T-square and triangle.

The same basic procedure is used for dividing vertical lines, as well as for dividing vertical and horizontal areas.

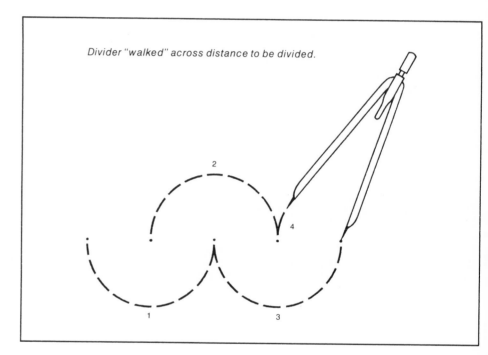

Divider "walked" across distance to be divided.

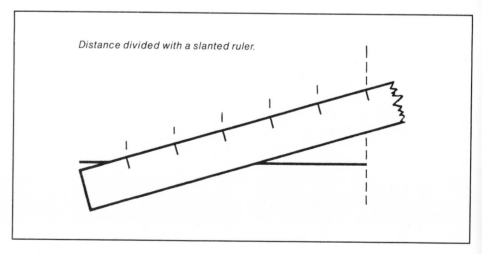

Distance divided with a slanted ruler.

BASIC CUTTING TECHNIQUES

Straight Cutting. A T-square (steel only) is used for making straight cuts. With the head firmly hooked over the edge of the drawing board, and with the blade firmly held by the fingers, there is minimal risk of the blade shifting through pressure of the cutting tool. Although the T-square is hooked to the side of the drawing board for ruling, it works better for cutting when hooked to the top or bottom of the drawing board. In this position, the cutting tool is pulled toward the body, which provides maximum control and leverage. This position is especially desirable for heavy materials such as illustration and mat board. A steel or steel-edged triangle may also be used for cutting, either alone or in conjunction with the T-square. Never use a steel ruler for cutting. Not only does it slip too easily, but the cutting tool might damage the engraved markings. Also, never use wood, plastic, or aluminum guides for cutting because they can be so easily nicked.

When cutting with a T-square, always check to see that the fingers holding the T-square blade are not near the cutting edge. The safest method is to place the tips of the two large fingers and thumb along the opposite edge of the T-square blade so that they rest partly on the blade and partly on the material being cut. Through feel alone, then, one can be sure that the fingers are the maximum distance away from the cutting edge.

When trimming artwork, the T-square blade should be placed on the "artwork" side of the line. In this position, the artwork, or piece to be used, cannot be damaged by a possible slip of the cutting tool. If the cutting tool slips, it will merely veer into the piece to be discarded.

An industrial razor blade is used to cut thin materials, and a mat knife is used to cut thick materials. For very precise cutting, a #1 X-acto knife with a #11 blade is used. When cutting thick materials a series of light cuts are better than one heavy cut. In fact, even a razor blade will successfully cut thick materials if a series of light cuts are made.

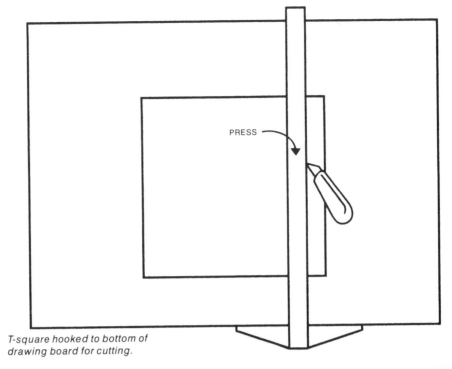

PRESS

T-square hooked to bottom of drawing board for cutting.

Cutting with a T-square. Note position of fingers on T-square blade.

Curve Cutting. Scissors are best for cutting thin, unmounted materials, and a frisket knife or #1 X-acto knife with #16 blade is best for cutting thin, mounted materials. Thick materials are very difficult to cut accurately. Use a #1 X-acto knife with #16 blade (a frisket knife is too delicate), and make many light cuts. If the resulting cut edge is frayed or bumpy, it can usually be smoothed with sandpaper.

Curves must be cut freehand. Although templates or irregular curves may have been employed to draw the curves, they should not be used as a guide for cutting, since the cutting tool would invariably nick them.

Circle Cutting. As described in the section on Cutting Tools (page 64), various types of compasses are available for cutting circles. All thin materials, and some thick materials, must be rubber cemented on to illustration board so that they don't shift during cutting. Usually one or two revolutions of the compass will cut thin materials, while many more are needed for thick materials. If the material inside the circle is to be used, the pivot hole made by the compass can be eliminated by rubber cementing or taping a small piece of cardboard over the center of the circle to be cut. Large circles, incidentally, can often be cut freehand, using one of the methods recommended for curve cutting.

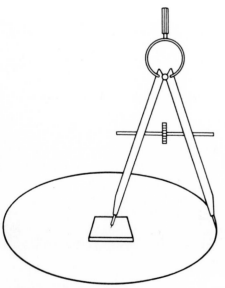

Cardboard affixed over pivot hole.

Butting and Insetting. Butting is the process of fitting two pieces of material tightly together, and insetting (also called inlaying or intarsia) is the process of fitting one piece of material into another. Insetting is used when it is desirable to eliminate the shadows and cut edges that occur when one piece of material is merely rubber cemented on top of another piece of material. Insetting is also used for transparent materials, such as color film and shading film. Butting and insetting are really the same, the only difference being that in butting, only one edge is involved, whereas two or more edges are involved in insetting.

To make a butt joint, rubber cement both pieces on to the mounting board, overlapping them at the intended joint. Cut through both pieces, holding the cutting blade vertically. Using a dispenser of rubber cement thinner, remove the excess strip of the overlapped piece, and lift the edge of the overlapped piece to remove the excess strip of the underlapped piece. Both pieces will now fit together perfectly. If the material being used is

white, the joint can be made virtually invisible by filling it in with white retouch or designers color applied by ruling pen. After it has dried, the paint ridge is removed by scraping with a razor blade. Use the whole blade, not just one corner, so as not to scratch the surface.

When insetting materials, it is usually necessary to first make a pencil overlay showing the exact position of each piece. Both pieces are then rubber cemented on to the mounting board, using the hinged overlay as a guide. Use the dry/wet method of rubber cementing (page 69), so the materials can be easily moved about for accurate positioning. After the rubber cement has dried, locate the cuts with pushpin holes through the overlay. Cut through both materials with a vertically-held blade, and remove excess pieces as described in butting.

Since color film and shading film are backed with low-tack adhesive, the foregoing rubber-cementing procedure would obviously be eliminated. When using film, don't burnish it until after the excess material has been removed.

Butting.

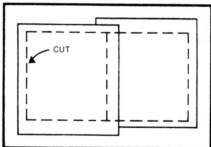

PIECES OF MATERIAL OVERLAPPED AND CUT

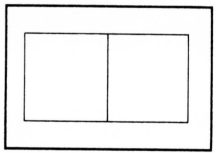

EXCESS MATERIAL REMOVED

Insetting.

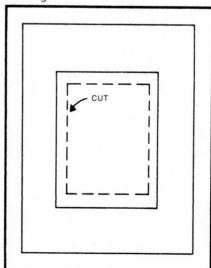

PIECES OF MATERIAL OVERLAPPED AND CUT

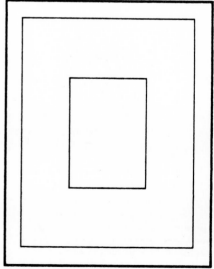

EXCESS MATERIAL REMOVED

RE-SPACING TYPE AND LETTERING

Type, photolettering, and hand lettering can easily be re-spaced by cutting it apart. If the original copy should not be cut, or if it was rendered on board thicker than 3-ply bristol, make a glossy photostat of it for cutting.

Mount the copy on illustration board or 2- or 3-ply bristol board. Use bristol board if the re-spaced copy is to be pasted directly on the mechanical; it is thick enough to withstand the cutting operation, but not too thick for pasting on the mechanical. Use illustration board if the re-spaced copy is to be photostatted for the mechanical. Tape or pin the mounting board on the drawing board, and use the dry/wet method of rubber cementing for mounting the copy. (Apply rubber cement to the back of the copy and let it dry. Then apply a generous coat of rubber cement to the mounting board and mount the copy on the wet cement.)

Re-spacing Letters and Words. As soon as the copy has been dry/wet mounted, carefully line up the base line of the letters with the T-square, and make a long horizontal cut above and below the entire line of letters. Press down firmly on the T-square so the copy doesn't shift. Use a razor blade or #11 X-acto blade, and cut through the copy but not the mounting board.

To re-space the letters or words, make a vertical cut at the right end of the cut strip and lift an inch or so of the strip so it can be grasped with the fingers. Then, starting at the left end of the line of lettering, open the spacing by vertically cutting the strip and sliding it to the right, or close the spacing by cutting a vertical segment from the strip and sliding it to the left. Vertical cuts are usually made freehand, but a steel-edged triangle is useful, especially when cutting thin segments away from the strip. Tweezers may also be use-

ful for removing thin segments if the fingernails prove inadequate. Because the cuts make it difficult to judge spacing, they can be obscured by viewing the lettering through tracing paper.

Work letter by letter from left to right. After each space has been adjusted, align the letters vertically and press down with the fingers. Use the point of the blade for adjusting and aligning the cut pieces, but don't jab the point into the letters themselves. The rubber cement will remain moist for some time under the large strip, but it will dry rapidly under the pieces that have been cut and pressed down. If the large strip dries out, take it off, remove the dried cement from both surfaces, and dry/wet mount it again.

The major feature of this method of re-spacing is that perfect horizontal alignment of the letters is maintained by the track cut in the paper. Therefore, not only must the track be perfectly aligned with the base line of the letters, but there must be enough surrounding paper so the track doesn't distort with the pressure of cutting.

PROOF, PHOTOSTAT, OR ORIGINAL ART

MOUNTING BOARD

Opening up letter or word spacing.

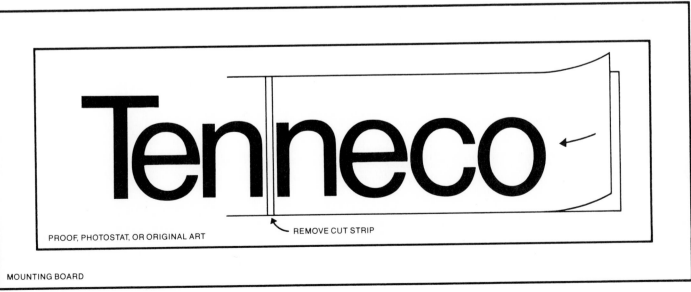

PROOF, PHOTOSTAT, OR ORIGINAL ART

REMOVE CUT STRIP

MOUNTING BOARD

Closing up letter or word spacing.

Re-spacing Lines. Before the copy is mounted, it is first necessary to draw base-line guidelines on the mounting board. To do this, first determine the new depth of the column and draw the base-lines for the first and last lines of the copy. Then use a divider to divide the intervening space into as many segments as there are lines of type, and draw these guidelines. (See Dividing distances into equal parts, page 90.) Finally, draw vertical guidelines indicating the width of the column. Draw all guidelines long enough to be visible after the copy is mounted.

Trim the copy of excess paper, and use the dry/wet method of rubber cementing to mount it, lining up the first line with the horizontal and vertical guidelines. If the copy is to be opened up, make a horizontal cut between every line and re-space the lines, working from the bottom up. If the copy is to be closed up, make double horizontal cuts between every line, re-move the cut segments, and re-space the lines, working from the top down. If the removed segments are exactly equal in width to the reduction in line spacing, the lines of type may simply be butted together. To find the width of the segments to be removed, use a divider to measure the difference between the copy base-lines and the new base-lines. Then transfer this measurement to the copy by puncturing the paper with the divider points. Use a spring bow divider so the setting can't be accidentally changed.

When cutting the copy, use a sharp razor blade or #11 X-acto blade, and hold the T-square firmly against the copy so that it doesn't shift. After the copy has been cut and re-positioned, don't remove the excess rubber cement for at least 15 minutes, since it may still be wet under the copy.

Display sizes of lower case type and lettering are frequently linespaced by visual estimation. Since every line consists of shapes of differing heights, mechanical measurements from base-line to base-line may result in very uneven spacing between lines. This is not a problem in body copy because the differences are too small to be discernible.

cigars for everyone

Line spacing adjusted to acknowledge ascenders and descenders.

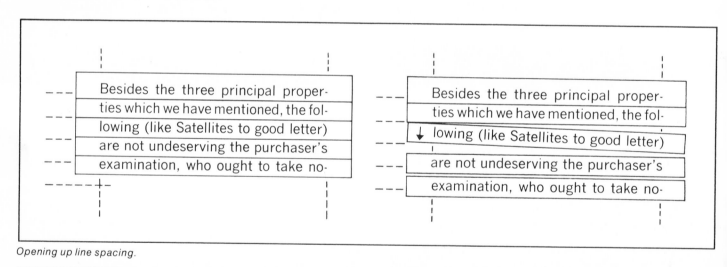

Opening up line spacing.

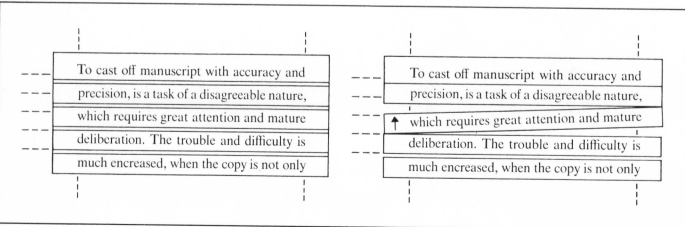

Closing up line spacing.

CUTTING MATS AND MOUNTS

The difference between matting and mounting is that matting involves the cutting of an opening in a piece of mat board and taping the artwork behind it, while mounting involves trimming the artwork and rubber cementing it on the surface of mat board. Artwork done on illustration board is usually matted to crop unwanted edges as well as to hide the thick edges of the board. Artwork done on bond paper, bristol board, photostat paper, or other thin, opaque material is usually mounted if it can be trimmed without damage, and if the exposed edges of the paper or board are not objectionable. Artwork done on transparent or translucent paper (such as tracing, layout, or visualizer paper), must usually be matted. If it were to be mounted, the tone of the underlying mat board would be visible through the paper, thus turning white areas to gray. When matting flimsy or translucent paper, it must be backed with opaque white paper or board. The paper may be adhered to the backing sheet with rubber cement or spray adhesive, or it may be simply taped around the edges.

When matting or mounting layouts and comps, the mat border should start right at the trim edge of the design. In a full-page magazine ad, for example, the mat should delineate the page size. A common mistake with beginners is to leave extra white space around the design, and delineate the trim size with a black line. This makes it very difficult to judge how the design will look when reproduced.

As mentioned in Studio Papers and Boards (page 78), only white, gray, or black mats should be used for graphic design work. As a general guideline, if the trim edges of the artwork are white, then a gray or black mat would probably be best; if the trim edges combine white and middle values of gray or color, then a black mat would probably be best; and if the trim edges combine middle and dark values of gray or color, then a white mat would probably be best. Since so many variables are involved, the proper choice of mat can only be determined by laying the artwork on white, black, and various gray mat boards and making a visual judgment.

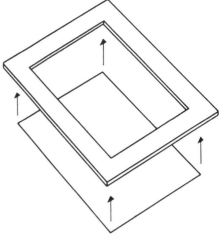

Mat. Untrimmed artwork taped to back of mat.

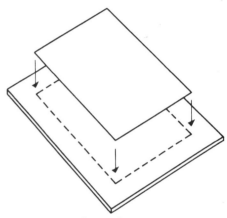

Mount. Trimmed artwork cemented on to mat board.

Mounting Procedure. Trim the artwork to size with a steel T-square and razor blade, lay it face down on a piece of mat board that is two or more inches larger on all sides, and rubber cement the back. Then put aside the artwork and rubber cement the mat. The area of mat board to be rubber cemented is marked by the cement that was brushed beyond the edges of the artwork. When both surfaces are dry, drop the artwork into position by eye. (If the artwork is on large, thin paper, it may have to be slip-sheeted. See Rubber Cementing Techniques, page 69.) Trim the mat to size with a T-square and mat knife or razor blade. The width of the mat border can be automatically measured by lining up the inner edge of the T-square blade on the edge of the artwork and then cutting on the outer edge of the T-square blade, thus producing a mat border that is the width of the T-square blade. Finally, remove the excess cement on the mat border. If cement has stained the mat board (which is not unusual with some

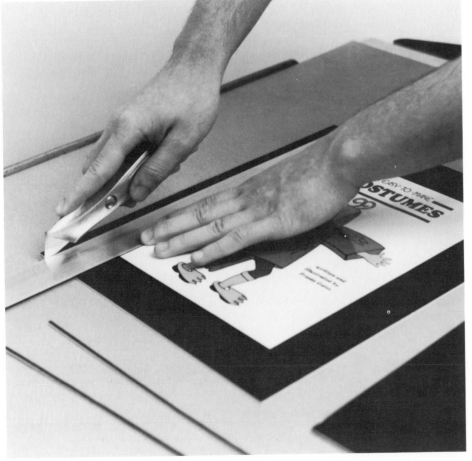

Cutting a mount.

types of mat board), cover the whole mat border with rubber cement and remove when dry. By staining the whole mat equally, the problem is masked.

Matting Procedure. Lightly tape a sheet of tracing paper over the artwork and draw the shape of the mat opening with a pencil, T-square, and triangle. Then place the tracing paper on a mat board, allowing three or more inches of board on all sides for borders, and mark the corners of the mat opening by puncturing through the paper into the board with a pushpin. Remove the paper, connect the pin holes with a lightly ruled pencil line, and measure and lightly rule the outer dimensions of the mat. A mat border of 2″ or 3″ on all sides is standard. Cut the mat opening first, using a very sharp mat knife and steel T-square. Place the blade of the T-square over the mat border so that if the knife slips it will merely veer into the piece of board to be discarded. To insure neat inside corners, start the cut at the corner and end it slightly short of the next corner. After all four sides have been cut this way, turn the board so that the cuts can be completed from the other direction. Beveled mats are not usually used in graphic design work. Not only are they difficult to cut, but the exposed white interior of the mat is often visually undesirable. After the mat is cut, inside and out, a piece of clean sandpaper from a sandpaper pad is used to clean up frayed edges. Finally, the mat is positioned over the artwork and held in position with a few pieces of drafting tape. The board is then turned over and the artwork is thoroughly taped on all four sides to the mat board. Use drafting tape so the mat can later be removed without damaging the back of the artwork.

General Rules for Matting and Mounting. When matting and mounting graphic design work, never make the mat borders larger than necessary (1½″ to 3″ is standard). Also, make all four borders equal in width, and use only white, gray, or black mat board. It is important to understand that the function of a mat is to crop, stiffen, and protect artwork, and to isolate it from environmental distractions. If the color or the shape of the mat is active (as opposed to passive or neutral), it will invariably interfere with the proper judgment of the artwork. Keep in mind that original art in graphic design is for reproduction, and that when reproduced, it will not be seen on a mat. Therefore, a mat that improves the artwork is just as bad as a mat that detracts from it.

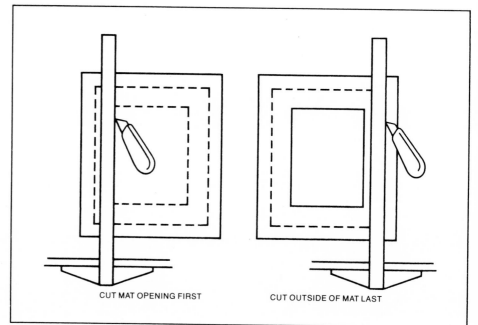

CUT MAT OPENING FIRST   CUT OUTSIDE OF MAT LAST

Cutting a mat.

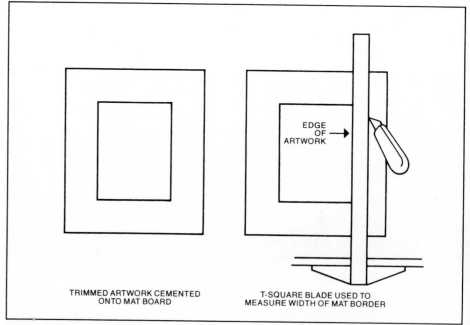

TRIMMED ARTWORK CEMENTED ONTO MAT BOARD   T-SQUARE BLADE USED TO MEASURE WIDTH OF MAT BORDER

EDGE OF ARTWORK

Cutting a mount.

FLAPPING ARTWORK

All finished art for reproduction should be flapped. This includes mechanicals as well as photographs, illustrations, and other copy being sent to the printer. It is usually not desirable to flap layouts, comps, and other forms of art that are not actually finished art for reproduction. Not only do they not need such protection, but the flap detracts from the visual presentation and also makes it difficult to quickly scan work in a portfolio. If normal mounting or matting is not sufficient protection for portfolio pieces, they should be covered with acetate (see page 80). Reproduced portfolio pieces are usually inserted, unmounted, into an acetate-folder presentation book, or laminated on a dry mounting press with Mylar laminating film.

When flapping finished art for reproduction, both a tracing paper overlay and a heavy paper cover are usually used. The tracing paper overlay is for indicating specifications, and should be easily removable in the event of changes in the specifications. The heavy paper cover is for protection, and should not be easily removable, either accidentally or intentionally.

Attaching the Tracing Paper Overlay.

The overlay is attached to the top front of the mounting board with drafting tape or white correction tape. Don't use transparent tape, since the stronger adhesive on this tape might damage the mounting board in the event of removal. The tracing paper should be larger than the mounting board, and is placed so that a ¼" to ⅜" strip of the top edge of the mounting board is exposed. When the tape is attached along the top edge of the mounting board, then, it will adhere to the exposed strip of board and top edge of the overlay, thus forming a hinge. If the tape is 2" to 3" wider than the board it is easier to handle, thus insuring accurate positioning and eliminating the possibility of wrinkles in the tape or overlay. Don't trim the excess tape and tracing paper until after the cover has been attached. At that time, all trimming can be performed in one operation.

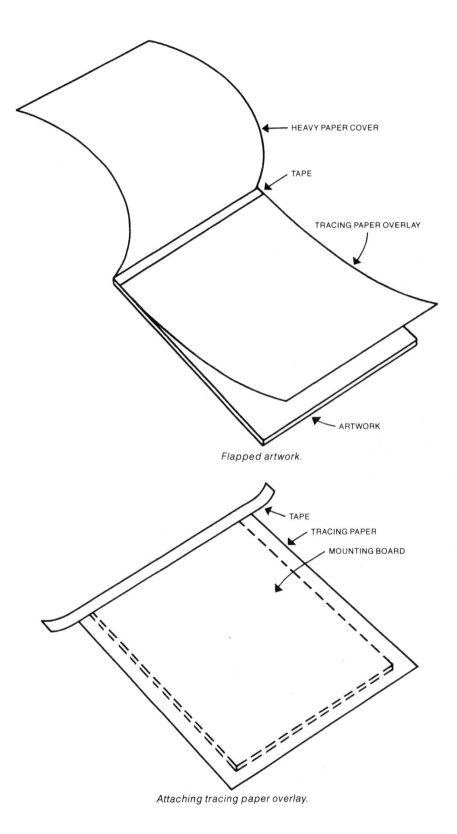

HEAVY PAPER COVER

TAPE

TRACING PAPER OVERLAY

ARTWORK

Flapped artwork.

TAPE

TRACING PAPER

MOUNTING BOARD

Attaching tracing paper overlay.

Attaching the Paper Cover. Medium or heavyweight brown wrapping paper makes a durable, neat, and inexpensive cover. For esthetic reasons, some designers use heavy cover stock, which is available in many colors and textures. The cover is attached to the top reverse side of the mounting board with rubber cement. Don't use tape, since the cover will not open and close properly and can be too easily removed, either accidentally or intentionally.

After the tracing paper overlay has been attached, but before it has been trimmed, place the mounting board face down on the sheet of cover paper. The cover paper should be larger than the mounting board on all sides, with a 1½″ to 2″ strip exposed at the top edge of the board. Hold the assemblage in position, and rubber cement the exposed strip and an equally wide strip along the top edge of the board. Still holding the assemblage in position, use a razor blade to make a freehand cut starting at each upper corner of the mounting board and running diagonally through the exposed strip of cover paper. After the rubber cement has dried, and still holding the assemblage in position, fold the trimmed tab of cover paper on to the mounting board.

After the cover has been attached, and while the assemblage is still face down, trim the excess tracing and cover paper with a razor blade. Press the assemblage down firmly along the edge being trimmed, and use the edge of the mounting board as a cutting guide. Hold the razor blade vertically so it doesn't cut into the mounting board. If the mounting board is not thick enough to properly guide the razor blade, use a steel T-square. Finally, remove the excess rubber cement from the back of the mounting board, and also from the inside fold of the cover.

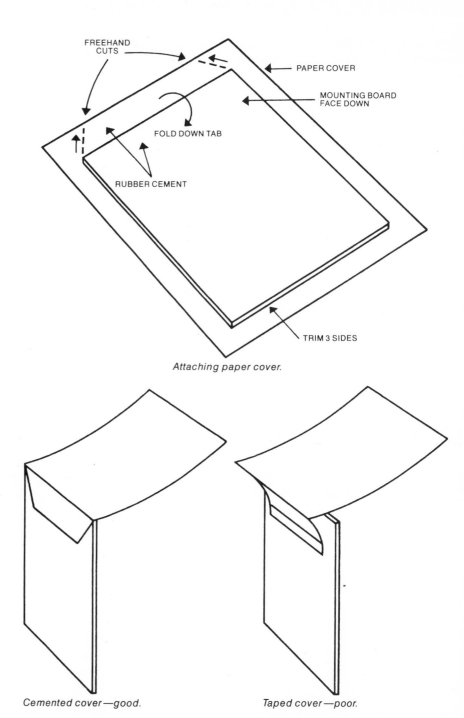

FREEHAND CUTS

PAPER COVER

MOUNTING BOARD FACE DOWN

FOLD DOWN TAB

RUBBER CEMENT

TRIM 3 SIDES

Attaching paper cover.

Cemented cover—good.

Taped cover—poor.

TRANSFERRING DRAWINGS

Graphite Transfer Method. This is the most commonly used method of transferring drawings from tracing, layout, or bond paper to bristol or illustration board. Graphite is applied to the back of the drawing, and a sharp, hard pencil is used to trace the outlines of the drawing onto the board.

The graphite can be applied with a regular drawing pencil, but a broad-lead sketching pencil is faster. Use a 2B pencil —it is soft enough to make a strong impression, but not so soft that it smudges. Apply graphite only to the image portion of the drawing. If the paper is too opaque to see the image, hold it up to the light occasionally to insure that all lines are being adequately backed up with graphite. After applying a substantial coat of graphite, smooth it with a facial tissue.

To speed up the process of applying graphite, some designers accumulate a supply of powdered graphite from sharpening their pencils, storing it in a small container with a cotton wad, cloth, or felt applicator. You can also buy powdered graphite.

To transfer the graphite-backed drawing, tape it to the bristol or illustration board, and firmly trace its outlines with a sharp 7H, 8H, or 9H pencil. Be careful that the pencil is not so sharp that it cuts through the drawing. After tracing one line, lift the tapes holding the lower edge of the drawing and check to see that the transferred line is sufficiently dark. If it is not, remove the drawing and apply more graphite. After the entire drawing has been traced, again lift the lower tapes and check to see that all lines have been traced, and are sufficiently dark. Don't remove the drawing completely until after making this check, since accurate re-positioning would be impossible.

When transferring a drawing to a dark-toned surface, use white or light colored pastel instead of graphite. If the pastel is too smudgy, spray it with a very light coat of fixative. (Too heavy a coat will not permit the pastel to transfer.)

Instead of applying graphite or pastel directly to the back of a drawing, a transfer interlay paper, as described on page 79, may be used. This not only saves time, but the absence of graphite on the back of the drawing makes it easier to align the drawing with underlying guidelines.

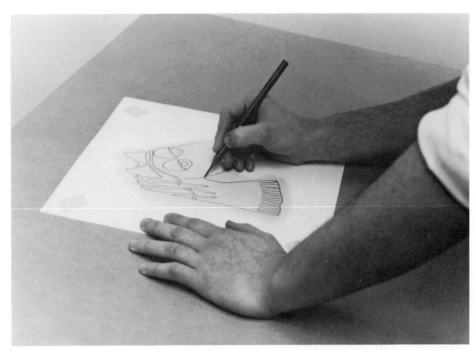

Tracing outlines of graphite-backed drawing.

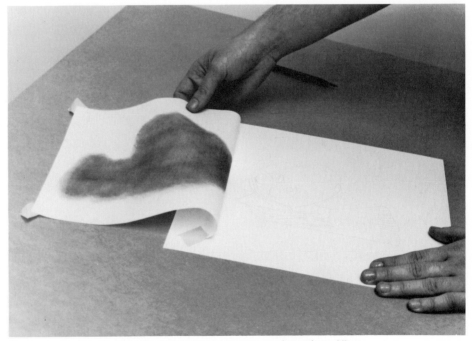

Tracing paper lifted to check quality and completeness of transferred lines.

Offset Transfer Method. If the original drawing was made with a fairly soft pencil, it can be transferred by this method. The drawing is taped, face down, on tracing or layout paper, and rubbed firmly and thoroughly with a hard pencil. This offsets the drawing, in reverse, on to the tracing or layout paper. The offset drawing is then taped, face down, on bristol or illustration board, and rubbed, thus offsetting the drawing once again, and reversing it back to its original orientation.

The advantage to this method is that both lines and shapes are transferred in their entirety, with no loss of fidelity. Also, in some cases it may be faster than the graphite transfer method. Its disadvantage, as mentioned previously, is that the original drawing must be strongly rendered in fairly soft pencil.

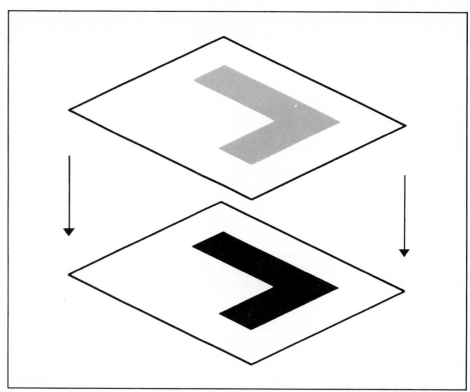

First step: Original drawing placed face down and rubbed, offsetting the image onto tracing paper.

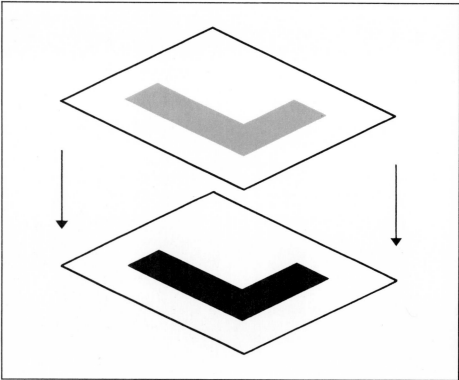

Second step: Offset image placed face down and rubbed, offsetting the image once again onto bristol or illustration board.

Tracing Box Transfer Method. The tracing box, as described on page 51, is very simple to use. The drawing is placed on the lighted surface, and a sheet of paper or bristol board is placed over it for tracing. Because the light must pass through both materials, they cannot be extremely thick or opaque. Illustration board cannot be used at all, and bristol board must be no thicker than 2-ply. Since finished art pasted on the mechanical is usually rendered on bristol board anyway, this is not a serious limitation.

The advantage to the tracing box transfer method is that it is clean and fast, and permits changes to be made during the tracing procedure. When tracing directly onto bristol board, don't use a pencil harder than 3H or it may score the board.

Using a tracing box.

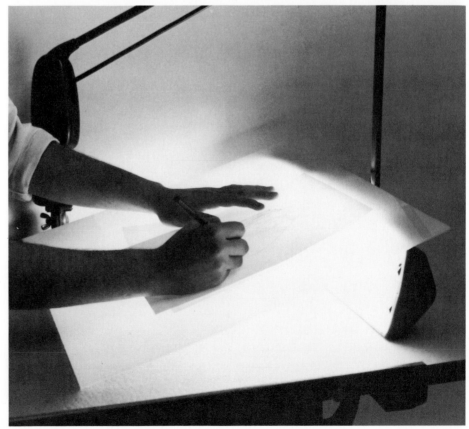

An inexpensive alternative to a tracing box: a translucent plastic sheet placed over an inverted drawing table lamp.

EMBOSSING

As explained in the section on Bindery Operations (page 49), embossing is the molding of paper or other material to form a raised image. In the reproduction process, embossing is done by pressing the paper between a brass female die and a male bed or counter. In the graphic design studio process, the embossing of comps and dummies is done in the following manner.

Make an accurate tracing paper drawing of the image to be embossed, including an outline of the total page. Place this drawing, face down, on a larger sheet of illustration board, and tape it along its upper edge. Then cut a piece of bristol board to an inch or two larger, on all sides, than the image to be embossed, and

firmly rubber cement it to the illustration board, using the flapped drawing as a positioning guide. The thickness of the bristol board determines the height of the embossed image (2- or 3-ply board will make a substantial embossment and is also fairly easy to cut).

Transfer the image to be embossed from the tracing paper to the bristol board. Because the tracing paper drawing is face down, it is necessary to use a graphite transfer sheet (see page 79), since the application of graphite to the back of the tracing paper would obliterate the drawing. Then cut out the image to be embossed with a #1 X-acto knife and #11 or #16 blade. Remove the cut-out pieces from the areas to be embossed, using rubber cement thinner, and remove the

excess cement with a rubber cement pickup. The resulting cut-out image is a female die, similar to the brass female die used in the reproduction process.

Place the paper to be embossed face down on the illustration board and tape it on all sides. The paper must be larger than the total page size and also of a quality and thickness that embosses well. Embossing creases and stretches the paper, and a poor-quality paper, or too thick a paper, cannot be worked properly. One-ply bristol board, 65 lb. cover paper, or 80 lb. text paper is ideal. Strathmore cover and text papers (Beau Brilliant and Grandee) are available in art supply stores in a wide variety of colors and textures. Whatever paper is used, make a test embossment first to see that it works

Female embossing die with tracing paper overlay and crochet hook.
Embossing die is made of bristol board cemented onto illustration board.

properly. Some designers dampen the paper to be embossed, but this is usually not necessary unless the paper fibers tend to break, which might happen with a very high embossment. The disadvantage to dampening is that it tends to warp the paper, and the embossed edges are not sharply defined.

After the paper is positioned, transfer the image to it from the flapped tracing paper overlay. (If the paper is dark-toned, use a light-colored pastel rather than graphite on the transfer paper.) Since the cut-out image is hidden, this guide is necessary to locate the areas to be embossed. While the overlay is still in position, also transfer the outline of the page, either by tracing the outline or by puncturing the corners with a pushpin.

The best tool for embossing is a small crochet hook (#3½ is ideal). Wrap the finger-holding area of the hook with drafting tape so it is easier to hold. The crochet hook is rubbed on the paper, following the cut edges of the bristol board. This creases the paper at the top of the cut edge and rounds it at the bottom of the depression, thus forming a perfect embossment when viewed from the opposite, or correct, side. If the paper being embossed is textured, the crochet hook will flatten the texture. This means that the entire embossed area, not just the edges, must be rubbed to flatten the texture equally.

After the image has been embossed, lift the tapes from one edge of the paper and carefully examine the embossing on the reverse side. Don't remove the paper entirely until this examination has been made, since it would be impossible to later re-position the paper accurately.

Multi-level embossing is done by rubber cementing pieces of bristol board on top of one another, and cutting out shapes from each. The shapes for all levels of embossing are drawn on a single tracing paper overlay, and then transferred as needed.

Debossing (depressed image) is done in a similar way to embossing. If a female die is used, then the drawing is not reversed, and the debossing is done on the front of the paper. The disadvantage to this method is that the tool marks of the crochet hook may be visible on the finished piece. Debossing may be done from the reverse side of the paper if a male die is used instead of a female die (that is, if the area to be debossed is raised rather than depressed). The dis-

advantage to this method is that the area surrounding the debossment is rubbed, which may flatten out a textured paper.

Lettering and/or other graphic images should be added after embossing. Since embossing (and often debossing) is done on the reverse side of the paper, it would be extremely difficult to accurately register the embossed image if the graphic images are rendered first.

Etching Press Embossing. Both embossing and debossing can be done on an etching press. The die can be made from pasted-up bristol and illustration board, or it can be an etched zinc or copper plate. Etched images may be hand drawn, or they may be photo-engraved from a film negative or positive.

The etching press method of embossing is superior for fine detail, but it doesn't produce images of particularly high or sharp relief. This is because the die is merely pressed against a felt blanket, whereas in the previously described method of embossing, the die is firmly rubbed with a crochet hook. The effect produced by a firmly rubbed crochet hook is more similar to the effect produced in commercial reproduction, where the male counter is a relief molding of the female die.

Image embossed on cover paper.

Layout Techniques

There are three stages in the process of designing a layout: thumbnail sketches, rough layouts, and the finished layout. If the finished layout is very carefully rendered, it is called a comprehensive layout, or comp. If the finished layout or comp is in 3-dimensional form, such as a booklet, folder, package, or display, it is called a dummy.

Each stage of layout design involves specific techniques and objectives, and each stage is extremely important in the development of a graphic communication. Beginners tend to rush through preliminary stages, believing that careful "noodling" of the finished layout or comp will somehow rectify design deficiencies. Just the opposite — the more careful the rendering, the more obvious the design deficiencies become. The result of this misconception is that the finished layout or comp will be unsatisfactory, and thus necessitate revision or re-execution.

To avoid this common beginner's error, it is necessary to pay particular attention to the preliminary stages of designing, which primarily involve research and experimentation. If these stages are carefully and thoroughly performed, the end result will be both competent and creative. The degree of creativity, of course, depends upon the individual, but as Thomas Edison so aptly put it, "genius is 2 percent inspiration and 98 percent perspiration".

Throughout the layout process, from thumbnails to roughs to finished layouts or comps, it is important to keep reproduction limitations in mind. For example, if the design specifications call for two colors, then only two colors, plus their mixtures, should be indicated on the layout. Always remember that the "work of art" in graphic design is the reproduced piece, not the finished layout or comp. This means, of course, that it is necessary to have a thorough knowledge of reproduction technology.

THUMBNAIL SKETCHES

Thumbnail sketches are so called because they are much smaller than reproduction size. Their primary function is to try out various graphic images, layout organizations, and color combinations in very rough form.

Thumbnail sketches begin to take form during the research stage of designing. This should include a careful analysis of the design specifications and copy, as well as a thorough investigation of related sources of information. For example, if the commission is for a tourism poster for London, then the research should include an investigation of London, as well as an investigation of poster design in general. Much of this investigation can be performed in libraries, but it usually also requires a visit to private sources of information, in this case a travel agency and/or the British bureau for tourism.

During the process of assimilating this information, certain images suggest that they might be usable as graphic devices. These should be jotted down in graphic form, much as one would jot down notes. If they prove to be good graphic images, they may be immediately tried out in a thumbnail layout sketch, or they may be saved for later layout experimentation.

Thumbnail sketches are usually made on layout or bond paper. While they are drawn smaller than reproduction size,

they must be proportionate in shape. If the design is to be in color, then the thumbnail sketches must also be in color. Many beginners tend to ignore color during the preliminary stages of designing. Color, however, is a very important element of design, and must not be treated as an afterthought. It is equal in importance to form, and in some cases may even be more important. Colored pencils, such as Prismacolor, or pointed-nib color markers are ideal for thumbnail sketching. For black and white sketching, any large, soft graphite pencil, such as a layout pencil, may be used.

It is important to keep in mind that the purpose of thumbnail sketches is to develop a good pattern of shapes and colors. The elements of the layout, such as the headline, the body copy, and one or more of the graphic images found in research, are indicated very roughly in regard to detail, but with much attention paid to size, position, and color. In the headline, for example, it is not necessary to indicate type style, or even to make the words legible, but it is necessary to indicate its overall size, weight, and position.

If the design involves body copy, it is usually necessary to make a rough estimation of its total area. The procedure for this is described in the section on Copyfitting, page 124.

Thumbnail sketches rendered with color markers (Russel Halfhide).

ROUGH LAYOUTS

After making a number of thumbnail sketches, one or more are selected for further development in rough layout form. Rough layouts are always drawn at reproduction size, the only exception being very large posters and displays that will not fit on normal sizes of paper or board. In that case, both the layout and the finished art are prepared at a scale specified by the printer. The printer, then, enlarges the finished art to reproduction size during the platemaking process.

Rough layouts are usually made directly on a pad of layout or visualizing paper. The reason for working directly on the pad is that it provides a resilient working surface, and the reason for using layout or visualizing paper is that it is sufficiently transparent to permit tracing shapes from an underlying layout. See the section on Studio Papers and Boards (page 77), for the method of working directly on a pad.

The first step in making a rough layout is to accurately draw the outside dimensions of the layout at reproduction size, and to then enlarge the thumbnail sketch to fit these dimensions. The thumbnail sketch may be enlarged with a Lacey-Luci projector, a camera lucida, or some other enlarging device, or it may be enlarged purely by visual estimation. The latter method is the more common practice; since the thumbnail sketch is very rough, it can only provide a general guide as to the size, shape, and position of design elements.

After the thumbnail sketch has been enlarged to reproduction size, the next step is to refine the basic pattern of sizes, shapes, and colors. This is a trial and error process, and usually requires a number of rough layout sketches. As each layout is produced, it is first analyzed, and then placed under a fresh sheet in the layout pad. New outline dimensions are drawn on the fresh top sheet, and the underlying layout is used as a guide for the next layout. By shifting the underlying layout, it is possible to adjust sizes and positions of design elements.

During this process, it is necessary to become more and more specific with typographic elements. In the beginning,

only general sizes, weights, and positions are important, but as refinement increases, specific typefaces and sizes must be indicated. They should not be accurately rendered in detail, but they should be reasonably accurate in regard to height, weight, line length, and column depth.

Since the purpose of rough layouts is to develop a good pattern of shapes and colors, it is important to indicate masses, not outlines of shapes. The best mediums for rapidly indicating masses are pastels and color markers. Color markers are preferred because they are cleaner to use and more brilliant in color. Pastels, on the other hand, are much less expensive and permit smoother modeling. Application techniques for both mediums are described in the section on Color Mediums (Color markers, page 75; Pastels, page 74). Colored pencils are not usually used for reproduction-size layouts because they cannot cover large areas rapidly or smoothly. For black and white layouts, both pastels and color markers are available in a complete range of grays. Graphite layout or sketching pencils may also be used, but they don't produce strong blacks.

Rough layouts rendered with color markers (Sharon Gresh).

FINISHED LAYOUTS, COMPS, AND DUMMIES

After the rough layout has been resolved as a pattern of shapes and colors, it must be refined—in regard to detail—for presentation to the client. If this detailed layout is rendered using layout techniques, it is called a finished layout. If it is rendered using techniques commonly employed for finished art, it is called a comprehensive layout, or comp. The difference between the two is merely a matter of degree of finish, and is usually determined by the type of design involved. For example, newspaper and magazine ads are usually rendered as finished layouts, while graphic design work such as posters, book jackets, record album covers, booklets, folders, and packages are usually rendered as comps. As mentioned previously, booklets, folders, packages, and other 3-dimensional designs are rendered in 3-dimensional form, and are called dummies.

The finished layout, comp, or dummy should be executed only after the design has been fully resolved in rough layout form. Since the final execution is very time-consuming, it should not need to be executed more than once because of inadequate preliminary planning.

Finished Layouts.

Finished layouts range from not much more than a rough layout to not much less than a comp. The degree of finish depends on the needs of the client. If the layout is to be judged by people not familiar with the graphic design process, such as marketing and sales personnel, then it probably should accurately simulate reproduction quality. If it is to be judged solely by advertising personnel, then it may not need to be much more than a rough. Sometimes the client will specify the degree of finish, but more often than not it can only be determined through experience with that client.

The finished layout is often executed with either color markers or pastels. Both mediums have certain advantages and disadvantages, which must be weighed against the objectives desired. For example, while color markers are clean to use and brilliant in color, they do not permit much modeling or re-working. Being limited to the indelible marks made by the various nib shapes, they are usually fine for rough and semi-finished layouts, but may not be adequate for highly finished layouts. Most mediums, such as charcoal, pastel, India ink, and designers color may be applied over color markers. White, light, and bright designers colors, however, must be isolated from the dye with a coat of bleed-proof white. Pastels, although less brilliant and more difficult to handle than color markers, permit extensive modeling and re-working, and can be combined with most other mediums. Also, they are much less expensive than color markers, and do not deteriorate in storage.

Finished layouts are often rendered directly on the pad of paper. Medium to heavy weight layout or bond paper is preferable for finished layouts because it is more opaque. Lightweight layout paper may be used, but it must be backed with white paper or board when matted for presentation.

The typographic elements in the finished layout must be rendered to the same degree of finish as the other elements. If the finished layout is quite rough, then the typographic elements must also be quite rough. If the finished layout is highly refined, then the typographic elements must also be highly refined. No matter what the degree of finish, however, the typographic elements should be accurate in regard to height, weight, line length, and column depth.

Finished layouts must usually be matted, not mounted. The reason for this is that even the heavier weights of layout and bond paper are not usually opaque enough to completely block out the tone of the underlying mat board. The opacity of the layout paper can easily be tested by placing a scrap of the mat board beneath it. If the tone of the mat board is the least bit visible, then the layout must be matted. The procedure for matting and mounting is described on page 95. Layouts are never flapped or otherwise covered, since this would detract from the presentation effect.

Highly finished layout rendered with airbrush, designers color, and ink. (Ted DeCagna)

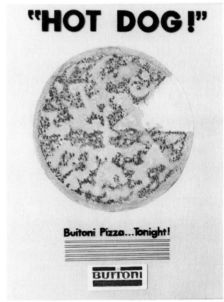

Highly finished layout rendered with pastel, designers color, and ink. (Michael Greer)

Comps.

Comps, or comprehensive layouts, are always highly refined. Their purpose is to simulate reproduction quality as accurately as posssible with hand rendering methods. Comps are usually rendered on illustration board, but may also be rendered on the paper to be used in printing if it possesses a color or texture that can't be simulated otherwise. If printing paper is used for the comp, it is usually rubber cemented on illustration board for durability as well as for ease in rendering.

The mediums and materials used for comps usually fall into the finished art category, such as ink, designers color, liquid dye, printing paper, color-coated paper, color film, etc. Layout mediums, such as pencils, color markers, and pastels are not usually used for comps because they are either not capable of fine detail, or cannot easily be re-worked or retouched. There are exceptions, however, which will be described later.

When determining materials, mediums, and techniques for comps, it is important to remember that whatever effect is achieved in the comp must also be achieved in reproduction. For example, if silver foil is used in the comp, the design must be printed on silver foil. Similarly, if a background is rendered in variegated colors, the design must be printed by four-color process, which is much more expensive than flat color printing.

Colored Backgrounds. Colored backgrounds for comps may be achieved with printing paper, color-coated paper, color film, designers color, liquid watercolor or dye, or pastel. The illustration board should be an inch or two larger, on all sides, than the trim size of the design, and the background color should usually extend beyond the trim size. (The mat, which is always cut to trim size, will cover the excess.) This not only saves time, but designers color and pastel can be applied more evenly if there are no borders to hamper broad application of the medium. Each background medium or material has certain advantages and disadvantages which are described below. The page on which the medium or material is described more fully is shown in parentheses.

Printing Paper (page 79). Printing paper is used for comps only when it is to be specified for reproduction, and when it possesses a color or texture that can't

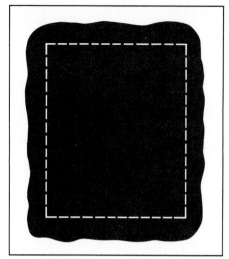

Background color extends beyond trim size.

be simulated otherwise. It must cover the entire design, and the other design elements must be rendered directly on it, just as would occur in printing. When using colored printing paper, keep in mind that printing ink colors, being transparent, will be affected by the paper color, and that white cannot be used at all. White printing ink can be printed on colored paper, but it will be a tint of the paper color. Pure white can only be achieved by screen printing.

Color-coated Paper (page 79). Color-coated paper, such as Color-Aid, is used to simulate printing ink colors. Its advantage over designers color is that it eliminates paint mixing and the possibility of streaking. Color selection is limited, however, and if lettering or other design elements are rendered directly on it, the color must be matched in designers color for retouching. If color-coated paper is to be applied to only a portion of the design, it is often better to adhere a piece larger than needed and then trim away the excess. For butting and insetting different colors of paper, see page 92. For transferring drawings to the paper, see page 99.

Color Film (page 80). Color film is more brilliant in color than color-coated paper, and therefore simulates printing ink more accurately. Being transparent, colors can be superposed to achieve mixtures that accurately simulate overprinting with printing ink. Lettering and other design elements may be rendered on color film with designers color, but retouching of the color film is difficult because the colors can't be matched in designers color. Designers color may be removed with a water-moistened cotton swab, or by scraping with an X-acto knife, but care must be taken so as not to damage the film color.

Designers color on dull gold paper.
(Ted DeCagna)

Designers color on color-coated paper.
(Joan Deprisco)

Drawings may be transferred on to matte color film, but when using glossy color film, the drawing must be transferred on to the illustration board before the film is adhered. Once the film is adhered, of course, the pencil lines can't be removed.

Designers Color (page 72). Designers color may be applied with an air brush or a ¾″ or wider sable or camel hair brush. To achieve a smooth, even coating with a wide brush, the designers color must be exactly the right consistency, rapidly applied, and brushed out thoroughly. If the color is the right consistency, one coat should cover without streaking. If a second coat is necessary, the first coat should be allowed to dry thoroughly.

As mentioned previously, the color should be brushed freely beyond the trim edge of the design, which permits rapid application and thorough brushing out. If the color is to be applied to only a portion of the design, frisket paper (page 79) is used to mask the areas to be left unpainted. Brush away from the edges of the frisket paper so that the brush will not pull up the edges. Don't use masking tape; not only doesn't it conform to curves, but the crepe paper permits paint to seep under, which results in ragged edges.

All large white, light, or brightly color foreground shapes should be masked. Even though designers color is opaque, it is difficult to entirely block out an underlying color unless it is substantially lighter. For example, if red is applied over anything but white, its brilliance will be diminished, no matter how many coats are applied. Small foreground elements, such as lettering, can be rendered over a colored background. Even then, however, bright colors need a base coat of white to isolate them from the underlying color. (This technique is explained in the section on Foreground Elements, page 110.)

The biggest advantage to designers color is that any color is possible, and once the color is mixed, it is available for later retouching. Also, it eliminates the need to buy special colors of paper or film for every job. Admittedly, it is difficult to apply large areas of designers color by brush, but if this cannot be mastered, the one-time investment in an air brush (which insures smooth coverage) is still cheaper than the continuing investment in color-coated paper and color film.

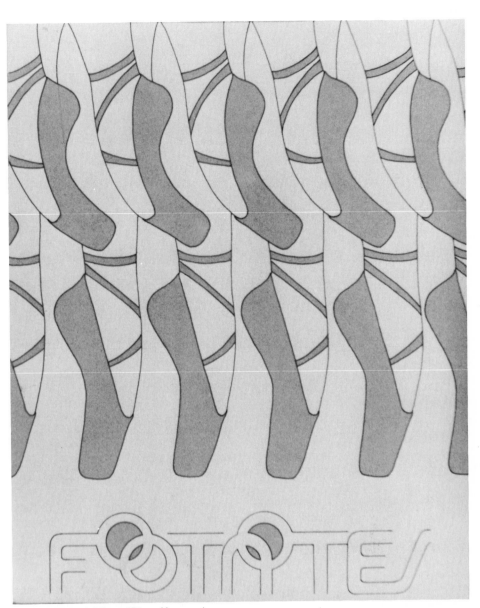

Color film over ink lines (Diane Vasquez).

Liquid Dye (page 74). Liquid dye, also known as concentrated water color, can be smoothly applied to large areas only by air brush. It is transparent and intensely brilliant, and colors can be superposed to simulate overprinting with printing ink. Most dye colors bleed through designers color, but bleeding can usually be prevented if a coat of bleed-proof white is applied first.

Dye colors are also available in spray cans, thus eliminating the need for an air brush. However, the colors cannot be mixed, which is a distinct advantage with bottled colors.

Designers color on illustration board. (Richard Hecht)

Pastel (page 74). Although pastel is not normally used for comp rendering, it is useful for applying background colors. It can be so smoothly blended that it resembles designers color, and designers color and ink may be applied over it after it has been fixed well. Foreground shapes can be masked with frisket paper.

Pastel illustration with designers color for type (Michael Greer).

Foreground Elements. Foreground elements may be rendered directly on the illustration board with designers color, ink, dye, etc., or they may be made from cut paper or film. Cut paper or film, however, can only be used when the foreground elements have simple, easy-to-cut contours. Detailed objects may be rendered on bond paper and then cut out and rubber cemented to the comp. The cuts must occur exactly at the outer contours of the object so they will be invisible on the comp. For the comp to accurately simulate reproduction quality, there must not be any signs of pasted-up elements, such as cut marks, shadows, patches, changes in paper texture, unintended changes in color tone or texture, etc.

When using designers color for large, flat-color foreground shapes, surrounding areas may be masked with frisket paper to permit rapid, broad-stroked coverage. Smaller shapes may be outlined with a brush and/ or ruling pen, and then filled in with as large a brush as possible. The secret to smooth, dense, onecoat coverage is to rapidly flood the outlined shape with as much color as possible, so that no part has a chance to dry before the shape is completed. This permits the color to level itself before it dries. Prior outlining is necessary to eliminate careful rendering during the flooding-in process.

When applying light or bright designers color over a dark background, the shape must first be rendered in white. After the white has dried, it is then covered with color. If the color is applied rapidly and without excess brushing, it won't pick up the underlying white. To insure against this possibility, acrylic white, which is waterproof when dry, may be used. Also, designers color white may be made waterproof with a coat of matte fixative. Make sure, however, that the fixative doesn't adversely affect surrounding areas. This procedure may sound like unnecessary work, but it is the only way to achieve clean, bright colors. Many beginners fail to heed this advice, and end up with muddy, dull colors, even after three or four applications of color.

Type is sometimes rendered on an acetate sheet that overlays the comp. This is usually necessary if the background surface is too rough, too delicate, or otherwise unsuitable for direct rendering. Either regular or prepared clear acetate may be used. Regular acetate is less expensive and has a harder surface, but won't accept designers color unless a plasticizing agent (page 74) is added to the paint. Prepared acetate is more expensive and has a more delicate surface, but accepts any medium (see Acetate, page 80).

To render the type, tape a pencil layout of the comp on to a white board and then tape the acetate over it. The type can be carefully drawn, in outline, on separate pieces of tracing paper, or it can be printed type clipped from reproduced work. In either case it is taped in position on the layout. Since it is difficult to use a ruling pen on acetate, the type is usually rendered entirely by brush. Large type is carefully outlined with a small brush, and then flooded in with a large brush. Small type is completely rendered in one operation. Since retouching is impossible on acetate, corrections are made by wiping off the paint with a saliva-moistened cotton swab, as described on page 76. For accuracy while rendering, press down the acetate with the handle end of a brush held in the left hand.

After rendering the type, position the acetate over the background rendering and tape it on one side. Then hinge it open, clean the back of it, mask around it with newspaper, and apply a light coat of spray adhesive. When the acetate is hinged shut, it will adhere to the background rendering, thus eliminating shadows around the type.

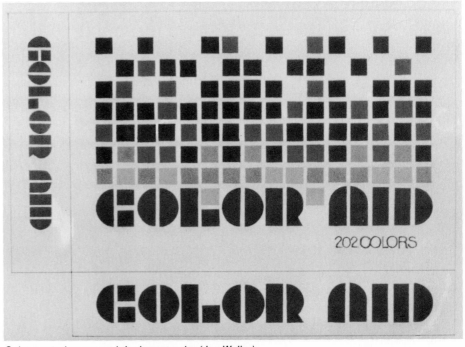

Color-coated paper and designers color (Joy Waller).

Using Photographs, Halftones, and Photostats in Comps. Photographic prints, reproduced halftones, and photostats are sometimes used in hand rendered comps. If such copy can be trimmed exactly at the edge of images, it can simply be rubber cemented on the comp and the cut edges will be invisible. If it can't be trimmed so that the cut edges are invisible, then it may be necessary to employ one or more of the super comp techniques, which are described in the following section.

Matting Comps. If the comp is rendered on illustration or other heavy board, it is usually matted. If it is rendered on paper or bristol board, mounting may be preferable. (See Cutting Mats and Mounts, page 95.) Comps should not be flapped, since the flap would detract from the presentation effect. If protection is desirable, the comp may be covered with acetate. A very thin acetate is used, and only the comp—not the mat—should be covered. See Acetate (page 80) for the procedure.

Super Comps.

Comps produced by photographic rather than hand rendering methods are called super comps. The preparation of a super comp is similar to the preparation of a mechanical, and usually all of the copy elements are of reproduction quality. Many of the copy elements, such as screen tints, type, symbols, patterns, and decorative devices are available in cut-out and dry transfer film. Type may also be used from already-printed pieces, and in some cases may even be set by a typographer. Veloxes are used for halftone copy, and photostats are used for enlarging or reducing both ready-made and hand-rendered elements to reproduction size.

Super comps are more expensive to make than hand rendered comps. In addition to the expense of preparing the original copy, there is the expense of producing the finished super comp, which involves the use of special equipment and materials. For the busy professional studio, however, these expenses are more than offset by the saving in creative time. Also, of course, the end result is superior.

There are a number of systems used to produce finished super comps. Some of these systems, such as Pinwheel, involve expensive equipment and specialized skills, and therefore can only be employed by graphic arts service companies. Others are inexpensive and simple enough to be employed in the design studio. The most common of these in-studio systems are described below.

Photostat Comps. For black and white super comps, photostats are usually the best choice because they are inexpensive and easily made. Photostats can also be used for color super comps if the color can be applied in such a way that it has a reproduced look, as with color film or air-brushed dye. The paste-up for a photostat comp is usually done in negative form on a black board, and is described in the section on Photostats (page 140).

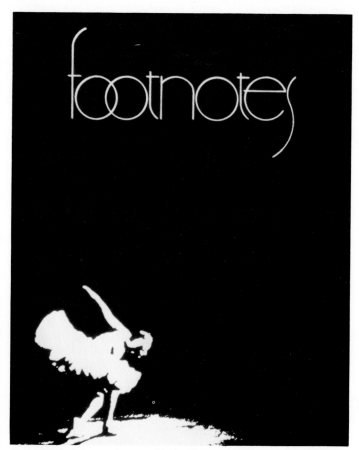

Posterized photograph assembled with type and then photostatted. (Sharon Gresh)

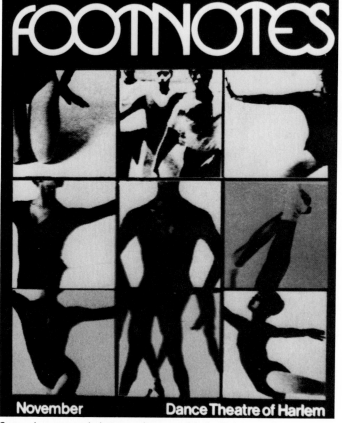

Coarsely-screened photographs assembled with type and then photostatted. Different colors of color film were applied to each of the nine panels (Joy Waller).

Photolith Film Comps. Photolith film, such as Kodalith, is a high-contrast orthochromatic film that is used in the photostat camera for reproducing line copy. Since the image area is black and the non-image area is transparent, it can be used for black and white super comps by simply taping it on a white board and attaching a mat. It can also be used for color super comps by applying color (film, dye, paper, etc.) to the board. The paste-up for a photolith film comp can be in either positive or negative form.

Blue Magic Comps. The limitation to both photostats and photolith film for color super comps is that the photographic images must necessarily be black. The Blue Magic process, which was developed by Schaedler/Pinwheel, overcomes this limitation. Working on a photolith film negative, Blue Magic Emulsion Remover is applied with a cotton wad, which removes the black-area emulsion but leaves the transparent-area emulsion intact. When liquid dye is applied to the film, then, it adheres only to the emulsion-coated areas. (Being a negative, the transparent or emulsion-coated areas are the positive images.) By using an underlying color layout as a guide, any number of colors can be applied to the film, and they can be butted by using frisket-paper masks. As with regular photolith super comps, the board to which the film is taped can be either white or colored.

I.N.T. Comps. This 3M "image 'n transfer" system enables the designer to make his own dry transfer sheets from any line copy, either ready-made or rendered. I.N.T. sheets are available in many colors, and may be transferred, by rubbing, to any type of material or shape. This makes them especially useful for folder, booklet, and package dummies, where film-backed imaging systems would be either undesirable or impossible to use.

I.N.T.'s are made by placing a film negative of the original copy in contact with an I.N.T. sheet and exposing it to strong ultraviolet light for about one minute, which hardens the coating in the image areas. The coating in the non-image areas is then washed away with a special chemical, and the sheet is ready to transfer.

Color-Key Comps. Color-Key is the 3M brand name for a polyester film with a light-sensitive color coating, which is available in more than 50 colors. It was originally designed for making pre-press color proofs (see Color Proofs, page 38), but has since been adopted by graphic designers for making super comps.

The preparation of a multicolor Color-Key comp is similar to the preparation of a multicolor mechanical: the copy for each color is placed on a separate board or overlay, and register marks may be needed for later positioning. A photolith film negative is then made for each color, placed in contact with a sheet of Color-Key, and exposed to an ultraviolet light source, which hardens the color coating in the image areas. The sheet is then washed in a developer to remove the coating in the non-image areas. After the copy for each color has been imaged on separate sheets of Color-Key, the sheets are overlayed—in register—and secured in position on a white or colored board or dummy.

Color-Key is available in 57 negative-acting transparent colors, 10 negative-

Color-Key comp in yellow, brown, and black.

acting opaque colors, and 9 positive-acting transparent colors. Additionally, opaque white Color-Key may be hand colored with special tube colors, which makes it possible to combine different colors on a single sheet.

The 3M Company makes a special light-source device for exposing Color-Key, but any type of contact printing frame will work. The most inexpensive method is to sandwich the copy and Color-Key behind a sheet of ¼" glass and expose it with a 500-watt photoflood lamp.

Color-Key materials with exposing unit.

Dummies.

Folders, booklets, and packages are the most common types of dummies encountered in the graphic design studio. Each involves special techniques, which are described below.

Folders. A folder is a sheet of paper that has been folded one or more times. (See Types of Folders, page 44.) It is usually printed on both sides, and may also be die-cut into an unusual shape. When designing a folder, a major design consideration is the tactility, or feel, of the design. This involves the paper itself, as well as the manipulation of the folded segments. Equally important, of course, is the relationship of the graphic design to the sequential unfolding of the segments.

For these reasons, a folder must be treated as a 3-dimensional entity from the very beginning. During the rough layout stage, the dummy may be made on any paper that is opaque enough for rendering on both sides, or, if layout paper is used, each side of the folder may be rendered separately and then rubber cemented on to a blank dummy made of heavier white paper. The second method makes it possible to re-do individual segments without re-doing the entire design.

It is also preferred when using color markers, which bleed through most papers, opaque or not.

The finished layout or comp dummy may also be made by rubber cementing individually rendered sides or segments on to a blank white dummy, but the more usual practice is to render it directly on the paper to be used for printing, particularly when the weight, texture, or color of the printing paper is important to the design.

The comp dummy should not be cut and folded until after the graphic elements have been rendered. This means, of course, that the accuracy of cuts and folds must have been verified in a trial dummy. To locate the position of the design on the opposite side of the paper, puncture the corners with a pushpin. After the graphic elements have been rendered, cuts are made with an X-acto knife, and folds are made by first scoring the paper with the end of a paper clip.

Since comp folders must be handled to be judged, they cannot be matted, and must be as impervious to injury as possible. For portfolio presentation, they are usually inserted in an acetate sleeve so that they may be easily removed for handling and viewing.

Booklets. A booklet is two or more sheets of paper that have been folded and bound together. Saddle-wire stitching is the usual method of binding, but other methods, such as side-wire stitching or mechanical binding are sometimes used. (See Binding Methods, page 46.)

A dummy is not always necessary in booklet design. If the booklet contains a great many pages, or if the paper stock and the page-to-page layout does not fall into the category of "high design," it may be rendered in finished layout form as separate sheets of double-page spreads. Most booklets encountered in the graphic design studio, however, such as promotional booklets and annual reports, are presented in comp dummy form, and are bound with saddle-wire stitching.

The rough layout dummy may be rendered on both sides of opaque paper and then bound, but the more practical method is to render each page on thin layout paper and then rubber cement it into a blank dummy made of heavier white paper. This makes it possible to later re-do individual pages. Before attaching the layout to the dummy, trim only the binding side of the layout. The other three sides are trimmed after it has been attached, using the dummy as a trimming guide. This may be done page by page, or after all the layouts have been attached.

The finished layout or comp dummy may also be made by rubber cementing individual pages into a blank white dummy, or it may be rendered directly on the paper to be used for printing. The second method is preferred when the weight, texture, or color of the printing paper is important to the design. When using printing paper, the cover is frequently of heavier weight than inside pages, and inside pages may vary in color, weight, and texture.

When rendering directly on the dummy paper, the rendering is done before the sheets are folded, bound, and trimmed. This means, of course, that the pages must be arranged in such a way that they will be in correct order when bound. To locate the sheet position on the opposite side of the paper, puncture the corners with a pushpin.

Folder dummy.

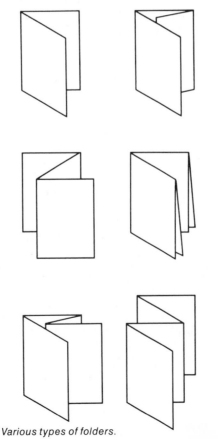

Various types of folders.

Making a Booklet Dummy. The procedure is the same for both blank and rendered dummies. When laying out the sheet, add exactly ½″ to its height and width. This provides ¼″ on all sides for trimming after the sheet has been folded and bound. In an 8½″x11″ booklet, for example, the sheet size would be 17½″x11½″. Draw the outline of these dimensions only, not the outline of the actual trim size. This is to avoid having to later erase the trim guidelines if the trimming isn't exact (as it won't be).

After drawing the sheet outline, accurately divide its horizontal dimension to find the location of the fold, and score the fold with a paper clip so it can be folded easily later. Then take a wire staple of the type used in a desk stapler, and use its legs to locate staple holes on the fold. On an 8½″ x 11″ booklet, the staples should be placed about 3″ from the top and bottom. Puncture the staple leg locations with a pushpin so the staples can later be inserted by hand when the folded sheets are assembled. Be very accurate when measuring staple hole locations, since even the slightest discrepancy will make it impossible to later insert the staples. If the booklet height and the staple hole locations are marked along the edge of a piece of paper, it can be used as a guide for all sheets. A special stapling machine, called a saddle stapler, may be used for stapling booklets. If this machine is available, then the staple holes do not need to be located or punctured beforehand.

After the sheet has been outlined, scored for folding, and punctured for staples, the procedure differs for blank and rendered dummies. With a blank dummy, the sheet is cut to outline dimensions and then set aside for assembly with other sheets. With a rendered dummy, the graphic elements are rendered on both sides before cutting to outline dimensions.

When rendering directly on the dummy, it is important to remember that the sheet dimension includes ¼″ extra margin on all trim sides. This margin remains fairly exact at top and bottom, but varies greatly at the left and right. This is because that when sheets are folded together and then trimmed, the inner pages will be narrower than the outer pages. In a thin booklet, the center pages may be only $1/32$″ narrower than the outer pages, but in a thick booklet, the center pages may be as much as $3/16$″ narrower. This variation in page width must be taken into account when designing.

After the sheets have been rendered, cut, and folded, the sheets are flattened, and staples are inserted through the cover and inside pages, sheet by sheet. When all sheets have been assembled, the staple legs are firmly bent over at the center spread, using a hard instrument to secure a tight binding. Finally, the assembled sheets are folded, the trim size is marked on the cover, and the booklet is trimmed with a steel T-square and a new razor blade or very sharp mat knife.

Inner pages of saddle-wire stitched booklet are narrower than outer pages.

Packages. Package design can be divided into two aspects: the design of the package itself, and the design of the applied graphics. When a new package is designed, both the package and the graphics are usually designed by a package design studio. When a new graphic design is applied to an existing package design, it is frequently done by a graphic designer.

The packages most frequently encountered in graphic design are the folding box and the set-up box. The folding box is the most common. It is usually made of one piece of white cardboard (called folding boxboard), and is designed in such a way that after it has been printed, cut, and scored by the box manufacturer, it can be shipped flat to the content manufacturer, where it is folded to its final shape for filling.

The set-up box is expensive to produce, and is therefore generally used only for expensive merchandise such as jewelry, cosmetics, candy, etc. It is a rigid container, usually having a separate base and lid, that is produced and shipped in 3-dimensional form ready to be packed with merchandise. The set-up box is made by cutting, scoring, and folding inexpensive gray boxboard (called chipboard) into a box shape, and the corners are "stayed" with paper, cloth, or metal reinforcements. Finally, the printed paper cover is wrapped around the box. If the cover paper is glued only at its edges, it is called a loose wrapping. If its entire surface is glued, it is called a tight wrapping. If padding is inserted between the paper and boxboard (as is frequently done with candy boxes), a loose wrapping must be used.

Making a Package Dummy. Professional designers are furnished with mechanical specifications for the package, and may also be furnished with unfolded or unassembled blank dummies for rendering purposes. If specifications or blank dummies are not available, a dummy can be made by disassembling an existing package and using it as a pattern for making a cutting and scoring layout. The layout should be extremely accurate, and should be drawn on tracing paper so it can be used for making both rough and comp dummies.

Ideally, the dummy should be made of the same board as the manufactured package. Folding white boxboard and chipboard may be obtained from box manufacturers, as well as from some

Booklet dummy.

paper merchants and printers. Art supply stores usually stock various weights of chipboard (also known as newsboard). Some may also stock folding white box-board. If they don't, heavy bristol board may be used as a substitute. In any event, make sure that the board is light enough to score and fold easily, and yet stiff enough to not warp after the box has been assembled.

To make a folding box dummy, transfer the cutting and scoring layout from the tracing paper to the sheet of boxboard or bristol board. Then render the graphic design upon it, making sure that bleed areas extend beyond the cut lines. Finally, score the folds with a paper clip, cut out the shape with an X-acto knife, and fold and glue it. Glue only the tabs that would be glued in the manufacturing process, and use an adhesive that is both fast-setting and strong, such as airplane cement (page 71) or two-sided tape (page 67). Don't use rubber cement, since it is not strong enough to withstand the stress that is inherent in folded elements. It may hold for the time being, but it will let go in a week or two.

Thumbnail sketches and preliminary rough layouts for a package may be rendered in perspective on layout paper, with the front, top, and one side of the package indicated. The fully-developed rough layout, however, should be rendered in dummy form so it can be judged in three dimensions. It may be rendered directly on the flattened dummy, or it may be rendered separately on layout paper and then adhered to the dummy. Since neatness isn't important at this stage, each side may be rendered and adhered separately, thus making partial revisions possible.

The comp should be rendered directly on the dummy whenever possible. If it is rendered separately on paper, it must be very firmly cemented to the dummy so it will not come loose after the dummy is cut and folded.

Because package dummies must be handled to be judged, they must be as impervious to injury as possible. For portfolio purposes, they should be recorded on slides, and the slides inserted into an 8½" x 11" plastic slide-viewing sheet. Use 2¼" x 2¼" slides if possible; 35mm slides are difficult to view without a projector. Make the slides as soon possible after the dummy is completed, since dummies deteriorate rapidly with age and handling.

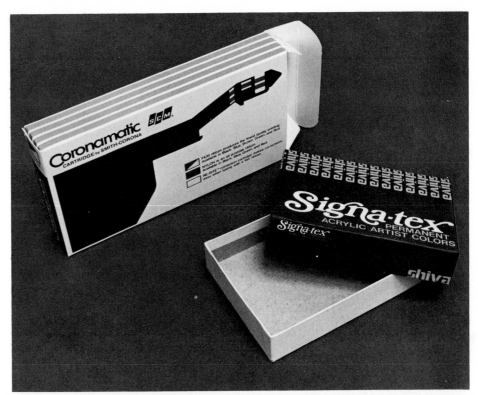

Folding box (left) and set-up box (right).

Folding box dummy; flat and folded. Folds are scored before folding.

COMP LETTERING

Comp lettering is the technique of simulating headlines and other display sizes of type and lettering on finished layouts and comps. Depending upon the effect and degree of finish desired, it can be rendered in various mediums, such as charcoal, pastel, ink, color marker, or designers color. Generally, only type and lettering 18 points and larger is comp lettered; smaller sizes are indicated with ruled lines, loops, or greeking (see Type Indication, page 120). In certain instances, however, such as in package design comps, small sizes of type must be comp lettered.

While this section explains the basic procedure for comp and layout lettering, full proficiency can only be developed through a thorough study of all aspects of letterform design. This includes structural systems, proportioning systems, and spacing, as well as the techniques for chisel-point and built-up lettering. The best way to learn the subject is through a course in lettering or letterform design at a design school. Recommended textbooks are *Lettering for Reproduction* by David Gates (Watson-Guptill), and *Lettering for Advertising* by Mortimer Leach (Van Nostrand Reinhold).

Many beginners like to believe that transfer type has made comp lettering obsolete. However, while transfer type may be employed for reproduction-quality comps (see Super Comps, page 111), it is not suitable for hand rendered layouts and comps. Its biggest drawback is that it is limited in faces, sizes, and colors (usually only black and white), which means that the designer must settle for a "good enough" typographic solution. Also, in addition to being expensive, it must be specially purchased for every job. And last but not least, it is of reproduction quality, which means that it is out of character with the techniques employed for other elements of the finished layout or comp.

The major reason that beginners favor transfer type, even when aware of its drawbacks, is that it looks better than their initial attempts at comp lettering. This may be true in regard to technique, but it is not true in regard to design. Comp lettering, no matter how crudely rendered, usually results in a superior design because it is custom tailored to fit the layout. This is as compared to transfer type, which is seldom exactly right in regard to letter design, size, and/or color.

Transfer type may look good enough to the beginner, but as his design sense develops, he will begin to discover its deficiencies. By that time, however, there's not much he can do about it if he has never learned comp lettering. Even worse, by continually settling for "good enough" typographic solutions, and by never becoming intimately involved in letterform design (which cannot be avoided in comp lettering), his typographic design sense remains undeveloped. For this reason, many design schools discourage the use of transfer type, at least until comp lettering proficiency has been acquired. By that time, of course, most students find its use unnecessary except for super comps and finished art, which is what it was designed for in the first place.

To do comp lettering, it is necessary to have a type specimen book that contains complete fonts of all major typefaces in one or more display sizes. It is desirable to also have specimen sheets of recently introduced typefaces, as well as catalogs of photolettering faces. Photolettering catalogs don't usually show complete fonts (to prevent pirating), but the letters not shown can be approximated well enough for comp purposes if one has a familiarity with letterform design.

The important thing to remember in layout design is that there are no size limitations with display type and lettering. Whatever size is indicated on the layout or comp can be achieved on the mechanical through photographic enlargement or reduction. In the case of type, for example, if the size indicated does not conform to available point sizes, the next larger size of type is ordered and then reduced by photostat for use on the mechanical. Since the type specimen is seldom the right size for the layout, the type must be indicated freehand, at least on the rough layouts. On the finished layout or comp, the type specimen may be enlarged or reduced by photostat or Lacey-Luci and then traced. If one has a good knowledge of letterform design, however, even the comp can be rendered by freehand methods.

*Type specimen book (*Type, *by David Gates).*

Pencil Sketching Techniques. During the thumbnail and preliminary rough layout stage of designing, only the overall size, weight, and position of display copy need to be indicated. This can be done with any layout tool, since individual letter shapes are not important. As the rough layouts are developed, however, the display copy must become more refined, which means that a typeface must be selected from a type specimen book, and rendered with a tool that quickly and easily simulates letter structures and details.

A soft graphite pencil with a chisel point is the best tool for laying out lettering. The chisel point is cut to the width of the thick strokes, which makes it possible to accurately indicate letter weights with a single stroke of the pencil. Depending on the way the pencil is held and manipulated, any style of lettering, such as Old Style, Modern, or Sans Serif, can easily be indicated. For narrower chisel widths, a round-lead drawing, layout, or sketching pencil is sanded to a chisel shape. For wider chisel widths, a flat-lead sketching pencil is used. See the section on Pencils (page 52) for the various pencils available and the method of making a chisel point.

Preliminary lettering sketches are usually made on separate pieces of tracing or layout paper. After the size, letter structures, and spacing have been resolved through a series of separate sketches, the final sketch is used as a guide for the rough layout, where it may be rendered in graphite, pastel, color marker, or designers color. Throughout this process, the lettering should remain rough in technique, but it should be fairly accurate in regard to size, weight, and spacing. Always use horizontal guidelines (base line, waist line, and cap or ascender line) to insure accurate height and alignment.

The technique of chisel-point lettering is very important to learn. Not only is it the fastest way to accurately simulate type and lettering, it makes it possible to render letters in any size, not just the sizes shown in the type specimen book. If the chisel-point technique is not employed, the only way to indicate layout lettering is by tracing the outlines of letters from a type specimen book, which is not only a very slow process, but limits letter sizes to those shown in the book. Of course, the type specimen can be enlarged or reduced by photostat or Lacey-Luci, but this is not desirable during the rough layout stage since it tends to stifle further experimentation with sizes and faces.

Above: sketching Old Style letters with a chisel-point pencil. Below: sketching Sans Serif letters with a chisel-point pencil.

Comp Lettering Techniques. The rough layout lettering usually needs further refinement before it can be applied to the comp or finished layout. This is done by making a careful drawing on a separate piece of tracing or layout paper and then transferring it to the comp, using one of the transfer methods described on page 99. The letters may be drawn freehand in chisel-point, using the type specimen book as a guide, or they may be traced in outline from the type specimen book. If the type specimen is not the right size, it can be enlarged or reduced by photstat or Lacey-Luci.

A variety of tools and mediums may be used for comp lettering. The choice depends on a number of factors, such as the medium employed for other elements of the finished layout or comp, the degree of finish desired, and the size and color of the lettering. Following is a description of the tools and mediums, and their typical applications.

Chisel-point Lettering. Chisel-point lettering is used for rough and finished layouts, but not for comps. It is used primarily on pastel layouts, but may also be used on color marker layouts if the color marker nib shapes are not suited to the letterforms being rendered. Charcoal or carbon pencil is used for black lettering, and pastel pencil is used for colored lettering. Graphite pencil may be used for rough layouts, but it is not black enough for finished layouts. Chisel-point pencil is the most rapid method for rendering small sizes of letters, but it requires a meticulous technique; charcoal, carbon, and pastel pencils are difficult to sharpen, wear quickly, and crumble easily. Also, great care must be taken to avoid smudging during execution, and the lettering must be sprayed with fixative when completed.

A sandpaper pad is used for sharpening chisel-point pencils. Since charcoal, carbon, and pastel pencils are so soft, however, minor re-sharpening is best accomplished by rubbing the pencil on a scrap of bond paper. This should be done every letter or two to insure crisp shapes. A needle-pointed pencil may be used in conjunction with the chisel-pointed pencil for fine lines and corners.

India Ink Lettering. India ink lettering can be used on both finished layouts and comps. It may be applied over pastel and color marker, but it cannot be applied over designers color because it will make the designers color chip off. Fine-line ink is used for small lettering and details, and extra-dense ink is used for large lettering. Because ink damages brushes, it should be applied by pen whenever possible. Large letters are usually outlined with a drawing and/or ruling pen and then filled in with a Speedball pen or brush. Small letters are usually blocked in, single stroke, with a Speedball pen, and then cleaned up with a drawing pen. In some styles of lettering, such as Modern and Engraved Script, small sizes of lettering are simultaneously outlined and filled in with a drawing pen.

When using a Speedball pen for blocking-in, try to select a nib shape and width that will render the desired shape in one stroke. B series pens are used for Sans Serif and Square Serif styles, and C series pens are used for Old Style.

Times Roman
Times Roman Ital.
Bodoni
Bodoni Italic
Helvetica

Chisel-point lettering in various styles. A chisel-point charcoal pencil was used for thick strokes, and a needle-point charcoal pencil was used for thin lines and details.

Century Expanded Italic

Ink lettering built up with a pointed drawing pen (Gillott 290).

Sequence of strokes used to build up the above letters.

Futura
Futura

Ink lettering first blocked in with a B-4 Speedball pen and then firmed up with a pointed drawing pen.

Designers Color Lettering. Designers color lettering is primarily used for comps, but it may also be used for white and colored lettering on rough and finished layouts. On rough layouts, letters are usually roughed in, single stroke, with a pointed or chisel-tipped brush. On finished layouts and comps, letters are usually outlined with a brush and/or ruling pen and then filled in. See Foreground Elements, page 110, for the method of outlining and filling in, as well as the method of lettering over dark backgrounds.

Designers color may be applied by drawing pen or Speedball pen if it is thinned slightly more than for brush application. This method is faster than outlining, and letter weights are more accurate. A second coat is usually necessary, however, and this should be applied by brush. To fill the pen, wipe a loaded brush against its side. Rinse and re-fill the pen frequently, since the designers color thickens rapidly.

Very small lettering can be rendered with a drawing pen or Speedball pen, or with a watercolor brush that has been trimmed to a chisel tip with a razor blade. The brush is preferable for lettering on painted backgrounds, since the pen would pick up the underlying color and clog. Also, the brush deposits a heavier coat of color, thus frequently eliminating the need for a second coat. For lettering directly on white or light colored paper or board, the pen is usually preferable because it controls weights better and is capable of finer details. Gillott drawing pens (page 54) are excellent for rendering very small letters.

Designers color symbol and lettering.

White designers color on black background.

Color Marker Lettering. Color marker lettering is used on rough and finished color marker layouts. It is seldom used in conjunction with other mediums or for highly finished comp lettering. The broad-nib color marker may be used like a chisel-point pencil, but the nib width isn't adjustable. Small letters and details are usually rendered with the pointed-nib color marker.

Cut-out Lettering. Large, simple letters may be cut out of paper or film. Usually, the letters are cut out after the paper or film has been adhered to the comp. With paper, however, it is also possible to cut out the letters separately and then adhere them. When cutting out the letters separately, rubber cement the paper to a scrap piece of illustration board to insure accuracy in cutting.

Cut-out letters have very sharp outlines and clean, smooth tones. This technique is not suitable, however, for small lettering, or for letters with fine lines or intricate shapes.

Folio Extra Bold

Ink lettering blocked in with a B-4 Speedball pen and firmed up with a pointed drawing pen.

Consort

Ink lettering blocked in with a B-6 Speedball pen and firmed up with a pointed drawing pen.

Caslon
Caslon

Ink lettering blocked in with a C-4 (chisel-shaped) Speedball pen and firmed up with a pointed drawing pen.

This mother wants the best for her children.

Your help is better than best.

Bide-A-Wee

Color marker lettering (Sharon Gresh).

AZUMA

Cut-out lettering (Sharon Gresh).

Frisket Paper Lettering. As with cut-out lettering, the frisket paper technique is suitable only for large, simple letters. The frisket paper is adhered to the comp. The letters are cut out and removed, and the color is applied by air brush or regular brush. See Frisket Paper, page 79.

TYPE INDICATION

Type indication is the technique of indicating body copy or text sizes of type on layouts and comps. It involves the use of ruled lines, loops, or greeking, and its purpose is to simulate the size and "color" of the line or lines of type without actually rendering letters individually. Type indication is used only when the type being indicated is so small that individual characters cannot be clearly discerned beyond a distance of 4' or 5', which includes most typefaces 14 points and smaller. Type and lettering 18 points and larger must be rendered letter by letter (see Comp Lettering, page 116).

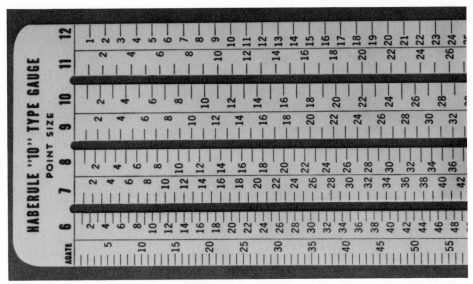

A type gauge is used for measuring line spacing.

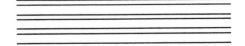

Lines.

Loops.

Greeking.

The first step in type indication is to fit the copy to the layout, as described in the section on Copyfitting (page 133). After the outer dimensions of the column of type have been drawn lightly in pencil on the layout, base-line to base-line measurements are ticked off along the left vertical guideline. For example, if the column is to be set in 11 point type with 2 points of leading between lines (11/13), the base-line to base-line measurement would be 13 points. The easiest method of measuring is with a Haberule Type Gauge (page 126). Otherwise, use a pica ruler that has a point scale, or a sample of type that has 13 point base-line to base-line spacing. When using a point scale or type sample, the measurement can be transferred to the layout with a divider, or it can be ticked off along the edge of a piece of bond paper and then transferred. Tick off about five lines on the bond paper so the paper doesn't have to be shifted so often when transferring the lines to the layout. Use a very sharp 5H pencil for measuring base-line spacing, since even the slightest discrepency would later be noticeable.

After the base-lines have been ticked off, then tick off the waist-lines or x-heights for each line. As explained on page 121, the x-height, or distance between the base-line and waist-line of lower case letters, is where most of the "color" occurs in body copy. In type indication, therefore, only the x-height is indicated. Of course, if the type is to be set in all caps, then base-lines and cap-lines should be indicated. Because capitals are so much larger than lower case letters of the same point size, however, all-capital copy larger than 10 points must usually be comp lettered.

The x-height can only be determined by measuring the lower case x or other letter of similar height in the typeface being specified, since this height varies with each typeface. The x-height can be transferred directly to the layout with a divider, or it can be added to the base-line measurements on the bond paper and then transferred.

After both the base-line and waist-line measurements have been ticked off on the layout, the next step depends on whether the type is to be indicated with ruled lines, loops, or greeking.

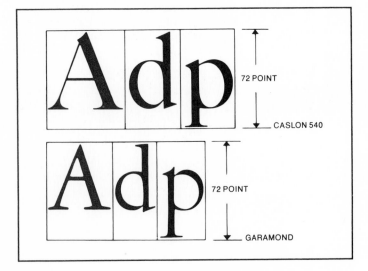

72 POINT — CASLON 540

72 POINT — GARAMOND

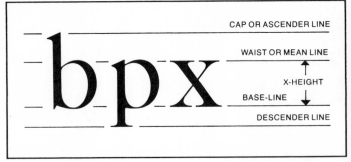

CAP OR ASCENDER LINE
WAIST OR MEAN LINE
X-HEIGHT
BASE-LINE
DESCENDER LINE

The distance between the waist line and base-line is the x-height.

Two typefaces of the same point size.
Note difference in x-height.

Step 1. Using a very sharp 5H pencil, T-square, and triangle, lightly draw the outer dimensions of the column of type on the layout.

Step 2. Measure the x-height of the type sample and transfer it to the left edge of the column, placing the waist-line measurement at the top corner.

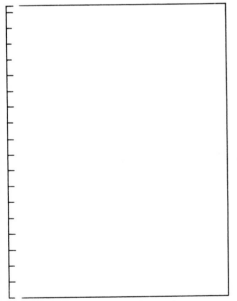

Step 3. Place the proper point scale of the type gauge (the base-line to base-line measurement) along the left edge of the column, align "line 1" of the scale with the transferred base-line measurement, and tick off the base-line measurements along the left edge of the column.

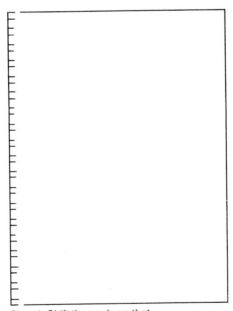

Step 4. Shift the scale so that "line 1" aligns with the transferred waist-line measurement, and tick off the waist-line measurements along the left edge of the column.

Method of applying type indication measurements to a layout using a type gauge.

The Ruled-line Method of Type Indication. The ruled-line method of type indication is the fastest and therefore the most common method. It is used for rough and finished layouts as well as comps. Lines may be ruled in graphite, carbon, or charcoal pencil, as well as ink or designers color.

Within its x-height area, a line of type is composed of certain percentages of black and white shapes, which, when optically mixed, produce a specific "color" or tone. It is necessary, therefore, for ruled lines to have the same black/white ratio, within the x-height area, as that of the typeface being indicated. This is done by adjusting the thickness of the ruled lines so the two lines, plus the white space in between, match the "color" of the type. The thickness of the ruled lines must occur within the x-height area. If the base-line and waist-line measurements are even slightly exceeded, the type indication will be oversized one or more points. Remember that 1 point is only $1/72$ of an inch.

Ruled Lines in Pencil. A 2B or HB graphite drawing pencil, or a charcoal or carbon pencil, is generally used for ruled lines in pencil. The pencil should be pointed, but should not be so sharp that it produces lines too thin to accurately simulate the "color" of the typeface being indicated. Guidelines delineating the copy block should be drawn very lightly, since they can't later be erased without also erasing the type indication.

The T-square must be used for ruling to insure accurate parallels. To insure flush margins, the lines should be drawn in two strokes; from left margin to center and from right margin to center. This is faster and more accurate than attempting to stop the stroke exactly at the right margin. Also, because of the added pressure at the beginning of strokes, both side edges of the copy block will be firmly delineated.

To simulate the type most accurately, it is desirable to break the copy into paragraphs of varying lengths. A paragraph is indicated by indenting the first line approximately one em, and by making the last line less than full width.

Another method of indicating body copy in pencil is to use a chisel-point graphite pencil cut to the x-height of the type being indicated. When using this method, only the base-line measurements need to be ticked off, and strokes are drawn the full width of the copy block, not edge to center as with the base-line/waist-line method. Chisel-point type indication is very accurate in regard to maintaining a consistent x-height, but it is less accurate in regard to "color." This is because its "color" is achieved by an actual gray value, not by an optical mixture of black and white as in type itself. Also, it can only be rendered in graphite pencil, which limits its use to graphite layouts.

When the pencil indication is finished, it should be cleaned and "fixed" immediately so it won't get smudged. Scrub the surrounding area with a kneaded eraser, using a scrap of bond paper as an erasing shield. If the lines are too dark for the type being indicated, they can be lightened by gently tamping with a flattened kneaded eraser. Before spraying with matte fixative, mask the surrounding area with scraps of bond paper held in position by hand.

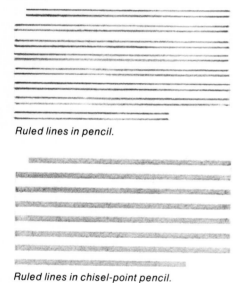

Ruled lines in pencil.

Ruled lines in chisel-point pencil.

Ink lines scraped with a razor blade to create texture and lighten "color."

Ruled Lines in Ink. A ruling pen, drawing pen, or technical fountain pen may be used for ruling lines in ink, The ruling pen is preferred because line thicknesses can be more accurately adjusted. However, if a good selection of pen point sizes are available, a drawing pen or technical fountain pen will usually suffice.

Because India ink is blacker than printing ink, ruled lines in ink, no matter what their weight, tend to look blacker than the type being indicated. To overcome this, many designers thin the ink slightly with water. This can be done in a palette, but the best method is to thin a partially used bottle of ink so that it can be saved for future jobs. (Make sure to label it so that it won't be used by mistake for other purposes.) Another method of achieving the right "color" is to scrape the completed copy block with a sharp razor blade. Place the blade flat on the paper and scrape lightly to avoid gouging. In addition to lightening the tone of the copy, this method will create a texture that is similar to that of type.

Ruled Lines in Color. If the layout was rendered in color markers, a pointed-nib color marker may be used for ruled lines. This is not a very accurate method, however, because the line thickness cannot be adjusted. The most accurate method of ruling lines in color is with a ruling pen and deisgners color. Don't use colored ink; being transparent, its tone will vary according to how heavily it is applied. Also, it very seldom matches the color used elsewhere in the design.

Ruled lines in ink.

The Loop Method of Type Indication. The loop method of type indication is halfway between ruled lines and greeking. Texturally, it is more authentic than ruled lines but less authentic than greeking, and timewise, it is slower than ruled lines but faster than greeking. These advantages and disadvantages, consequently, must be weighed in terms of the layout or comp requirements and objectives.

After the x-height measurements have been ticked off along the left edge of the copy block, guidelines are extended across the entire block with a T-square and 5H pencil. These guidelines should be very light, particularly for pencil loops, which would make their later erasure impossible.

A certain amount of practice is required to produce loops that have the general characteristics of type. The loops should have the same rhythm as the type being indicated. with shapes and spaces that are neither too condensed nor too expanded. The loops should be generally vertical; otherwise they will indicate either a backhand or an italic face.

Loops may be drawn entirely freehand, staying generally within the x-height area (the occasional stroke that slips above or below this area can be considered an ascender or descender), or they may be drawn using the T-square as a base-line guide. If the T-square is positioned at the base-line as a lower limit for the pencil or pen, the looping procedure is not only speeded up, but the ensuing loops will more accurately represent the mechanical quality of type. An occasional slip above the waist-line will represent an ascender, and the lack of descenders will never be noticed.

Loops should be broken into typical word lengths of one to ten characters, and the space between words should be one character, or one loop, in width. Also, paragraphs of varying lengths should be indicated. To indicate a paragraph, indent the first line and shorten the last line.

Loops in Pencil. Pencil loops may be rendered with a pointed charcoal, carbon, or 2B or HB graphite pencil. The degree of pointedness depends on the weight of the type being indicated. The cleaning and fixing operations are the same as for ruled lines.

Loops in Ink and Color. Ink loops may be rendered with a drawing pen, such as a Gillott 170, or a technical fountain pen, such as a Rapidograph. The pen point size should match the weight of the type being indicated.

Color loops may be rendered with a drawing pen, or with a small watercolor brush cut to a chisel tip. When using a drawing pen, the designers color must be thinner than for brushing, and the pen is filled by wiping a loaded brush against the side of the nib. Rinse and re-fill the pen frequently, since the paint thickens rapidly. For most purposes, the pen is preferred to the brush because it maintains weights better. However, the brush is better for painted or dark surfaces because it applies a thicker coat, and doesn't pick up the underlying paint.

Pencil loops drawn freehand.

Ink loops using the T-square as a base-line guide.

The Greeking Method of Type Indication. The greeking method of type indication most accurately simulates the texture and "color" of type. Greeking takes longer to execute than ruled lines or loops, and is therefore used only on highly finished layouts and comps. Even then, it is not practical for very lengthy copy.

The objective in greeking is to simulate typographic letter shapes without creating recognizable words (thus the name, "greeking"). For that reason, only common letterstrokes are used. Uncommon strokes, such as are found in a, c, f, g, k, r, s, t, x, y, and z are not usually used because they can be too easily identified as belonging to specific letters. To further insure the abstractness of word patterns, the letterstrokes are never joined together. The resulting shapes can be likened to Bodoni with the thin strokes removed. Ascenders and descenders should be used in greeking, but guidelines are not necessary for them. It is important, however, that their length should never exceed the x-height of the type being indicated. Capital letters can be indicated in greeking, but because of the unique shapes of capitals, it is much more difficult to create an authentic pattern without using identifiable letterstrokes.

As with loops, greeking should be broken into typical word lengths of one to ten characters, and the space between words should be one character in width. Paragraphs of varying length should be indicated by indenting the first line and shortening the last line. The first letter in the paragraph is usually capitalized, but caps are not used otherwise.

The layout procedure for greeking is exactly the same as for loops; the x-height measurements are ticked off along the left edge of the copy block, and light guidelines are extended across the entire block with a T-square and 5H pencil. For greeking in pencil, see Loops in Pencil, and for greeking in ink and color, see Loops in Ink and Color.

Common letterstrokes used in greeking.

Greeking in pencil.

Greeking in ink.

Copyfitting

Copyfitting, also known as copy casting, is the process of converting written words, or copy, into typographic form. The copy, which is usually prepared and/or written by a professional copywriter, is furnished to the designer, along with other specifications, at the time that he receives the design commission. It is always typewritten, and is variously referred to as the copy, the typescript, or the manuscript. It contains every word that is to be printed, such as the headline, the sub-head(line), and the body copy or text.

Copyfitting is done during the layout stage of designing. Using the manuscript as a guide, the designer experiments with various styles, sizes, and arrangements of the typographic elements, taking into account their relationship to the entire design. When he has arrived at a good solution, he writes his specifications on the manuscript and sends it to the typographer for typesetting. If the specifications are complicated, it is also necessary to include a pencil layout.

The typographer sets the type and makes a trial proof on inexpensive paper. This trial proof, called a first proof, rough proof, or galley proof, is sent to the designer for checking and approval. The designer marks the errors and alterations, if any, and returns the proof to the typographer for corrections. A final, or reproduction, proof is then made on high-quality paper. This reproduction proof, commonly called the repro, is sent to the designer for pasting on to the mechanical.

While the beginner may find this process bewildering, it cannot be disregarded. Every printed piece contains typography of some kind, and every graphic designer, therefore, must be capable of doing copyfitting. The remainder of this chapter describes each aspect of the process in detail.

It will be seen that even though metal typesetting has largely been replaced by phototypesetting, its characteristics are frequently used in this chapter to describe certain aspects of typography. The reason for this is that metal type, being 3-dimensional, is easier to comprehend in regard to measurements. Also, many typographic terms originated in metal typesetting, and they make more sense if one is aware of their source. Leading, for example, refers to the thin strips of lead that are placed between lines of metal type.

TYPE SPECIMEN BOOKS

To do copyfitting, it is necessary to have a type specimen book that contains complete fonts, in all sizes, of at least the major typefaces. A complete font includes capitals, lower case letters, figures (numbers), and punctuation marks. The book should also contain charts showing the number of characters per pica for text or body sizes.

Many typographers have type specimen books containing complete showings of their typefaces. Being expensive to produce, however, they are usually only available to good customers. A number of type specimen books are available at art supply stores, but not all meet the preceding specifications. Recommended books are *Type,* by David Gates (Watson-Guptill), and *Type and Typography,* by Ben Rosen (Van Nostrand Reinhold). While either of these books will serve the beginner's needs, they must be supplemented with other typographic reference material as proficiency develops, such as specimen sheets of recently introduced faces, photolettering catalogs, etc. From the very beginning, therefore, it is important to make a habit of acquiring anything and everything that relates to typographic design, and storing it in such a way that it is readily available for reference.

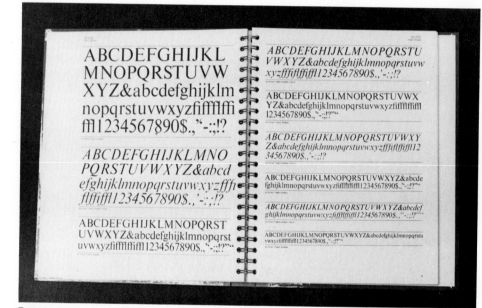

Type specimen book (Type, *by David Gates*).

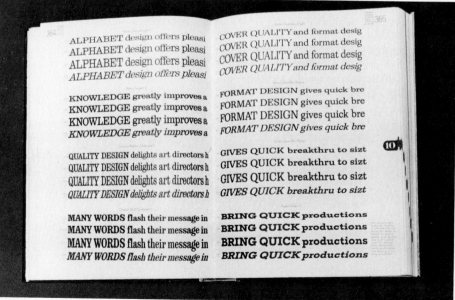

Photo lettering catalog (Photo-Lettering, Inc.).

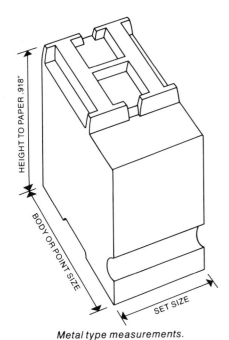

Times Roman
Times Roman Bold
Times Roman Italic

Size	6	7	8	9	10	11	12	14
Picas								
10	36	33	31	29	27	25	23	22
12	43	40	37	34	32	30	28	26
14	50	46	43	40	37	35	32	30
16	58	53	49	46	42	40	37	34
18	65	59	55	51	48	45	41	39
20	72	66	61	57	53	50	46	43
22	79	73	67	63	58	55	51	47
24	86	79	73	68	64	60	55	52
26	94	86	79	74	69	65	60	56
28	101	92	85	80	74	70	64	60
30	108	99	92	86	80	75	69	65

*Character count chart
(Haber Typographers, Inc.).*

Metal type measurements.

HEIGHT TO PAPER .918"

BODY OR POINT SIZE

SET SIZE

TYPE MEASUREMENTS

The basic units of measurement in typography are points and picas. Twelve points equal 1 pica. (As a matter of comparison, one point is approximately $1/72''$, and one pica is approximately $1/6''$. It is not important to remember this, however, since typographic measurements are always made in points and picas, never inches.)

1 INCH
*12 points equal 1 pica.
6 picas equal .996 inch.*

A special unit of measurement, the agate, is used to measure column depth in newspaper and magazine advertising. Fourteen agate lines equal 1″. This unit of measurement is not used in copyfitting.

Points are used to designate typeface sizes, as well as the amount of added space (or leading) between lines. Picas are used to designate the width of the line or column of type, as well as the length of strip materials such as rules and borders.

The point size of a typeface refers to the vertical dimension of the top surface of the type body, not to the vertical dimension of the letters themselves. Because of design differences between typefaces, such as longer or shorter ascenders and descenders, typefaces of the same point size will differ in actual letter size. For example, Caslon 540 letters, having very short ascenders and descenders, are much larger than Garamond letters of the same point size. Consequently, the only way to determine the point size of a typeface after it has been printed is to refer to a type specimen book.

TWO POINT SYSTEMS

The didot point, which is used in most European countries, is slightly larger than the pica point used in Britain and the United States. The didot point measures .0148 of an inch, whereas the pica point measures .0138 of an inch. 12 didot points equal 1 *cicero* or *douze*, which measures .178 of an inch.

While the didot point system is not frequently encountered in the United States, it is sometimes used in photolettering and printed alphabet sheets to size European typefaces.

.4980"

36 POINT PICA

.5328"

36 POINT DIDOT

The x-height of a typeface refers to the height of the lower case letters without ascenders and descenders. The lower case x is used to designate this height because its horizontal top and bottom makes it easier to measure than other letters. The x-height measurement is very important in typography. Since type is usually set in upper and lower case, and since capitals as well as lower case letters with ascenders and descenders are in the minority, it is the x-height of the lower case letters that establishes the size, legibility, "color," and texture of a line of type. As mentioned in the last paragraph, if a typeface has short ascenders and descenders, its x-height will be larger than in a typeface of the same point size that has longer ascenders and descenders.

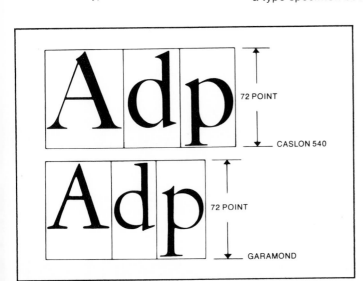

72 POINT

CASLON 540

72 POINT

GARAMOND

Two typefaces of the same point size. Note difference in letter sizes.

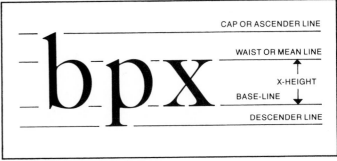

CAP OR ASCENDER LINE

WAIST OR MEAN LINE

X-HEIGHT

BASE-LINE

DESCENDER LINE

Letter measurements.

A pica ruler is necessary for typographic measurements. A 24″ stainless steel ruler with inch, pica, and agate scales is ideal, since it can be used for both graphic and typographic design purposes. As stated in the section on Rulers and Scales (page 58), some brands of steel rulers, such as the Gaebel Printers Comparative Scale, also have a point scale. While the point scale is not a necessity in typographic design work, it can be very helpful.

A line gauge, such as the Haberule Type Gauge, is used to measure line spacing and column depths. It has scales for measuring 6, 7, 8, 9, 10, 11, 12, 13, and 15 point lines, as well as a scale for character counting manuscript copy. It is not a necessary tool, but is very desirable since it eliminates mathematical calculations.

24″ steel ruler—front and back.

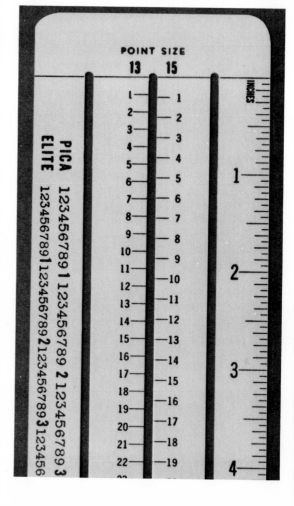

Haberule type gauge—front and back.

WORDSPACING

The space between words is normally determined by the typographer. However, if more or less than normal wordspacing is desired by the designer, he must specify this on the manuscript. In handset type, wordspacing is done by inserting pieces of metal, called quads and spaces, between words. The basic unit of spacing materials is the em quad, and it is a square of the type size being used. For example, an em quad for 12 point type is 12x12 points, an em quad for 24 point type is 24x24 points, etc. Similarly, 2-em and 3-em quads are, respectively, two times and three times the width of an em quad.

Em quad is the square of the point size of the type.

The en quad is one-half the width of the em quad. For example, a 12 point en quad is 6 points wide, a 24 point en quad is 12 points wide, etc.

Spacing materials thinner than em and en quads are called spaces, not quads. Standard widths are 3-em, 4-em, and 5-em ($\frac{1}{3}$ em, $\frac{1}{4}$ em, and $\frac{1}{5}$ em). Spaces thinner than 5-em are called thin spaces, and are measured in points rather than fractions of the em. Thin spaces are frequently used in letterspacing but rarely in wordspacing.

The space between words is usually 3- or 4-em, depending on the style and size of type. Larger and/or narrower typefaces require less wordspacing, and smaller and/or wider typefaces require more wordspacing. When a line of type must be made equal in length to other lines, then the space between words must be adjusted. This is called justifying the line. As long as the adjustment is not excessive, the varying wordspacing from line to line will not be noticeable. If it is too noticeable, the designer should request the typographer to improve the wordspacing by re-setting one or more lines.

Paragraphs are usually indented one em. If unusual indentation is desired, the designer should specify so on the manuscript. (See Proofreaders' Marks, page 137, for the method of specifying indentations.)

In addition to the normal use of the em unit of measurement for wordspacing, it is also used to designate the width of dashes. The dash is wider than the hyphen, and is frequently used to denote a span of time, such as 1900–1950, or in place of parentheses. The appropriate length of dash may be left up to the typographer, or it may be specified by the designer. An en dash is usually used to denote a span of time, an em dash is usually used to set off parenthetical matter, and a 2-em or 3-em dash is used to indicate omitted words, phrases, etc. The method of specifying dash lengths is shown in Proofreaders' Marks (page 137).

The em measurement is also used in phototypesetting, the main difference being that divisions of the em are expressed in units rather than fractions of the em or points, as explained in the Unit System of Measuring (page 13). In an 18-unit (to the em) phototypesetting system, for example, 6 units would be the same width as a 3-em ($\frac{1}{3}$ of an em) space in metal type.

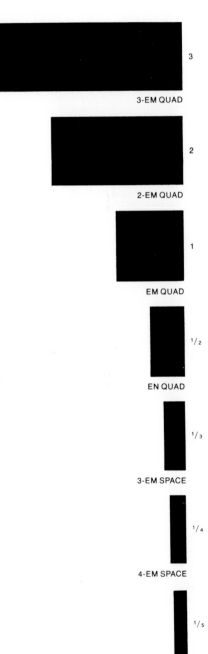

3

3-EM QUAD

2

2-EM QUAD

1

EM QUAD

$\frac{1}{2}$

EN QUAD

$\frac{1}{3}$

3-EM SPACE

$\frac{1}{4}$

4-EM SPACE

$\frac{1}{5}$

5-EM SPACE

Quads and spaces.

The present popularity of the old style has encouraged French type-founders to revive other early printed forms, but

3-em wordspacing.

The present popularity of the old style has encouraged French type-founders to revive other early printed forms, but

Wordspacing adjusted to justify lines.

LETTERSPACING

In handset type, the normal space between letters is automatically determined by the "set" or width of the type body of each letter. There are occasions, however, when the space between letters must be increased (it can't be decreased). This is done by inserting metal spaces between the individual pieces of type, and is called letterspacing.

In phototypesetting, since there is no metal type body to contend with, the normal space between letters can be decreased as well as increased. Decreased spacing is called minus letterspacing. Letterspacing is expressed in units-to-the-em, such as −1, +1, or N (normal). Both letterspacing and minus letterspacing can be automatically applied between all letters, or it can be selectively applied between certain letter combinations to achieve more even spacing. When all letters are spaced consistently tighter than normal it is called minus letterspacing, and when only selected letter combinations are spaced tighter than normal it is called kerning.

For best legibility, the smaller the type, the more open the letterspacing should be, and the larger the type, the tighter the letterspacing should be. There should be enough letterspacing to make every letter element perceptible, but not so much that letters are perceived as individual entities rather than as "word pictures." When copyfitting, therefore, it is usually better to increase or decrease the area of a copy block by changing the point size of the type, rather than by drastically altering the letterspacing.

But while maximum legibility is of utmost importance in text sizes and/or lengthy copy, it is less important in display sizes and/or brief copy. If individual letters can be clearly seen at 2′ or 3′, their graphic "entertainment" qualities are more important than legibility. At such sizes, letters can be very openly or tightly spaced, or even overlapped. So long as the resulting design is sufficiently satisfying, conceptually and/or aesthetically, the observer is willing to expend the effort needed to decipher it.

Many phototypesetting systems are capable of setting display sizes of type. At sizes above 36 point, however, the inadequacies of mechanical letterspacing become apparent, and it is usually necessary to cut and re-space the type proof by the method described on page 93. For this reason, it is often advantageous to use photolettering for display

type. As explained on page 15, most photolettering systems are capable of very accurate letterspacing because it is done visually rather than mechanically.

Printed alphabet sheets (page 17) are also commonly used for display type. Not

only are they inexpensive, but accurate letterspacing is easy to achieve. Also, they can be used in ways that would be difficult, expensive, or impossible with phototype and photolettering, such as the butting or overlapping of letters.

LARK LARK

Normal spacing.   Letterspaced to improve spacing.

Typography

TOUCHING

Typography

VERY TIGHT

Typography

TIGHT

Typography

NORMAL

Typography

TV SPACING

Photo lettering with various letterspacing (Photo Typositor).

LINE SPACING (LEADING)

Line spacing is the amount of vertical space between lines of type. A certain amount of line spacing is automatically provided when one line of type is butted (set solid) against the next line of type, but this is not usually adequate for optimum legibility. Depending on the size, style, and line length of the type, line spacing must usually be increased one or more points. In handset type, this is done by inserting thin strips of metal between the lines of type. These strips of metal are called leads (pronounced ledds), and the process is called leading.

In phototypesetting, leading is achieved by keyboard command. Leading can be increased by ½-point increments, and because there is no type metal to contend with, it can also be decreased (minus leading). Minus leading is frequently used for setting caps and display type, but its use in normal text typesetting usually damages legibility.

The basic rule for leading is that it should be increased as the length of line increases. The reason for this is that the longer the line, the more difficult it is for the eyes to follow the line, and also to locate the succeeding line. Additional space between the lines makes this easier. Generally, a 12-pica column is leaded 1 or 2 points, a 20-pica column is leaded 2 or 3 points, and a 30-pica column is leaded 3 or 4 points. A typeface that has a large x-height (see page 125) requires more leading than a typeface that has a small x-height.

While this guideline is adequate for the beginner, optimum leading can only be achieved by comparing sample columns of type having differing amounts of leading. Since the style and size of type influences the amount of leading needed, the sample columns, ideally, should be set in the style and size of type being used. Comparison charts for leading are available in some type specimen books, and are a worthy addition to the type reference library.

When specifying the amount of leading between lines, the usual procedure is to first state the point size of the type, and then state the point size of the type plus the leading. For example, if 10 point type is to be leaded 2 points, the specification would be 10/12 (orally expressed as "10 on 12"). If there is to be no leading (set solid), then the specification would be 10/10.

To determine the amount of leading in a column of printed type, first find the point size of the type by referring to a type specimen book, and then find the distance between lines by measuring from one baseline to another. Subtract the point size of the type from the distance between lines to find the amount of leading. For example, if the type is 10 points, and the distance from one baseline to another is 12 points, there are 2 points of leading.

THE BEST AND THE MOST DURAB
$\frac{9}{9}$ The best and the most durable fashi ons quickly become dated whenever styles change. There are perhaps m

THE BEST AND THE MOST DURAB
$\frac{9}{10}$ The best and the most durable fashi ons quickly become dated whenever styles change. There are perhaps m

THE BEST AND THE MOST DURAB
$\frac{9}{11}$ The best and the most durable fashi ons quickly become dated whenever styles change. There are perhaps m

THE BEST AND THE MOST DURAB
$\frac{9}{12}$ The best and the most durable fashi ons quickly become dated whenever styles change. There are perhaps m

9 point Helvetica Regular with various line leading.

The reason for using the baseline of letters as a point of measurement is because it is common to all letters, both capital and lower case. This is as compared to cap or ascender lines, waist lines, and descender lines, which are not common to all letters.

The ideal tool for measuring line spacing is the Haberule Type Gauge. If this gauge isn't available, line spacing can be measured with a point scale. If a point scale isn't available, a fairly accurate estimate of points can be made with a pica scale.

---

1 POINT LEAD

2 POINT LEAD

3 POINT LEAD

4 POINT LEAD

6 POINT SLUG

8 POINT SLUG

12 POINT SLUG

18 POINT SLUG

*Leads—under 6 points.
Slugs—6 points and over.*

_____ *sick poor in the said hospital, free of charge for*
_____ *diet, attendance, advice, and medicines, and*
_____ *shall make the same appear to the satisfaction*
_____ *of the speaker of the Assembly for the time be*
_____ *ing, that then it shall and may be lawful for the*
_____ *said speaker and he is hereby required, to sign*

*12 point Future Bold Italic
with 2 point leading.
Measurement from base-line to
base-line is 14 points.*

COLUMN WIDTHS

For good legibility, the width of the column should be proportionate to the size of the type. As a general rule, there should be 30 to 60 characters per line, with 40 to 50 providing optimum legibility. This is not a hard and fast rule, and may be modified to a certain extent.

As mentioned in the section on Line Spacing, too wide a column makes it difficult for the eyes to follow a line, and also to locate the succeeding line. If a column must be widened beyond normal limits, additional leading may help to retain good legibility. Too narrow a column makes rapid scanning impossible, and an excessive number of words must be broken at the ends of lines. Also, if the column is justified (set flush left and right), wordspacing will be very uneven from line to line.

The symbol "X" is used to specify column widths. For example, the specification "X20" means a column 20 picas wide.

Too narrow a column makes rapid scanning impossible, and an excessive number of words must be divided at the ends of lines. Also, if the column is justified (set flush left and right), wordspacing will be very uneven from line to line.

Too narrow a column.

For good legibility, the width of the column should be proprotionate to the size of the type. As a general rule, there should be 30 to 60 characters per line, with 40 to 50 providing optimum legibility. This is not a hard and fast rule, and may be modified to a certain extent. As mentioned in the section on spacing, too wide a column makes it difficult for the eyes to follow a line, and also to locate the succeeding line. If a column must be widened beyond normal limits, additional leading may help to retain good legibility.

Too wide a column.

COLUMN ARRANGEMENTS

Flush Left and Right (Justified). This is the most common column arrangement. As explained in Wordspacing (page 127), lines are justified (made equal in length) by adjusting wordspacing.

Flush Left/Ragged Right. In this arrangement, the lines are not justified. This means that the wordspacing remains consistent from line to line. Also, few if any words need to be divided at the ends of lines. When specifying a flush left/ragged right arrangement, it is desirable to indicate minimum and maximum line lengths. In a narrow column, line lengths should normally not vary more than 2 picas, while in a wide column, line lengths could vary as much as 4 or 5 picas.

Flush Right/Ragged Left. This arrangement is not usually used for large amounts of copy because it is difficult for the eyes to locate line beginnings. It is frequently used for captions, however, since the flush right/ragged left arrangement often makes a better composition with the photograph or illustration.

Centered. The centered column arrangement is primarily used for titles and headings. In order to achieve a pleasing combination of line lengths, it is necessary to make a word-by-word character count, and to indicate the line breaks on the manuscript.

Asymmetrical. In this arrangement, lines of varying lengths are staggered over one another in such a way that the total column is balanced, either in itself or in relation to other layout elements. In addition to indicating the line breaks on the manuscript, the typographer must be provided with a layout indicating line positions.

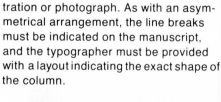

Runaround. In this arrangement, the column is shaped to fit around an illustration or photograph. As with an asymmetrical arrangement, the line breaks must be indicated on the manuscript, and the typographer must be provided with a layout indicating the exact shape of the column.

TYPING THE MANUSCRIPT

The manuscript copy should be typed on 8½" x 11" opaque white paper, one side only, using double spacing. Always make a carbon copy for reference. The margins should be at least 1" wide, and the lines of body copy should be as equal in length as possible. The title or description of the job should appear at the top of every page, and every page should be consecutively numbered.

The standard typewriter type sizes are pica and elite. The pica size produces 10 characters per inch, and the elite size produces 12 characters per inch. Type-writers with proportional spacing, such as the IBM Executive, should not be used for typing manuscript copy because the number of characters per inch varies, thus making accurate character counting impossible.

The manuscript copy should be as legible and uncomplicated as possible. Handwritten corrections and changes may be made in the copy, but if they become excessive, the copy should be re-typed. Neat copy not only minimizes typesetting errors, it minimizes type-setting costs.

CHARACTER COUNTING THE MANUSCRIPT

Copy that is to be set in 18 point or larger type does not need to be character counted. This is because large sizes of type are rendered letter by letter on the layout, using the type specimen book as a guide. 14 point and smaller type is not rendered letter by letter on the layout. Rather, it is indicated with ruled lines that represent the type height, line length, and number of lines. To determine the line length and number of lines for a specific size of type, it is first necessary to character count the manuscript.

The total number of characters in a body of manuscript copy is found by multiplying the number of characters per line by the number of lines. Since it would be extremely time-consuming to count the number of characters in every line, the following method of averaging is used.

At the end of a line of average length, draw a vertical guideline through the copy. Then count the characters in the line of average length, including periods, commas, spaces, etc. If a pica typewriter was used, there will be 10 characters or space units per inch, and if an elite typewriter was used, there will be 12 characters or space units per inch. Multiply the number of characters in the average line by the number of lines to find the total number of characters in the copy. Count the short lines at the end of paragraphs as full lines, since there will be similar short lines in the type.

This method of character counting is fairly accurate, and is adequate for most applications. However, if the line lengths vary greatly, or if greater accuracy is desirable, add all the characters that fall beyond the guideline, and subtract all the blank spaces in lines that fall short of the guideline.

When counting the characters in a line, a ruler can be used to speed up the process. For example, if the line measures between 6" and 7", multiply the characters per inch (either 10 or 12) by six, and then add the characters that fall beyond the 6" mark.

```
                                    Copyfitting   p. 1


Copyfitting
                                                      50
Copyfitting, also known as copy casting, is the

process of converting written words, or copy, into

typographic form.  The copy, which is usually pre-

pared and/or written by a professional copywriter,

is furnished to the designer, along with other

specifications, at the time that he receives the

design commission.  It is always typewritten, and

is variously referred to as the copy, the typescript,

or the manuscript.  It contains every word that is

to be printed, such as the headline, the sub-head

(line), and the body copy or text.

    Copyfitting is done during the layout stage of

designing.  Using the manuscript as a guide, the

designer experiments with various styles, sizes, and

arrangements of the typographic elements, taking

into account their relationship to the entire design.

When he has arrived at a good solution, he writes

his specifications on the manuscript and sends it -

plus the layout - to the typographer for typesetting.  19


                                    950
```

This copy averages 50 characters per line. Multiplied by 19 lines, the total character count for the page is 950.

The Haberule Type Gauge (page 126) contains a scale for counting both pica and elite type. Such a scale is essential for line-by-line character counting, which is necessary when fitting type into certain column arrangements, such as centered, asymmetrical, or runaround (see page 130). If a Haberule Type Gauge is not available, a character counting scale can be made with a typewriter that matches the size of the manuscript type. Starting at the top left edge of an 8½" wide sheet of paper, type the numerals 1 through 9, followed by an underlined 1. Then type the numerals 1 through 9 again, followed by an underlined 2. Repeat this process across the entire sheet, each time increasing the underlined number by one digit. The underlined numbers; 1, 2, 3, etc., represent 10, 20, 30, etc.

The character count for a block or page of copy should be indicated at the bottom of the block or page. If every line is character counted, the character count should be indicated next to each line in the right margin. If line breaks for typesetting are indicated in the manuscript, the character count should be indicated at the end of the line to be set, preceding the mark that is used to indicate the line break. Since character counts are used only by the designer for copyfitting, and not by the typographer for typesetting, they should be written in pencil so that they can be erased before the manuscript is sent to the typographer. This is usually only necessary when the character counts tend to interfere with the copy and other specifications.

If line breaks for typesetting are indicated in the manuscript, 64/ the character count should be indicated at the end of the line to be set, 74/ above and preceding the slash mark that is used to indicate 60/ the line break. Since character counts are used only by the designer 70/ for copy-fitting, and not by the typographer for typesetting, they 67/ should be written in pencil so they can be erased before the manuscript 71/ is sent to the typographer.

Method of indicating line breaks and characters per line.

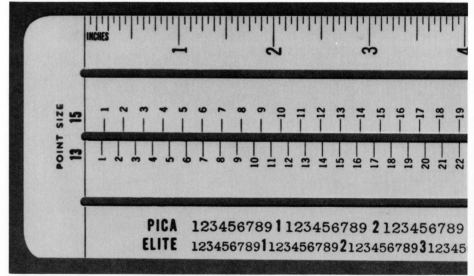

Haberule Type Gauge showing scale for counting pica and elite typewriter copy.

PICA TYPEWRITER SCALE

Handmade typewriter character count scale.

COPYFITTING

Copyfitting is the process of converting typewritten manuscript copy into typographic form to fit the layout. As mentioned in the section on character counting, copy that is to be set in 18 point or larger type is rendered letter by letter on the layout, while copy that is to be set in 14 point or smaller type is indicated with ruled lines that represent the type height, line length, and number of lines. Copyfitting large sizes of type is purely a graphic process and is explained in the section on Comp Lettering (page 116). Copyfitting small sizes of type involves character counting, character count charts, and mathematics, and is described in this section.

In order to copyfit small sizes of type, it is necessary to use character count charts, which are available for all keyboard-composition typefaces. These charts are included in some type specimen books, but may also be purchased separately. The Haberule Copy Caster book (not to be confused with the Haberule Type Gauge) contains charts for all typefaces and sizes.

The purpose of character count charts is to find the average number of typeface characters that will fit into a specific line or column width. The number of typeface characters per line is then divided into the total number of characters in the manuscript copy to find the number of lines in the column. For example, if the amount of manuscript copy (say 1,150 characters) and the layout design suggest that a 20-pica-wide column of 11 point Times Roman is appropriate, a glance at the character count chart for Times Roman will show that there are an average of 50 characters of 11-point type in a 20-pica

line. Divide 50 into the 1,150 characters of manuscript copy, and the answer of 23 is the number of lines in the column.

To find the pica depth of the above column, multiply the number of lines (23) by the point size of the type (11). This gives an answer in points (253), which is then divided by 12 to find the answer in picas (21 plus). If the lines of type are leaded, then the leading must be added to the column depth. For example, if the above 11-point type is leaded 2 points (11/13), multiply 23 lines by 13 points per line to find the point depth of the column (299), and divide by 12 to find the pica depth (24.9).

An easier way to find the depth of a column is to use the Haberule Type Gauge. This device contains scales for measuring 6, 7, 8, 9, 10, 11, 12, 13, and 15 point linespacing, thus eliminating arithmetical calculations.

If the above procedure results in a column depth that is either too short or too long for the layout, various adjustments can be made, either individually or in

combination. These adjustments might involve the column width, the point size of the type, or the amount of leading between lines, but they should never be so severe that legibility is damaged. If the type cannot be fitted to the layout without damaging legibility, then the layout design must be altered.

It is important to remember that typeface characters, as opposed to typewriter characters, vary in individual width. The number of characters per pica in a character count chart, therefore, is only an average. This means that even with very careful character counting and copyfitting, the typeset column might be a line shorter or longer than was estimated. Always take this possibility into account when fitting copy to a layout.

During the preliminary layout stage, only the outline of a column of type needs to be indicated. For the finished layout or comp, however, every line of type must be indicated with ruled lines. This is called type indication, and is explained in the section on Layout Techniques (page 120).

Times Roman								
Times Roman Bold								
Times Roman Italic								
Size	6	7	8	9	10	11	12	14
Picas								
10	36	33	31	29	27	25	23	22
12	43	40	37	34	32	30	28	26
14	50	46	43	40	37	35	32	30
16	58	53	49	46	42	40	37	34
18	65	59	55	51	48	45	41	39
20	72	66	61	57	53	50	46	43
22	79	73	67	63	58	55	51	47
24	86	79	73	68	64	60	55	52
26	94	86	79	74	69	65	60	56
28	101	92	85	80	74	70	64	60
30	108	99	92	86	80	75	69	65

*Character count chart
(Haber Typographers, Inc.).*

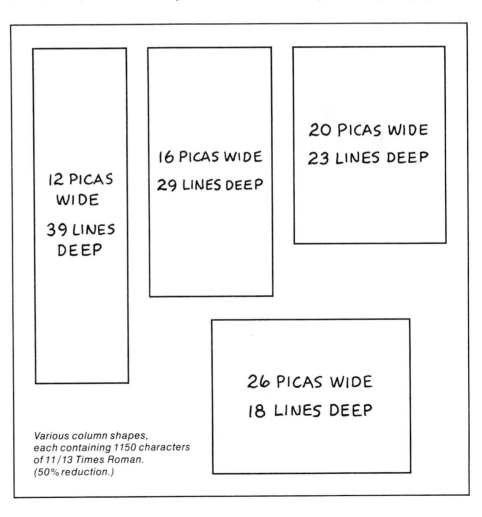

Various column shapes, each containing 1150 characters of 11/13 Times Roman. (50% reduction.)

TYPE SPECIFICATIONS

The process of writing type specifications on the manuscript copy is variously termed "marking up the copy," "specifying the type," or "specking the type." Type specifications should be clearly written or printed, preferably in the left margin, with lines pointing to or bracketing the copy being specified. If possible, use a colored pencil or pen for specifications so that they can easily be seen and also cannot be confused with copy corrections. Specifications should be both concise and precise, using standard terminology, abbreviations, and symbols. Symbols for making copy changes are known as proofreaders' marks, and are listed on page 137. Following is a checklist of specifications.

Typeface Name. The full typeface name should be written just as it appears in the type specimen book. Make sure to include any number that appears in the typeface name, since this usually denotes a specific version or weight of the typeface.

Capitalization. If the copy is to be set in all capitals, write "caps" after the typeface name. If the copy is to be set in upper and lower case, write "U. & l.c." after the typeface name.

Typeface and Line Leading Size. If, for example, 10 point type is to be leaded 2 points, write "10/12" before the typeface name. The first number is the typeface size, and the second number is the typeface size plus the leading. If the 10 point type is to be set solid (no leading), write "10/10." When specifying a display size of type that has no leading, such as a headline, simply write the point size (for example, "48 pt. Helvetica U. & l.c.").

Column Width and Arrangement. If the column of type is to be justified (set flush left and right), write the pica width of the column after the typeface/line-leading size, placing an "X" before the pica measurement. For example, in the specification of "10/12 X20", the "X20" means a column 20 picas wide. The word "justified" is usually written at the end of the other specifications.

If the column of type is to be flush left/ragged right, write the minimum/maximum line width, plus the specification "flush left/ragged right," at the end of the other specifications (for example, "18-22 picas flush left/ragged right").

A flush right/ragged left column arrangement can be specified in a similar way to a flush left/ragged right arrangement. All other column arrangements, however, such as asymmetrical or runaround, can only be specified with a layout. If a layout is necessary for typesetting, write as many specifications as possible on the manuscript copy, followed by the notation, "see layout".

CORRECTING MANUSCRIPT COPY

On the typewritten manuscript, copy corrections are made in ink between the lines at the point of correction. Corrections may also be placed in the margins if they don't fit between the lines. Encircled words written in the margins denote specifications to the typographer or questions to the author that are not part of the copy to be set. If the corrections are unduly complicated or extensive, the page should be re-typed. Proofreaders' marks are listed on page 137.

COPYFITTING FOR PHOTOTYPESETTING

Since the design and capabilities of every phototypesetting system vary greatly, it is necessary to use the type specimen book of the manufacturer for copyfitting. In addition to containing all typeface specimens and character count charts for that system, it contains a description of the system's capabilities.

Most systems are capable of tightening the space between letters and lines. This is called minus letterspacing and minus leading or interlinespacing. Also, most systems are capable of setting larger sizes and wider columns than metal machine-setting systems. All of these factors are obviously of great importance when copyfitting.

The copyfitting procedure for phototypesetting is basically the same as for metal typesetting, but some of the terminology may differ. For example, flush left, flush right, and centered are called quad left, quad right, and quad center. Also, leading is called interlinespacing, and a proof is called a photoproof. It is not important for the designer to use these terms, however, since the typographer is also familiar with metal typesetting terms.

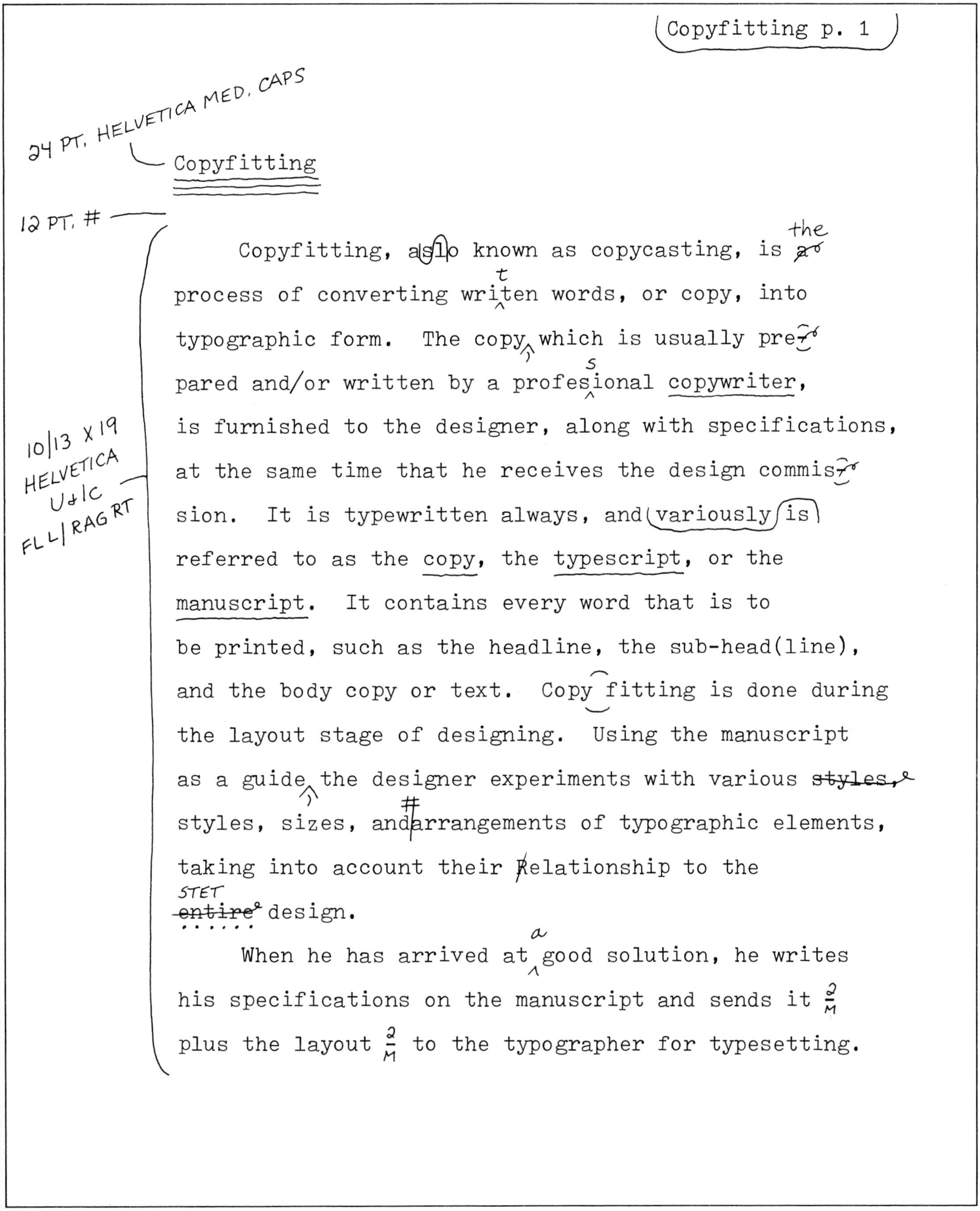

Copyfitting p. 1

24 PT. HELVETICA MED. CAPS

Copyfitting

12 PT. #

10|13 X 19
HELVETICA
U & lc
FL L | RAG RT

Copyfitting, also known as copycasting, is the
process of converting written words, or copy, into
typographic form. The copy which is usually prepared and/or written by a professional copywriter,
is furnished to the designer, along with specifications,
at the same time that he receives the design commission. It is typewritten always, and variously is
referred to as the copy, the typescript, or the
manuscript. It contains every word that is to
be printed, such as the headline, the sub-head(line),
and the body copy or text. Copy fitting is done during
the layout stage of designing. Using the manuscript
as a guide the designer experiments with various styles,
styles, sizes, and arrangements of typographic elements,
taking into account their relationship to the
STET
entire design.

When he has arrived at a good solution, he writes
his specifications on the manuscript and sends it $\frac{2}{M}$
plus the layout $\frac{2}{M}$ to the typographer for typesetting.

Manuscript copy with type specifications and copy corrections.

CORRECTING GALLEY PROOFS

As described at the beginning of this chapter, a trial proof is pulled after the type is set. This is called the first, rough, or galley proof, and is sent to the designer for checking and approval. In addition to checking typesetting specifications, it is important to look for broken letters, mis-alignments, and "typos" (typesetting errors in spelling, punctuation, etc.). Sometimes the galley proof is also checked by the copywriter or editor.

Corrections and alterations are marked on the proof, using standard proofreaders' marks. If an error was made by the typesetter, an encircled PE (printer's error) should be written beside the correction. The designer's, copywriter's, or editor's errors and/or alterations are indicated with an encircled AA (author's alteration). The cost of making AA's is added to the typesetting bill.

Copy corrections are made in ink in the margins, with a mark in the text at the point of correction. Always make corrections in the margins, even if there is room to make them in the text, since the typographer may otherwise overlook them. Corrections are usually made in the right margin, but the left margin, or both margins, may also be used. Some proofreaders make corrections for the left half of the column in the left margin, and corrections for the right half of the column in the right margin. This is useful when there are many corrections in one line.

Each person proofreading the copy should initial the upper righthand corner of each proof to indicate that he or she has proofread it.

COPYFITTING

Copyfitting, also known as copycasting, is the process of converting written words or copy, in to typographic form. The copy, which is usually prepared and/or written by a professional copywriter, is furnished to the designer, along with specifications, at the same time that he receives the design commission. It is typewritten always, and is variously referred to as the copy, the typescript, or the manuscript. It contains every word word that is to be printed such as the headline, the subhead(line) and the body copy or text. Copyfitting is done during the layout stage of design. Using the manuscript as a guide, the designer eperiments with various styles, sizes and arrangements of typographic elements, taking in to account their relationship to the entire design.

When he has arrived at a good solution he writes his specifications on the manuscript and sends it—plus the layout—to the typographer for typesetting.

First or galley proof with errors indicated.
Errors shown are for demonstration purposes only,
and would not be so excessive in normal typesetting.

Copyfitting

Copyfitting, also known as copy casting, is the process of converting written words, or copy, into typographic form. The copy, which is usually prepared and/or written by a professional copywriter, is furnished to the designer, along with other specifications, at the time that he receives the design commission. It is always typewritten, and is variously referred to as the *copy,* the *typescript,* or the *manuscript.* It contains every word that is to be printed, such as the headline, the sub-head(line), and the body copy or text.

Copyfitting is done during the layout stage of designing. Using the manuscript as a guide, the designer experiments with various styles, sizes, and arrangements of the typographic elements, taking into account their relationship to the entire design. When he has arrived at a good solution, he writes his specifications on the manuscript and sends it—plus the layout—to the typographer for typesetting.

Final or reproduction proof
with errors corrected.

PROOFREADERS' MARKS

Correction desired	Marginal mark	Mark in text at point of correction
Comma	⋀	⋀
Semicolon	;/	⋀
Colon	⊙	⋀
Period	⊙	⋀
Apostrophe	⌄	⋀
Open quotes, close quotes	⌄⌄	⋀
Hyphen	=/	⋀
Dash—show length	$\frac{1}{N}$ $\frac{1}{M}$ $\frac{2}{M}$	⋀
Brackets, parentheses	[ ] ( )	⋀
Delete	℘	/ or ℘ or ——— through characters
Substitute or insert character(s)	new character(s)	⋏ through or between characters
Insert omitted copy	out-see copy	⋀
Disregard correction—let stand as printed	stet	dot under each character to be retained
Paragraph	⁋	⋀
Flush paragraph	fl ⁋	⋀
Indent (show no. of ems)	□ ▢ ▭	⌐
No paragraph, or run in	no ⁋ or run in	⌒
Move right or left	⊐ or ⊏	⊐ or ⊏
Raise or lower	⊓ or ⊔	⊓ or ⊔
Center	ctr	⌐ ⌐
Flush left or flush right	fl L or fl R	[or]
Align horizontally	══	lines above and below defect
Align vertically	‖	lines to the left and right of defect
Transpose	tr	had first miss or hit
Insert space	#	⋀
Equalize space	eq sp	⋀ ⋀ ⋀
Close up	⌢	⌢
Wrong font	wf	encircle
Lower case	lc	/ through characters, or encircle
Capitals	cap	triple underline
Small capitals	sc	double underline
Roman	rom	encircle
Italic	ital	single underline
Bold face	bf	jagged underline
Superior or inferior character	⌄2 or ⌃2	⋀
Broken type	X	encircle
Invert type	↺	encircle
Push down type	⊥	encircle
Spell out	spell out or sp	encircle
Query to author	(who?)	⋀ or encircle
Line break	break	∫ between characters

Photostats

Photostats, or "stats," are black and white photographic prints made with a photostat camera. There are two photostat systems in common use; the standard negative-positive system and the newer direct-positive system. In the standard system, a negative print of the original copy is made on photographic paper, and the negative print is then used to make a positive print on photographic paper. Since both negative and positive prints are on paper, and since it is sometimes difficult to tell which is the negative and which is the positive, the negative is called the "first print," and the positive is called the "second print."

Original copy.

First print (negative).

Second print (positive).

In the direct-positive system, a positive paper print is made directly from the original copy. Although no negative is needed to make a positive, it is possible to make one if the original copy is to be reversed.

Most large stat houses use both the standard and the direct-positive systems, whereas most small stat houses and in-studio installations use the direct-positive system. Because standard photostats are much less expensive, per print, than direct-positive photostats, and because negatives are so often needed in graphic design work, the standard system is used in this chapter to describe the procedures involved in ordering and using stats. Most of these procedures also apply to the direct-positive system, the main difference being that negatives are not made unless specifically needed.

Although both photostat systems are generally adequate in themselves, there are advantages and disadvantages to each. Thus, while this chapter primarily describes the standard photostat system, the differences between the systems are also described.

Types of Photostat Paper. The major use of photostats is to reduce or enlarge line copy. For this purpose a high-contrast paper is used, which in the standard system has a glossy finish and is called a "glossy" stat, and in the direct-positive system has a low-luster finish and is called either a "glossy" or a "line" stat. Because no paper internegative is used in direct-positive stats, they are sharper than standard stats and are therefore preferable where extremely fine detail is involved. On a mechanical, if detail is too fine to be held on a photostat, use the stat "for position only," and request the printer to shoot directly from the original copy.

Regular-contrast paper is available for shooting continuous-tone copy. In the standard system the paper has a matte finish and is called a "matte" stat. In the direct-positive system the paper has a low-luster finish (just like line paper) and is called a "tone" stat. Matte and tone stats are used for indicating the size and position of photographs and other continuous-tone copy in mechanicals, but they are not as high in fidelity as regular photographic prints and therefore are not normally used as shooting copy. Matte stats are also commonly used for comps and presentations; they not only hold

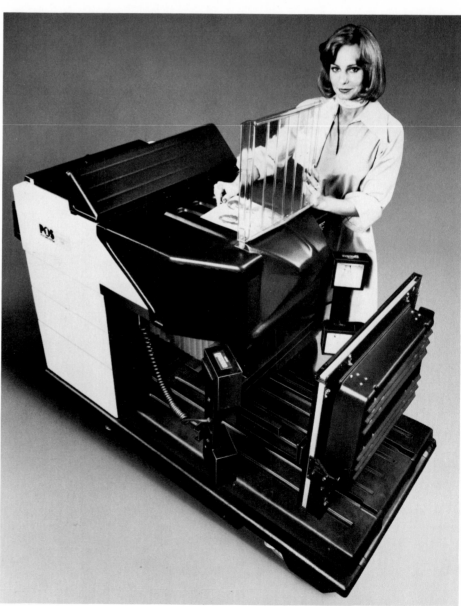

Photostat camera suitable for in-studio use (Visual Graphics Pos One).

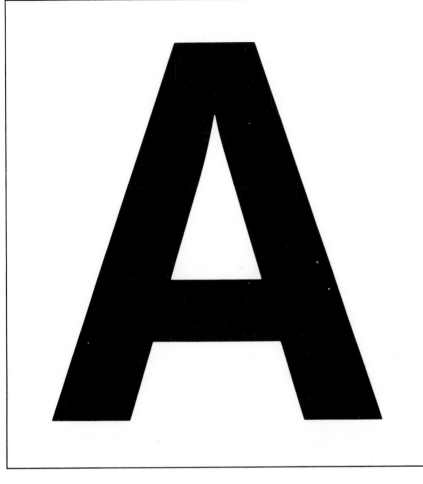

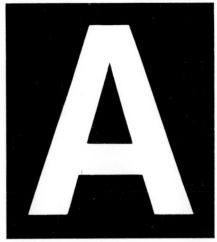

50% first print.

50% second print.

Original copy.

tonal graduations well, but the matte finish looks like studio or printing paper and accepts most mediums (see Making a Negative Paste-up, page 140).

Photostats are priced according to paper size, and in most standard systems these sizes are 8½″ x 11″, 11″ x 14″, 14″ x 18″, and 18″ x 24″.

Reducing and Enlarging Photostats. In the standard photostat system, the maximum reduction is 50%, and the maximum enlargement is 200%. However, each subsequent print can be further reduced or enlarged. For example, if the first print is reduced to 50%, and the second print is again reduced to 50%, the second print will be 25% of the original copy. Similarly, if the first print is enlarged to 200%, and the second print is again enlarged to 200%, the second print will be 400% of the original copy. Greater enlargements or reductions can be made with additional prints, or by special lenses or techniques. Enlargements larger than the normal maximum of 200% are called "easel shots." They are not as sharp as regular enlargements, however, and are also more expensive per print.

Other Photostat Capabilities. When reducing line copy, thin lines may become too thin for good reproduction. This can be avoided by requesting the camera operator to "hold thin lines" or "heavy up" the stat.

Photostat paper does not normally record blue, and red records as black. If it is necessary to photostat blue copy, or if red and black copy must be separated into different tones, the camera operator can be requested to do this with filters.

Original copy can be reversed left to right (mirror image) by ordering a "flopped" stat.

Other Uses of a Photostat Camera. Most photostat cameras can be used to make veloxes and line conversions from continuous-tone copy, and also to make photolith film negatives and positives. Some direct-positive systems can make color prints and transparencies from either opaque or transparent originals.

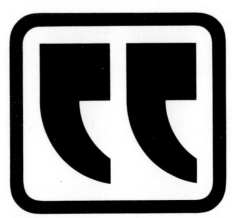

Original copy.

Flopped photostat.

MAKING A NEGATIVE PASTE-UP

When original line copy must be re-worked for use in a mechanical, or when a number of pieces of original line copy must be re-sized and fitted together, it is often desirable to perform these operations using negative or first print photostats. A positive print made from a negative paste-up is not only neater and easier to handle, it permits further retouching without the hindrance of cut edges. Also, the negative paste-up can be larger than the reproduction size of the mechanical, making it easier to do retouching.

The negative stat or stats are rubber cemented on to heavy, smooth, black bristol or cover stock for performing the necessary cutting, fitting, and retouching operations. Use red pencil for guidelines; it is easy to see on the black stock but will not be visible when photographed. After all cutting and fitting has been performed and the rubber cement is thoroughly dry, remove the excess cement and blacken all cut edges. Use India ink and a split-nib drawing pen, such as a Gillot 170. A pen works better than a brush because it is easily guided by the cut edges. If ink gets on the white images, it can be wiped off with a water-moistened cotton swab. Cut edges may also be blackened prior to pasting up, using India ink and a brush.

The negative paste-up method is also useful for comps and presentations. Matte negative stats must be used for continuous-tone copy, and either matte or glossy negative stats may be used for line copy. (Glossy stats will provide greater sharpness.) The positive print, as mentioned previously, is always made on matte paper. In addition to holding tones better, its texture is similar to studio paper or board, and it accepts most color mediums.

The original copy can be rendered, but already-printed material, such as type, logos, symbols, and product illustrations can also be used. Photographic situations can often be created by statting various parts of photographs to the right size and then combining and retouching them. (See Making a Photomontage, page 152.)

If elements of the comp or presentation are to be in color, apply a diluted India ink wash or air brush spray to those elements on the negative. By toning down the white of the negative to a dark gray, it will print as light gray on the positive, thus making it easy to cover with color. Opaque designers color is usually used for line copy, while liquid dye or color markers are usually used for photographs and continuous-tone illustrations. Matte color film can be used for flat areas of color. If line copy such as type was not toned down on the negative, it can be toned down on the positive with a wash coat of casein or acrylic white. Being waterproof when dry, this white will not be picked up when color is applied over it. It doesn't have to be carefully applied, since it blends into the white of the matte stat paper. Never attempt to apply designers color directly over black. Even though designers color is opaque, the colors will be muddy and dull no matter how many coats are applied. Also, every speck of black must be covered, thus making it much more painstaking to cover than light gray, which is so close in value to the white paper that it doesn't require perfect coverage.

Color illustrations and renderings are frequently not included in the negative paste-up. Rather, they are rendered separately on thin paper and pasted on the positive stat. To avoid a pasted-up look, the paper must be trimmed exactly at the outer contours of shapes so that the cut edges will be invisible.

ORDERING PHOTOSTATS

The quality and facilities of photostat companies vary greatly, and it is therefore important to use a company that is recommended by graphic design professionals. A company that is familiar with the needs and practices of the graphic design profession not only produces better work, it is an invaluable source of information and advice. Overnight service is customary, but one- or two-hour service is possible if the shop isn't too busy.

If the copy to be photostatted is on paper, it should be taped or rubber cemented onto stiff white or black board. This protects the copy from damage, and also provides a margin for writing specifications. Use red pencil for writing on black bristol board; it is easy to see and will not photograph. Fragile artwork should be flapped.

When ordering photostats, the following specifications must be provided:

1. Number of prints.

2. Type of print, either first print (negative), second print (positive), or direct-positive. Also specify if the print is to be flopped or heavied-up.

3. Type of paper, either glossy or matte for standard photostats, or line or tone for direct-positive photostats.

4. Area of copy to be statted. If extra paper is desired around the imagery, indicate the area with crop marks and specify "shoot to crop marks."

5. Size of print, either same size (SS), or the size of reduction or enlargement. Reductions and enlargements can be specified by various methods. The easiest method is to state the size of one dimension of the original copy (usually the overall height or width), followed by the size to which it is to be reduced or enlarged. For example, if the original copy is to be reduced in width from 8″ to 6″, write 8″ to 6″ in the margin of the original copy. Similarly, an enlargement in width from 8″ to 10″ is written as 8″ to 10″. From these measurements, the photostat camera operator determines the percentage of reduction or enlargement with a proportional scale. This percentage is then used to set the camera.

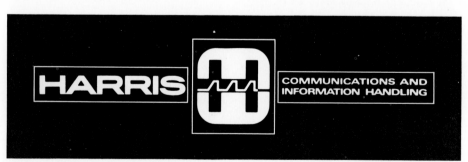

Negative paste-up. White edges of stats must be blackened.

A second method of specifying size is to indicate one set of dimension marks in the margin. The dimension marks should be accurately extended from the copy with a T-square, triangle, and sharp pencil. The two marks are then connected by a dimension line with arrowheads, and the reduction or enlargement size is written above or below the line; for example, 6″ BM (between marks). The camera operator measures between marks to find the size of the original copy, and then uses both figures to find the percentage of enlargement or reduction on the proportional scale.

A third method of specifying size is to indicate the percentage of enlargement or reduction. Use a proportional scale to find the percentage (see Circular Proportional Scale, page 85). This method is preferred by most designers since it eliminates the possibility of error by the camera operator. (Camera operators also prefer it, of course, because it saves them

time.) It is particularly advantageous when many pieces of original copy are involved. If two or more pieces are found to be the same or very close in percentage, it is often possible to group them together on one board, thus reducing the number of photostats that need to be made.

Ordering photostats by percentage can be confusing. For example, "reduce to 25%" means that the photostat is to be reduced to 25% of the original copy size, whereas "reduce 25%" means that the photostat is to be reduced to 75% of the original copy size. To avoid possible confusion, use only the percentage figure that is shown on the proportional scale. No other words should be added, since the camera operator understands that it means "percentage of original size," as is stated on the proportional scale itself. For example, an 8″ to 6″ reduction would be stated as "75%," and an 8″ to 10″ enlargement would be stated as "125%."

Following are a number of examples of typical standard photostat specifications:

1 GLOSSY 2ND PRINT 8″ TO 6″

The camera operator makes a glossy first print 8″ to 6″ or 75%, and from that makes a same size glossy second print.

1 GLOSSY 1ST PRINT SS
1 GLOSSY 2ND PRINT 8″ TO 6″
1 GLOSSY 2ND PRINT 8″ TO 10″

If different sized second prints are needed, it is less confusing if the first print is the same size as the original copy.

1 GLOSSY 2ND PRINT 25%
(8″ TO 2″)

Because 25% is an unusually large reduction, the camera operator might wonder if you mean "25% of the original size," or "25% off." ("25% off" is the way that some people order a stat that is to be 75% of the original size.) To avoid a possible misunderstanding, therefore, the reduction size can also be indicated in inches.

1 MATTE POSITIVE 1″ TO 6″
(ORIGINAL IS POSITIVE)

Since the maximum enlargement on the photostat camera is 200%, a number of prints must be made for a 1″ to 6″ enlargement. Instead of specifying first, second, third, and fourth prints, it is usually simpler to merely order a positive or negative print to the desired size, and indicate whether the original copy is positive or negative.

To make the above photostat, four prints are required. The first print is 200% of the original copy (1″ to 2″), the second print is 200% of the first print (2″ to 4″), and the third print is 150% of the second print (4″ to 6″). Although the third print is the desired reproduction size, it is negative rather than positive. A fourth positive print the same size as the third negative print is therefore necessary.

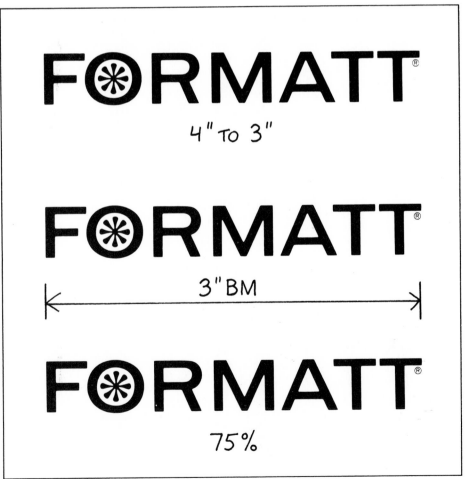

Three methods of specifying print size for copy that is to be reduced from 4″ to 3″ wide.

Line Copy

Line copy is any original art composed of solid blacks and whites with no intermediate gray tones, such as type or pen and ink drawings. To reproduce line copy, the printer simply makes a photographic line negative, which is then used to image the printing plate.

To minimize the printer's task, all line copy is assembled in position on the mechanical. Some line copy, such as body type, is produced at reproduction size and can be pasted directly on the mechanical. More often than not, however, the line copy is produced larger than reproduction size and must be photostatted for use on the mechanical. (Copy to be reversed is also usually photostatted.) Glossy stats are sharp enough for most line copy, but for extremely fine detail, it may be necessary to use the stat "for position only," and request the printer to shoot directly from the original copy (see Photostats, page 138).

Hand-rendered line copy, such as hand lettering, symbols, and illustrations, is usually rendered 20% to 50% larger than reproduction size. When reduced to re-

Wax crayon illustration (Gerry Contreras).

Pen and ink illustration (Gerry Contreras).

production size, such a reduction range eliminates minor imperfections but still retains details. The amount of reduction must be taken into account when rendering fine lines. If fine lines are not made proportionately heavier, they may break or disappear when reduced. Fine white spaces must also be made proportionately wider or they will fill in when reduced.

RENDERING TECHNIQUES

Any tool, medium, or material that results in solid black and white patterns may be used for rendering line copy. This includes pen and ink, brush and ink (or opaque black paint), scratchboard (see page 78), printed metal, wood, or linoleum cuts, and black paper or color film adhered to white board.

Textures or gradated tones may be

Hand lettering (Ray Barber).

achieved by applying a dense black medium, such as charcoal, conte crayon, wax crayon, or dry-brushed ink, to textured paper or board. Any textured paper or board may be used, but a special stippled board (page 78) will produce finer and more even gradations. The medium is deposited on the high spots of the paper or board, while the low spots remain white, thus resulting in halftone-like textures or tonal gradations. Printed textures and patterns are available on adhesive-backed film and dry transfer film (see page 80).

Screen tints may be achieved with adhesive-backed shading film (page 80), or with a special bristol board which is printed with two invisible screen tints, one light and one dark. Special chemicals are applied by pen or brush to develop the tints (see page 78). Screen tints applied to the original copy are less expensive than screen tints applied by the printer. Also, they permit re-working by the artist. However, the finest screen available is 85-line, which limits their use to coarser forms of reproduction.

RULED LINES AND FORMS

The most common method of making ruled lines, boxes, borders, etc., is with ink and a ruling pen or technical fountain pen (see Ruling, page 86), or with pressure-sensitive tape that is printed with lines, dashes, etc. (see Tapes, page 67). In tables and charts, if the type elements are set in layout position, the ruled lines can be applied to the type proof. Since it is difficult to rule on type proofs, the lines can also be ruled on a drafting film overlay, and the printer will combine the type and ruled lines in the stripping operation. If the type elements are not set in layout position, the ruled form is made on a separate board and the type elements are cut apart and pasted in position.

Another method of making ruled lines and forms is by having the stripper scribe the lines into the negative with a special scribing tool or machine. The position and weight of the rules are indicated on an overlay. This is often the best method for complicated forms. In addition to producing very sharp, accurate lines, it minimizes the work of the designer.

Some phototypesetting systems are capable of setting rules. Both vertical and horizontal rules can be set in position in one operation.

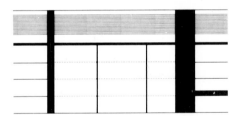

The Diatronic "S" phototypesetting system sets type together with vertical and horizontal rules in position.

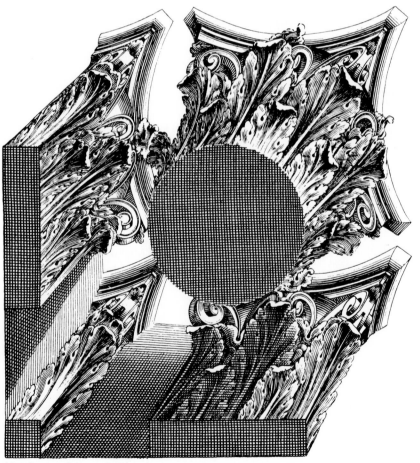

Metal engraving.

VELOXES AND LINE CONVERSIONS

A velox is a halftone reproduction of continuous-tone copy that has been printed on photographic paper. Being opaque line copy, the velox can be pasted on the mechanical. This is less expensive than having the printer make the halftone and strip it into the negative of the mechanical. Also, it permits re-working by the designer. For example, highlights and shadows can be strengthened by painting out the halftone dots in those areas with retouch white or black, and the definition of details can be improved by converting dot patterns to solid lines and shapes. A magnifying glass is advisable for these operations.

As with conventional halftones, veloxes can be made in square, silhouette, or vignette form, and line copy can be surprinted or dropped out on them. Veloxes are available in 55- to 120-line screens, which generally limits their use to coarser forms of reproduction.

Line conversions are similar to veloxes, the difference being that special screens are used to convert the continuous-tone copy to line copy. These screens are available in a variety of patterns, such as concentric circular lines, horizontal or vertical lines, pebbled, woodgrain, linen-weave, and crosshatch.

This page: Velox prints (courtesy Mask-O-Neg, Inc.).

Opposite page: the top six prints are camera line conversions. The bottom three prints are laser-scanned line conversions and a velox. This new process is both versatile and inexpensive (courtesy Schaedler/Pinwheel).

65-line screen.

85-line screen.

100-line screen.

110-line screen.

120-line screen.

Velox with re-worked highlights and shadows.

Vertical Straightline—85-line.

Circleline—60-line.

Mezzotint—75-line.

Crosshatch Posterization—50-line.

Steel Engraving—50 line.

Woodgrain Walnut Posterization—50-line.

Laserline 4-tone Posterization—65-line.

Laserline Aztec—24-line.

Laserline 55-line velox—60% condensed.

Continuous-tone Copy

Continuous-tone copy is any original art containing gradated or blended tones, such as photographs and pencil, pastel, oil, acrylic, watercolor, and gouache illustrations. To reproduce continuous-tone copy, the printer must photograph it through a halftone screen. This converts the tones to minute dots of varying sizes which, when printed, optically mix with the white of the paper to simulate the tones of the original art.

Full-color, continuous-tone copy may be reproduced in black and white, or it may be reproduced in full color by four-color process. This section describes black and white reproduction, but the copy preparation for four-color process is basically the same. There are, however, certain color factors that must be considered when the copy is to be reproduced in full color. These are described in Color Printing—Process Color, page 36.

Pencil drawing by Gerry Contreras. This is a dropout halftone, which means that the black dots in the background have been eliminated.

Photograph by Ken Korsh.

Because the halftone screen reduces tonal contrasts and makes details less distinct, the original art should be bolder than is desired in the halftone reproduction. (Just how much bolder depends upon the fineness of the halftone screen; a fine screen will hold tones and details better than a coarse screen.) In addition to stronger details, highlights, and shadows, the difference between tones should be distinctive. Less than a 10 percent difference would most likely be indistinguishable when reproduced.

To insure an adequate difference between tones, a gray scale should be used. The standard gray scale ranges from white to black in 10 percent gradations. Such a scale can be made with retouch grays, or with mixtures of black and white designers color. It can also be purchased from an art or photo supply store.

For best reproduction, continuous-tone copy should usually be 20% to 50% larger than reproduction size. When reduced to reproduction size in the halftone, such a reduction range eliminates minor imperfections but still retains details. If the reduction is larger than 50 percent, there is the risk of losing details.

Because the halftone reproduces tonal values, everything that is visible in the original art will be visible in reproduction. Even the lightest guidelines must either be thoroughly erased or blocked out. If blocking out or retouching is necessary in an illustration, use the same medium, and the same brand of medium, that was used originally. Even though the tones of different mediums or brands look correct on the original art, they may photograph differently. Avoid ridges in the paint, which could cast shadows under the lights of the printer's camera. For photograph retouching, see page 151.

Continuous-tone copy is referred to as "shooting copy" because it accompanies the mechanical to the printer for the shooting of a halftone negative that will later be combined with the negative of the mechanical in a process called "stripping." Because it will be handled by many people, it must be sturdily mounted or matted, and flapped with both a tracing paper overlay and a heavy paper cover. Remember that continuous-tone copy, such as illustrations and retouched photographs, is usually both fragile and expensive, and sometimes even irreplaceable.

Gouache illustration by Gerry Contreras.

The remainder of this chapter deals specifically with photography, the most common form of continuous-tone copy. However, it will be seen that many of the procedures, such as mounting, scaling, cropping, and marking are also used in preparing continuous-tone illustrations for reproduction.

0%

10%

20%

30%

40%

50%

60%

70%

80%

90%

100%

Gray scale.

TAKING THE PHOTOGRAPH

When a photograph is reproduced in halftone, even the strongest blacks are grayed with white dots, and even the strongest whites are grayed with black dots. Consequently, the reproduced photograph is less "contrasty" than the original print. To minimize this problem, it is desirable to shoot for as high a contrast as possible without losing required detail in either the dark or the light areas.

PRINTING THE PHOTOGRAPH

In printing photographs, keep in mind that the qualities desirable in an exhibition print are not necessarily the qualities desirable for halftone reproduction. It is not how the print looks to the eye, but how the print will look when screened for reproduction.

For maximum contrast and detail legibility in halftone reproduction, a glossy, white print with either a neutral or brown-black tone image is best. Of course, if a soft or low contrast image is desired, then a textured or matte surface print might be preferable. If the photograph is taken and/or printed by a professional photographer, it is important to indicate its specific use, such as newspaper reproduction or offset reproduction.

HANDLING THE PHOTOGRAPH

Never use paper clips directly on photographs; they will leave indentations that might show up in reproduction. If a paper clip must be used, pad the print with a piece of folded cardboard.

Never write on the back of a photograph with a hard instrument. Again, this will leave impressions that might reproduce. If writing is necessary, place the print on a hard surface and use a very soft graphite pencil or china marker. The best method is to write on a label that can then be affixed to the back of the print. Use a label with a pressure-sensitive adhesive, since the label should be easily removable in the event that the print must later be mounted. If the label is not removed, it will create a raised surface on the front of the mounted print.

Never touch a retouched area with the fingers or hands. A retouched surface is extremely delicate, and even the slightest bit of dirt or oil will damage it.

When mailing prints, always place them between heavy sheets of stiff cardboard. Never lay prints face to face, since the hard emulsion surfaces might scratch each other. The rolling of prints

should be avoided. If it can't be, roll the print with the emulsion side out. If a slight crack occurs in the emulsion, then, it will most likely close up when the print is flattened.

Never crop a photograph by cutting the print to size. This makes it impossible to correct an error in scaling, and also makes the print unusable for other applications.

MOUNTING THE PHOTOGRAPH

Photographs for reproduction are almost always mounted on board. The only exception might be in editorial work for magazines and newspapers. Smooth illustration board or mounting board (which is cheaper than illustration board) should be used, with a 1″ to 2″ border on all sides for crop marks, specifications, etc. Don't use pebbled or heavily textured board. Also, don't make the border too wide, since this will make it difficult for the printer to gang up photographs that are to be shot at the same focus.

Because photographs have a tendency to warp, particularly during retouching, it is important that they be very securely mounted. Dry mounting, which is a heat-bonding process involving the use of thermosetting adhesive tissue and a heated press, provides the strongest bond. This process is described on page 71. If dry mounting is desirable and a press is not accessible, most custom labs will provide this service.

The 3M Company makes a spray adhesive called Photo Mount that is formulated especially for mounting photographs. It is quick-bonding, very strong, and permanent.

Rubber cement also makes a good bond, providing that both surfaces have been thoroughly coated and dried before bonding. The drawback to rubber cement is that it will eventually fail as an adhesive, and may also stain the photo. The method of dry bonding with rubber cement is described on page 69. As this method describes, fairly flat photographs can be merely dropped onto the mounting surface for adhering, while curled or buckled photographs require the use of a slip sheet. Severely curled photographs should be wetted and then blotted to a damp condition before cementing and adhering. A pad of newspaper, large sheets of blotting paper, or paper towels can be used to remove excess water.

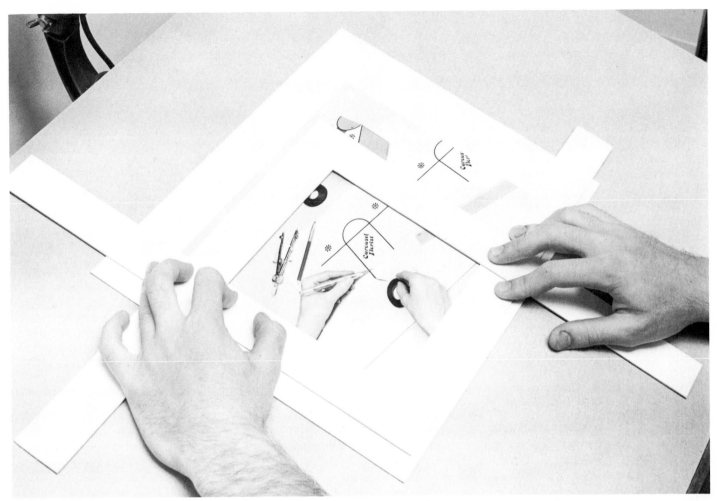

Cropping frames being positioned on photograph.

CROPPING AND SCALING

Photographs and other forms of continuous-tone original copy are usually larger than reproduction size. Additionally, only a portion of the original copy is usually selected for reproduction. The process of reducing (or enlarging) the original copy to reproduction size is called scaling, and the process of selecting the right portion of a photograph or illustration for reproduction is called cropping.

Cropping and scaling is a combined operation which must be resolved during the layout stage. Sometimes it is the design of the layout which determines the size and shape of the photograph or illustration, and sometimes it is the content or composition of the photograph or illustration which determines its size and shape in the layout. More often than not, both factors must be taken into consideration, which means that a good amount of back and forth juggling of sizes and shapes is necessary before the best solution is found.

Methods of Cropping. The simplest method for cropping is to cut two L-shaped frames from mat or illustration board. Each arm should be 12″ to 15″ long and 1½″ to 2″ wide. The cropping frames are laid on the mounted copy and moved about until the best composition is delineated by the inside edges of the two frames. The resulting framed area does not have to be parallel to the outside edges of the copy, but the inside meeting corners of the two frames should be as square as is possible by eye. When the best composition is found and the inside meeting corners are squared by eye, the cropping frames are taped in position with a few pieces of drafting tape. The tape should be placed on the outer edges of the cropping frames, preferably in the border of the mounting board. The mounted copy, with cropping frames attached, is then taped onto the drawing board, using the T-square to align the inner horizontal edge of one of the cropping frames. After one cropping frame

has been aligned and the mounted copy taped to the board, the other cropping frame can be adjusted so that both are perfectly square with each other.

When the framed area of the original copy has been squared, pencil crop marks are drawn in the border area of the mounting board, using the inner edges of the cropping frames as guides. The cropping frames are then removed, and the crop marks are extended to opposite sides, using the T-square and triangle. The foregoing procedure is usually performed during the layout stage of design, and the pencilled crop marks should therefore not be inked in until all corrections have been made and the mechanical is being produced. At that time, the crop marks should be inked in with a fine ruling pen line.

As mentioned previously, photographs for magazine and newspaper editorial work are often not mounted. For ease in handling an unmounted photograph during the cropping and scaling process, it

Diagonal-line scaling combined with cropping.

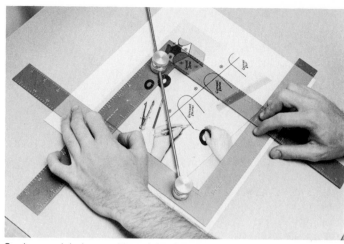

Scaleograph being positioned on photograph.

should be temporarily taped onto a scrap piece of board. The crop marks are drawn directly on the photograph, either in the border or in an unused portion of the photograph itself. A red china marking pencil is used to draw crop marks. Not only is this easy to see on a black and white print, it is easy to remove from the print emulsion with a facial tissue moistened with rubber cement thinner.

If the original copy must conform to a pre-determined layout shape, take a piece of tracing paper that is at least 3″ larger on all sides than the original copy, trace the layout shape about 3″ in from one corner, and draw a diagonal line through two corners of the shape, extending it across the entire tracing paper. Tape one cropping frame to the tracing paper, aligning its two inner edges with the two outer edges of the layout shape. Place the tracing paper and attached cropping frame on the original copy, and position the other cropping frame so that its inside corner coincides with the diagonal line, and its arms are parallel to the arms of the attached cropping frame. By maintaining this alignment, any size rectangle delineated by the cropping frames will be in proportion to the layout shape. (See Diagonal-line Scaling, page 82.)

This method of combining diagonal-line scaling and cropping in one operation can also be achieved with a Scaleograph, the brand name for a device comprised of two plastic L-shaped frames, a diagonal connecting rod, and two tightening knobs.

To use the Scaleograph, loosen the knobs, line up the inside edges of the L frames on the perimeter of the area to be scaled, and tighten the knobs. The device is now locked into a height/width ratio, and the L frames may be expanded or contracted to new sizes that are in exact ratio to the original setting. Both L frames are engraved with inch measurements for measuring copy as well as for squaring up the two frames.

In addition to scaling and cropping original copy to fit a pre-determined layout shape, the Scaleograph is also used in the reverse way. The original copy is first cropped for best composition, and the resulting cropped shape is then scaled to layout size. As mentioned previously, the process of cropping and scaling is usually a back and forth juggling of sizes and shapes to achieve the best composition of the original copy and the best design of the layout. The ease with which this is accomplished with the Scaleograph makes it an extremely useful tool.

Methods of Scaling. The methods of scaling are described in the section, Enlarging and Reducing (page 82). Following is a list of the methods that are used specifically for scaling photographs and other forms of continuous-tone copy.

Diagonal-line Scaling (page 82). The simplest and most commonly used method of scaling. It is fairly accurate and doesn't require the use of arithmetical calculations. As described in the section, Methods of Cropping, it can be combined with the cropping operation.

Arithmetical Scaling (page 82). The most accurate method of scaling. The formula for the solution of a proportion is not difficult to understand or remember, and this method is often used when the original copy does not need to be cropped. It is also more practical than diagonal-line scaling where great reductions or enlargements are involved.

Circular Proportional Scale (page 85). An inexpensive plastic device comprised of two rotating discs. This method is as accurate as arithmetical scaling and also much faster, since no calculating is involved.

Scaleograph. The brand name of a device for scaling and cropping in one operation. This device is described in the section, Methods of Cropping.

Scaling can also be done by photostat, camera lucida, Lacey-Luci projector, or pantograph (all described in the section, Enlarging and Reducing). However, these methods are only used when it is necessary to indicate the details of the original copy. In fact, when using these methods, the outer dimensions of the shape are usually first determined by one of the four methods previously described.

MARKING THE PHOTOGRAPH

Crop Marks. As described in the section, Cropping the Photograph (page 149), crop marks should remain in pencil during the layout stage of cropping and scaling. Only after the mechanical is completed should they be converted to ink.

Bleed Marks. When a photograph or other art runs off the edge of a printed piece, an extra ⅛″ must be provided to allow for possible variations in trimming. This is called bleed, and the width of the bleed area is indicated on the original copy with bleed marks placed outside the crop marks. If the original copy is larger than reproduction size, the bleed area must therefore be proportionately wider than ⅛″. This need only be a rough (but generous) estimate, since the bleed marks on the original copy are merely used to call attention to the existence of a bleed, so that both the retoucher and the printer know to include a sufficient extra portion of the original copy in their operations.

Sizing. The size that the original copy is to be reduced to for reproduction is indicated by drawing a pencil dimension line, with arrows, between two crop marks, and writing the reduction size above or below it. The actual size between marks, and the indicated reduction size, are converted by the printer to a percentage figure for setting the camera. This conversion, which requires the use of a circular proportional scale (page 85), can also be performed by the designer. In that case, only the percentage figure is written on the original copy.

Keying. If more than one photograph or other form of continuous-tone copy is used in a design, each piece must be identified with a key letter and/or number that also appears in the proper location on the mechanical. The layout or dummy is usually also keyed, particularly if only the outlines of the continuous-tone copy have been indicated. The key is usually an encircled A, B, C, etc., and it should appear in the same position on all original copy. If the design is multi-paged, both the page number and a letter are used, such as 5-A, 5-B, 6-A, 6-B, etc.

Mounted photo showing crop marks, bleed marks, percentage of reduction, and key number and letter.

FLAPPING THE PHOTOGRAPH

After the photograph has been mounted, scaled, cropped, and marked, it should be flapped with a tracing paper overlay, and preferably also with a heavy paper cover. (The flapping procedure is described on page 97.) If the photograph is to be retouched, attach an easily removable tracing paper overlay and omit the cover. Not only is it easier to retouch an unflapped photograph, but the overlay and cover would get so soiled and creased during retouching that they would have to be replaced anyway. After retouching, of course, the photograph should be immediately flapped with an overlay and cover to protect it from dust, fingerprints, and other hazards.

RETOUCHING THE PHOTOGRAPH

In photography for reproduction, retouching is often necessary to improve contrasts, alter details, or eliminate imperfections, as well as to silhouette or vignette figures or objects. Retouching is a very difficult and meticulous process that is generally performed by a photo retouching specialist. However, most graphic designers are capable of doing minor retouching, and some can do much more.

Detail alterations and silhouetting can be performed with a red sable brush, but vignetting and more extensive retouching require the use of an air brush (page 66). Retouch colors are used for both brush and air brush application, and the various types are described on page 73. Frisket paper (page 79) is used to mask out areas during air brushing. Cotton wads and swabs (page 76) are used for cleaning prints and wiping off retouch colors.

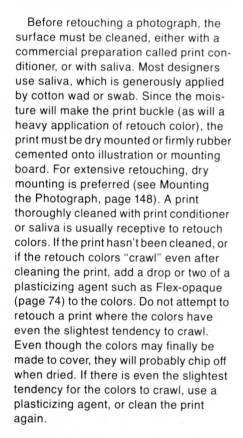

Silhouetted photograph.

Vignetted photograph.

Before retouching a photograph, the surface must be cleaned, either with a commercial preparation called print conditioner, or with saliva. Most designers use saliva, which is generously applied by cotton wad or swab. Since the moisture will make the print buckle (as will a heavy application of retouch color), the print must be dry mounted or firmly rubber cemented onto illustration or mounting board. For extensive retouching, dry mounting is preferred (see Mounting the Photograph, page 148). A print thoroughly cleaned with print conditioner or saliva is usually receptive to retouch colors. If the print hasn't been cleaned, or if the retouch colors "crawl" even after cleaning the print, add a drop or two of a plasticizing agent such as Flex-opaque (page 74) to the colors. Do not attempt to retouch a print where the colors have even the slightest tendency to crawl. Even though the colors may finally be made to cover, they will probably chip off when dried. If there is even the slightest tendency for the colors to crawl, use a plasticizing agent, or clean the print again.

Silhouetting. The removal of a background from around a figure or object in a photogaph is called silhouetting or outlining. This is a fairly easy procedure that doesn't require the services of a professional photo retoucher. A pointed sable brush and retouch white are used, and only a ¼" band of white around the figure or object is necessary for the platemaker's needs. If the original print must not be retouched, the silhouetting may be done on a firmly taped acetate overlay. To insure accuracy when silhouetting on an overlay, hold the acetate tightly against the immediate area being silhouetted, using the handle end of a brush held in the left hand. Also, use a scrap of paper under the working hand to avoid damaging the acetate or retouching.

Silhouetting can also be done by the printer if he is provided with a tracing paper overlay containing a pencil outline of the area to be silhouetted. However, not only does this entail an extra printer's charge, it leaves open the possibility of inaccuracies, particularly in areas where there is little or no contrast between the subject and the background.

Vignetting. When a photograph or illustration gradually fades away to white around its edges, it is called a vignette. In photography, vignetting is done with an air brush and retouch white. If the entire background is to be faded, the foreground subject matter must be masked with frisket paper.

MAKING A PHOTOMONTAGE (COMPOSITE PHOTOGRAPH)
When two or more photographs are combined into one image, it is called a photomontage or composite photograph. A photomontage can be made by projecting parts of negatives onto photographic paper, but the usual method is to make a paste-up of photographs and then retouch the joints.

A layout is necessary to determine the composition and sizes of the various photographic elements to be combined. A Lacey-Luci projector or camera lucida is useful for enlarging or reducing the various elements. After the sizes have been determined, new prints are made to the layout size, and then cut and fitted together in a paste-up. When cutting unmounted prints, scissors are best for curves, and a steel T-square and knife are best for straight cuts. When cutting mounted prints, a low-angled blade, such as a frisket knife or #16 X-acto blade is best for both curved and straight cuts, and the #11 X-acto blade is best for fine details (see Cutting Tools, page 64). To minimize shadows, photographs must be very firmly mounted with rubber cement. Shadows can be further minimized by feathering the reverse edges of the photographs with sandpaper before mounting.

In simple photomontages, it is sometimes possible to use the paste-up itself as shooting copy. (In that case, it is particularly important to minimize shadows.) More often than not, a photographic copy of the paste-up must be made to properly retouch the detail at joints.

Unretouched photo.

Retouched photo (courtesy Belart Associates, Inc.).

Photomontage (George Lois, art director).

Photomontage (George Lois, art director).

Preparing the Mechanical

The final step in the graphic design process is the mechanical assembly of the finished art elements. This mechanical assembly, called the mechanical or paste-up, is used to make the printing plate or plates. It is executed at reproduction size, whenever possible, and contains all line copy pasted into printing position. Continuous-tone copy is not pasted on the mechanical because it must be photographed separately by the printer. However, its position must be accurately indicated so that it can later be stripped into the negative of the mechanical. The base, or key, mechanical is executed on illustration board, and one or more acetate overlays may be needed for additional colors, screen tints, etc.

The major objective in preparing a mechanical is to assemble the elements in such a way that it minimizes hand work by the stripper. It is usually easier and less expensive to perform the necessary operations on the mechanical rather than on the stripper's negatives. There are exceptions to this, however; sometimes the stripper's method provides greater accuracy, and sometimes the designer just doesn't have the time to do it himself.

This chapter describes the preparation of the mechanical for offset lithography, which is the printing method most often encountered in the graphic design studio. The mechanical preparation for other methods of printing, such as letterpress, gravure, or screen printing, is generally the same, but may differ in certain aspects. Once the procedure for preparing mechanicals has been mastered, however, specifications for other methods of printing can easily be acquired through consultation with the printer. (Basic specifications are described in the section on Printing Processes, page 18.) In fact, no matter what the method of printing, the printer must be consulted before preparing the mechanical. There are many ways of preparing a mechanical, and only the printer can determine which is best in regard to budget and his particular platemaking and printing facilities.

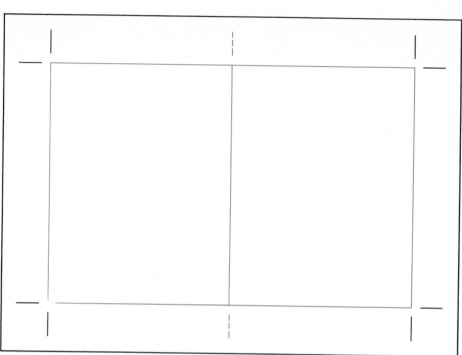

Illustration board with layout for mechanical. Black solid lines are crop or trim marks, and red (or black) dash lines are fold marks. Light blue guidelines indicate the trim size and the fold.

LAYING OUT THE MECHANICAL

Smooth illustration board, such as Bainbridge 172, is generally used for mechanicals, particularly if ruled lines are involved. Medium surface board may also be used, but rough surface board should be avoided. Cut the illustration board to about 2″ larger, on all sides, than the trim size of the mechanical, and attach it to the drawing board, using the T-square to align it horizontally. Pushpins are better than masking tape for attaching illustration board because there is less danger of the board shifting. Only two pushpins at the upper corners are needed. If masking tape is used, it should be applied to all four corners.

Use a sharp 5H pencil, ruler, T-square, and triangle to measure and draw the guidelines. Be very accurate, and do not score the board with the pencil. The basic guidelines are the outer dimensions or trim size of the printed piece, plus the folds, if any. Guidelines may also be used for positioning various elements of the mechanical, such as type, drawings, and photographs. The measurements for these elements can be transferred from the layout and/or the finished art with a divider, or with tick marks placed along the edge of a scrap of paper. Don't use a ruler, since the ruler graduations seldom coincide with the layout measurements. Guidelines for these elements are not

always either necessary or desirable, however, particularly when the finished art differs slightly from the layout in size and/or position. In that case, exact positioning can best be determined by visual judgment at the time that the element is being pasted up. Extend all guidelines well beyond their normal lengths so that the ends of the lines remain visible during the paste-up process.

To avoid having to later erase graphite pencil guidelines, some designers use light blue pencil or ink, which doesn't reproduce. Pencil lines may be drawn with a special non-reproducing light blue pencil, or with any colored pencil that is light blue and holds a sharp point, such as an Eagle Verithin Sky Blue pencil. Ink lines may be drawn with a special non-reproducing light blue ballpoint pen, or with a ruling pen and watered-down blue ink. Even when the erasing of graphite lines is not considered an inconvenience, light blue lines are sometimes used because they help in making a visual judgment of the completed mechanical. For example, if the trim size and folds are delineated with light blue lines, it is much easier to judge the spatial relationship of design elements. Incidentally, light blue pencil or pen may also be used for writing specifications directly on the reproduction area of the mechanical.

After the guidelines have been drawn,

thin black crop (or trim) marks and fold marks are drawn about ⅛″ outside the trim dimensions with a T-square, triangle, and ruling pen or technical fountain pen. Crop marks are solid lines about ½″ long, and fold marks are dash lines about ½″ long. These marks must be very accurate, since even the slightest discrepancy will result in a printed piece that is out of square. Also, the crop marks are used as an alignment guide if the mechanical is removed and then re-positioned on the drawing board. For this reason, they should be ruled in as soon as the guidelines have been drawn. Some designers rule fold marks in red ink, but this is not a necessity.

RENDERING LINE COPY ON THE MECHANICAL

Ruled lines, dashes, boxes, and other basic shapes are usually rendered directly on the mechanical. They should be executed before the paste-up assembly to insure the cleanest possible working surface, as well as to avoid extra work in the event that a major mistake or accident in inking necessitates re-doing the mechanical. The various tools and techniques for ruling lines, dashes, boxes, etc. are described in the section on Ruling (page 86). Also see Line Copy (page 143), for other methods of achieving ruled lines and forms.

Basic line elements may also be ren-

dered separately on bond, vellum, or bristol board and then cut out and pasted up. If a mistake or accident occurs in inking, then, no harm is done to the mechanical. Also, separately rendered elements may be easily removed or re-positioned on the mechanical, and rendering may be done on paper better suited for ruling than the mechanical itself. This method is also used to correct elements already rendered on the mechanical. Re-execution is usually faster, more successful, and neater than making extensive repairs.

Black shapes may be outlined with fine line ink and then filled in with extra dense ink, or, if they have simple contours, they may be cut from red color film. Black paper is not commonly used because its edges tend to fray, either during cutting or during later mechanical operations. Black paper may be used, however, to cover the central area of large shapes that have first been outlined with a broad band of ink.

Ink should be used for rendering line copy whenever possible. Being waterproof, it will not discolor retouch white applied over it. Poster or designers color black is sometimes used for filling in large shapes, but the outlines should be inked. Use a good-quality retouch white (page 73) for retouching details. If a large area needs to be blocked out, paste opaque white paper over it rather than attempting to cover it with paint. White correction tape (page 67) or self-adhesive labels may also be used for blocking out. Any amount of retouching or patching is permissible on the mechanical, so long as the line copy itself is clean, sharp, and accurate. As mentioned previously, however, re-execution of the mechanical, either in whole or in part, is usually faster, more successful, and neater than making extensive repairs. This is particularly advisable for beginners, who usually need to include mechanical samples in their portfolios. While a patched up mechanical might reproduce properly, its use in a portfolio could suggest a lack of craftsmanship and/or experience.

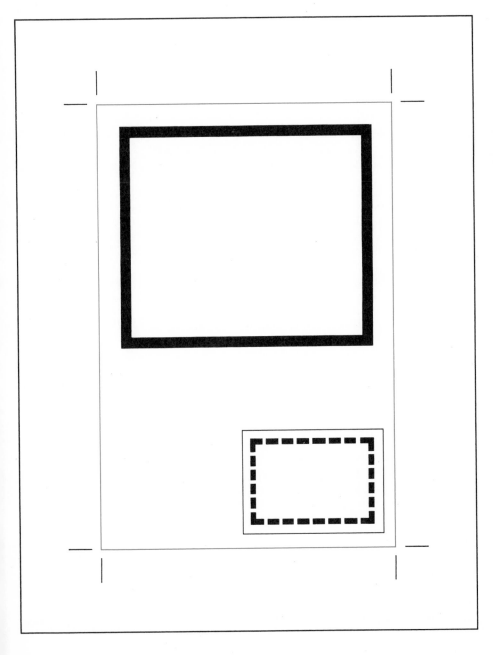

Solid-line box drawn directly on the mechanical.
Dash-line box drawn on bristol board and pasted on the mechanical.

PASTING UP LINE COPY

Line copy to be pasted up includes type, lettering, line illustrations, velox prints, etc. (See Line Copy, page 142.) Glossy photostats may be used to alter the sizes, reverse the tones, or reverse (flop) the images of the original copy. If the original copy was rendered on illustration board (which is too heavy for pasting up), it can be photostatted, or the face paper can be stripped from the backing (see Illustration Board, page 78).

When trimming the paste-up elements, leave at least $1/16''$ of paper around the images if possible. Cut marks sometimes reproduce on the stripper's negative, and if they are very close to the images, they cannot easily be opaqued. Free-form shapes may be trimmed with scissors, but squared-up shapes should be trimmed squarely with a razor blade, T-square, and metal-edged triangle. If the cut marks are not aligned perfectly with the copy, the copy will appear crooked when it is pasted up, thus making the visual judgment of the paste-up very difficult. Since the mechanical is attached to the drawing board, cutting must be done on a piece of cardboard placed on top of it. Any thick, dense cardboard will do, such as the back of a pad or a piece of chipboard.

Free-form shapes can be trimmed with scissors. Try to make at least one accurate vertical or horizontal cut so that the shape can be easily aligned on the mechanical.

Squared-up shapes should be trimmed squarely so they can be easily aligned on the mechanical.

Adhesives used for paste-ups are rubber cement, one-coat rubber cement, wax adhesive, and spray adhesive (see Adhesives, page 68). Rubber cement is recommended for beginners because it is easy to use, inexpensive, and has many other studio applications. Its only disadvantage is that the removal of dried cement is time-consuming, which makes it less practical than the other adhesives for high-volume mechanical production. The tools and techniques of rubber cementing are of great importance in paste-up work, and are fully described starting on page 68. The dry/wet method of rubber cementing is generally used for paste-ups. (Apply rubber cement to the back of the copy and let it dry. Then apply a generous coat of rubber cement to the mechanical and mount the copy on the wet cement.) Very large copy, or copy on very thin paper, however, may need to be dry bonded with a slip sheet. Use the back of a pad or other scrap piece of cardboard for applying rubber cement to the copy. Don't use the cutting board, because dried cement on the cutting board would make it impossible to trim copy that has already been backed with a coat of cement.

When positioning the paste-up elements, the previously drawn guidelines are used as a basic guide, and the T-square and triangle are used for exact alignment. Since guidelines are generally used only for the positioning of major elements, a divider is necessary for posi-

tioning minor elements (see Drawing Instruments, page 60). In lieu of a divider, transfer the measurements from the layout to the mechanical with tick marks placed along the edge of a scrap of paper. If an element is difficult to position because of its large size or irregular shape, make an outline tracing of the layout position of the element and tape it on to the mechanical for use as an overlay guide when pasting up.

While individual elements must be aligned mechanically, the alignment between elements, as well as the space surrounding elements, must be adjusted by visual judgment. When centering an element, for example, it is the spatial area between elements that must be equalized, not the linear distance. Since most elements have irregular contours, and since optical center is higher than mechanical center, space between elements can only be judged by visual estimation. If the cut marks make it difficult to judge the space accurately, they may be obscured by placing a sheet of tracing paper over the mechanical.

After all the elements have been pasted up and the excess rubber cement has been removed, the cut edges of negative photostats must be blackened, using ink and a split-nib drawing pen (see Photostats, page 140). Cut edges may also be blackened before the elements are pasted up, using ink and a brush.

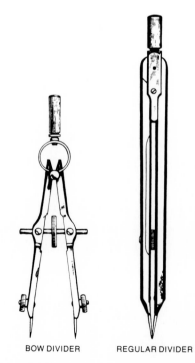

BOW DIVIDER   REGULAR DIVIDER

Use a divider to transfer measurements from the layout to the mechanical.

PASTING UP TYPE PROOFS

Type proofs are also line copy, but they require special handling and techniques. Ink-printed (not photographic) type proofs are easily smudged when freshly printed. For this reason, they should be sprayed with a light coat of acrylic spray coating, such as Crystal Clear Krylon. Don't use matte fixative, since it may cause the ink to spread. Typewriter composition proofs, such as VariTyper and IBM Composer, are particularly susceptible to ink spread, even with acrylic spray coating, and should be sprayed very lightly. Smudging may also be prevented with a dusting of talcum powder, but the powder must be thoroughly removed with a cotton wad to achieve good reproduction.

Photographic type proofs cannot be smudged, but some types of paper can be stained by moisture on the hands. If this happens, spray the proofs with two light coats of Crystal Clear Krylon.

Since all the type elements are usually printed on one sheet, it is easier and faster to rubber cement the entire proof before cutting out the individual elements. After the rubber cement has dried, place the proof on the cutting board (the board must be free of dried cement) and make all the horizontal cuts with a razor blade and accurately aligned T-square. The cuts should extend an inch or so beyond the type, but not the full width of the

proof. By leaving the ends of the strips attached to the surrounding proof, the type elements will remain in alignment for the vertical cuts.

The vertical cuts can be made all at the same time, or as each element is to be pasted up. The second method is better when many small elements are involved, since it insures against the mixup or loss of elements. Vertical cuts can be made with the T-square and metal-edged triangle, or, if the cutting board is turned 90°, with the T-square alone. If the type elements are only one or two lines in depth, the vertical cuts can be made with the metal-edged triangle alone, which eliminates the need to accurately position the cutting board on the drawing board. This is not a very accurate method, but the cuts are so short that a slight inaccuracy will not be disturbing. As mentioned previously, if cut marks are not aligned perfectly with the copy, the copy will appear crooked when it is pasted up, thus making it difficult to position the elements by visual judgment. (With experience, very accurate positioning can be done by visual judgment, the T-square being nec-

TIFFANY

Crooked cut marks make it difficult to align type by eye.

Blue lines drawn on the type proof and mechanical to facilitate the positioning of the type.

essary only for the final, minor adjustments.)

When aligning type with guidelines drawn on the mechanical, it is helpful to draw light blue alignment marks on the top left edge of the type proof, one indicating the left edge of the type, and the other indicating the top edge of the type.

If a glassine type proof was furnished by the typographer, it may be used to check the type against the layout. It may also be used as an overlay guide when positioning the type on the mechanical.

If re-spacing of the type is necessary, it is usually done on a separate piece of bristol board, not on the mechanical itself. In this way, if the type needs to be later re-positioned on the mechanical, the entire assembly can be moved in one piece. The methods for re-spacing letters, words, and lines are described on page 93.

After the type has been pasted up and the excess cement has been removed, it should be carefully inspected for broken hairlines and other minor imperfections. (Major imperfections, such as seriously broken letters and misaligned letters and lines, should have been found at the time of proofreading and the proof returned to the typographer for corrections.) Minor imperfections can be corrected with retouch white, lampblack watercolor, and #1 watercolor brushes (one for each color). The sprayed surface can be made receptive to retouching by rubbing with a kneaded eraser, or a plasticizing agent may be added to the paint. A magnifying glass (page 65) is very helpful for such minute retouching.

Cutting a type proof with a T-square, metal-edged triangle, and razor blade.

INDICATING CONTINUOUS-TONE COPY

As mentioned previously, only the size and position of continuous-tone copy is indicated on the mechanical; the copy itself is submitted separately to the printer. (See Continuous-tone Copy, page 146, for the methods of preparing continuous-tone copy for reproduction.)

If the continuous-tone copy has a geometric outer shape, such as square, rectangular, or circular, it is indicated on the mechanical with either an outline or solid shape. A solid shape is usually preferable because it makes a transparent window on the negative into which the halftone negative can be stripped, whereas with an outline, the window must actually be cut out of the film, using the transparent outline as a guide. There are times, however, when an outline is preferable, such as when a matte photostat of the continuous-tone copy is pasted within the outline as a positioning guide, or when the continuous-tone copy abuts another element on the mechanical.

Outlines are usually ruled in red ink. Red reproduces as black, but on the mechanical a red line indicates a "holding line" which is not to be printed. Black may be used for holding lines, but the words "holding line" must be written on the mechanical (either in red or black inside the halftone area, or in light blue outside the halftone area). If this is not done, the stripper will assume that the halftone is to have a black border, since black normally indicates line art that is to be reproduced. If a matte photostat of the continuous-tone copy is pasted inside the holding lines as a positioning guide for dropouts, surprints, etc., it should be trimmed so that there is about 1/16" of space between the stat and the holding lines.

Solid shapes for indicating continuous-tone copy are usually cut from black paper or black or red color film. Red film is best because underlying guidelines can still be seen after it is applied, thus making trimming easier. (As mentioned previously, red reproduces as black.) Black paper is least desirable because its edges tend to fray. The one advantage to black paper is that it can be cut to size before it is adhered, which is helpful when the exact position of the halftone can best be determined by visual judgment.

Result when printed.

Red holding line drawn on mechanical.

Red film applied to mechanical.

Red holding line drawn on mechanical, with photostat of copy pasted up to show subject matter and cropping. Photostat must not cover holding line. Mark photostat "for position only."

Red film applied to photostat and then cropped to size and pasted on the mechanical. Subject matter and cropping are visible to the eye, but the red film makes a blank transparent window on the negative.

Result when printed.

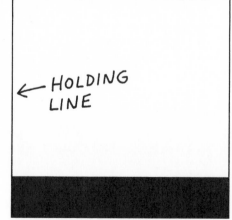

Red or black holding line must be used when continuous-tone copy abuts another element on the mechanical.

Irregular-shaped continuous-tone copy, such as a silhouetted photograph, is indicated on the mechanical with a matte photostat. The stat should be dark enough so that the outer edges will be visible on the stripper's negative. A red holding line may also be used for irregular-shaped copy, but this is usually too time-consuming a method to be practical.

When using a photostat to indicate position, write "for position only" on the stat, in either red or black wax crayon, so that it won't be used as shooting copy for the halftone negative. Also, if there is more than one piece of continuous-tone copy, key the original copy to the mechanical with an encircled letter and/or number (see Keying, page 151). Use red or black wax crayon inside the halftone area, or light blue pencil outside the halftone area.

Result when printed.

Photostat pasted on mechanical and marked "for position only."

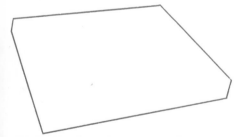

Red holding line showing size and position of silhouetted copy.

BLEED

The portion of a printed image that runs beyond the edge of the trimmed sheet is called a bleed. Since trimming is seldom exact, the bleed must extend at least ⅛" beyond the crop marks to insure that the image doesn't end short of the trimmed edge.

Result when printed and trimmed.

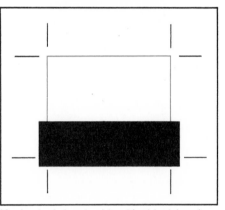

Mechanical showing bleed for black band.

INDICATING DIE-CUTS

If the cut is straight and on the outside edge of the printed piece, it is usually trimmed on a paper cutter. In that case, crop marks placed outside the printing area are used as a cutting guide. If the cut is irregular in shape or a hole in the paper, the shape is indicated with a thin, accurate, red or black ink line on the mechanical and marked "die-cut." When the die-cut falls over a printed area, it must usually be indicated on an overlay. In some cases, however, it may be better to draw the die-cut on the key mechanical and position the printing copy on an overlay.

Result when trimmed and die-cut.

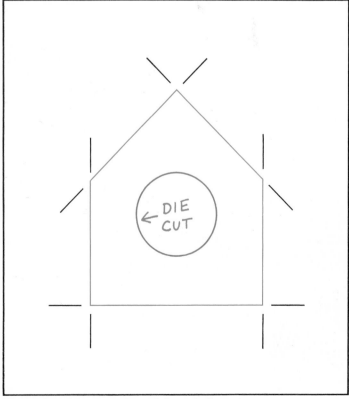

Mechanical with crop marks and die-cut indicated.

SCREEN TINTS

Screen tints, sometimes called Benday screens, are flat tints of black or color. They can be applied to the mechanical with shading film (page 80), or they can be applied by the stripper. The shading film method is least expensive, and also permits retouching or re-working of the dot pattern by the designer. However, the finest screen available is 85-line (85 lines per inch), whereas the stripper can lay screens as fine as 150-line, and some-times even finer. The use of shading film, therefore, is generally limited to newspaper and other coarse forms of reproduction.

Shading film being applied to a line drawing on the mechanical (Formatt).

If the stripper is to lay the screen tint, its size and position is indicated on the mechanical in the same way as continu-ous-tone copy: either as a red outline or as a solid red or black shape, depending upon the situation. This provides a win-dow on the stripper's negative for strip-ping in a piece of film containing the screen tint in negative form. If the screen tint abuts another element of the same color, it is usually indicated with a red holding line. If it abuts another element of a different color, it may be indicated with a red holding line, or it may be indicated on an overlay (see Multicolor Mechanicals– flat color, page 165).

Screen tints must be specified by per-centage on the mechanical, such as "30% tint," "50% tint," etc. In order to specify screen tints accurately, it is necessary to use a scale which contains printed screens ranging from 10 to 90 percent in 10 percent gradations.

In multicolor printing, screen tints of different colors may be overprinted to achieve a great range of color/tint com-binations (see Specifying Flat Color, page 168).

Result when printed (50% tint).

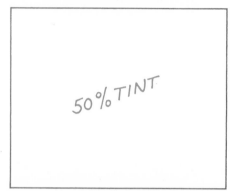

Red holding line on mechanical.

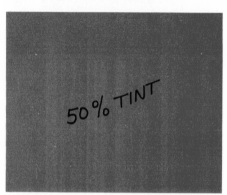

Solid red (or black) shape on mechanical.

Result when printed (60% tint).

Except for screen tint specification, black type requires no special procedure on the mechanical.

Result when printed (black and 30% tint).

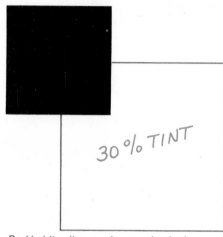

Red holding line used on mechanical to separate black and tint areas.

Result when printed (black and 40% tint).

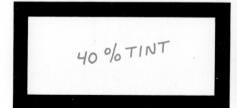

Tint area on mechanical is completely delineated by black shape. No special mechanical procedure is required except screen tint specification.

Note: see page 32 for chart showing screen tints, dropouts, reverses, and surprints.

DROPOUTS AND REVERSES

If line copy is dropped out of a halftone or screen tint, it is called a dropout. If it is dropped out of a solid background, it is called a reverse. The difference between the two is that a reverse results in a single line negative, whereas a dropout requires the combining of the line negative and the screened negative in the stripping operation.

A reverse is prepared by simply pasting a glossy negative stat of the line copy on the background shape and blackening its edges. If the line copy is too fine in detail for photostatting (such as very small type), paste the original, positive copy in position—making sure not to cover the outer edges of the background shape—and let the printer reverse it. If the line copy is to print in positive on one part of the design and reverse where it overlaps the background shape, also paste up the positive copy: the printer will reverse the portion that overlaps the background shape. As long as the background shape is straight-edged, and the line copy doesn't obscure too much of it, the line copy may be pasted directly onto it: the portion that is obscured can be completed by the stripper. Otherwise, the line copy must be pasted on an acetate overlay.

A dropout is prepared in a similar way to a reverse. If the halftone or screen tint is indicated with a solid black or red shape, simply paste a negative of the line copy in position and blacken its edges. This results in a window in the line negative which contains a black image of the line copy. The halftone or screen tint negative is stripped into the window, and when the printing plate is made, the dot pattern is eliminated or "dropped out" of the portion of the screen where the line copy occurs. If the halftone or screen tint is indicated with a red holding line or matte photostat, or if the line copy is to be partly in positive and partly dropped out, follow the procedure described in the preceding paragraph. Line copy may be

Reverse—printed result.

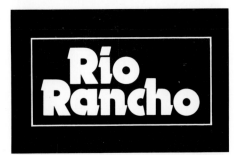
Solid black shape with negative stat of type on mechanical. Blacken edges of stat.

Solid black shape with positive type on mechanical.

Dropout—printed result.

Solid red (or black) shape with negative stat of type on mechanical. Blacken edges of stat.

Red holding line with positive type on mechanical.

pasted directly over holding lines or matte photostats so long as key elements of the halftone or screen tint shape and position remain visible. Also, even though silhouette halftones have irregular contours, they may be partially obscured because the mechanical is used only for position; the exact shape of the silhouette is derived from the separate shooting copy. If there is any doubt about pasting line copy directly over halftone, screen tint, or solid background shapes, use an acetate overlay.

Because the edges of the dropped out line copy are defined solely by the dots of the screened background, small and/or delicate line copy requires a finely screened background. Also, there must be sufficient contrast between the dropout and the background. With halftones, this may require retouching the original copy.

Note: see page 32 for chart showing screen tints, dropouts, reverses, and surprints.

Dropout—printed result.

Red holding line with positive type pasted over it on mechanical.

SURPRINTS

A surprint is line copy superimposed over screened copy on the same printing plate. This is not to be confused with overprinting, which is the printing of one color over another and requires two printing plates. For example, black type on a black screen tint is a surprint, whereas black type on a red screen tint is an overprint.

The preparation of a surprint is similar to the preparation of a dropout. The positive line copy is pasted directly over the halftone or screen tint indication, or, if it obscures too much of the underlying indication, it is pasted on an acetate overlay. In the stripping operation, the line negative and the screened negative are combined photographically into a single negative and stripped into the goldenrod layout, or flat. A less commonly used method is to expose each negative separately on the printing plate; first the screened negative and then the line negative.

As with dropouts, small and/or delicate surprint copy requires a finely screened background, and there must be sufficient contrast between the surprint and the background.

Note: see page 32 for chart showing screen tints, dropouts, reverses, and surprints.

A.   Surprint. Type and screen tint
(or halftone) are combined on one plate.
B.   Overprint. Type and screen tint
(or halftone) are on separate plates.

Printed result (black and 30% tint).

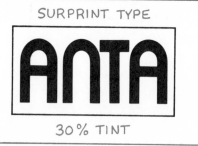

Red holding line with positive type on mechanical.

Solid red (or black) shape with positive type on mechanical.

Printed result.

Type proof obscures screen tint shape on mechanical. One element must therefore be put on an acetate overlay.

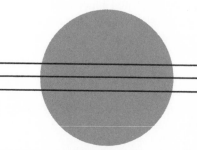

Printed result.

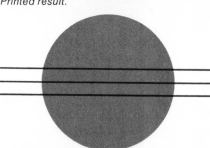

Black and red will both photograph transparent on the platemaker's negative. One element must therefore be put on an acetate overlay.

MORE INSIGHT

Printed result.

MORE INSIGHT

SURPRINT TYPE

Red holding line with positive type pasted over it on the mechanical.

ACETATE OVERLAYS

Acetate overlays are used to separate colors in flat color printing, to separate line copy from screened backgrounds for dropouts and surprints, to indicate screen tints and die-cuts, etc. Either clear, frosted, or prepared acetate may be used, depending on the mediums to be applied to it (see Acetate, page 80). Heavy tracing paper (vellum) may be used for loose register overlays, but it is not dimensionally stable enough for tight register (it stretches or shrinks with changes in humidity).

The overlay is cut 1″ to 1½″ larger, on all sides, than the trim dimensions of the mechanical, and hinged to the mechanical with drafting tape along its top edge. Don't use cellophane tape, since this may damage the board when the overlay is removed. To hold the opposite edge of the overlay tightly against the mechanical, attach two drafting tape tabs. If one end of each tab is folded over on itself, the tabs can easily be grasped when lifting the overlay. Don't remove the tabs completely when lifting the overlay; just detach the portion that is adhered to the board. If more than one overlay is required, hinge each one to different sides of the board. In this way, any overlay can be brought into direct contact with the key mechanical or other overlay, which is necessary to achieve accurate register of elements. If the overlays are all hinged on the same side, or if more than four overlays are involved, the interlying overlays must be completely detached to achieve direct contact.

The register of the overlays with the key mechanical is achieved with register marks, which are fine, crossed ink lines, about ½″ long, located about ¼″ outside the trim dimensions. At least three register marks are necessary, and they should be spaced as far apart as possible around the periphery of the mechanical. First draw the register marks on the key mechanical, using a T-square, triangle, and ruling pen or technical fountain pen, and then accurately trace the marks onto each overlay, which must be firmly taped down and in direct contact with the key mechanical. Printed register marks are available on clear, self-adhesive cellophane tape. Being fast and easy to apply, they are used by most designers. Crop marks and fold marks need not be applied to the overlays, since only those on the key mechanical will be recorded on the printed sheet.

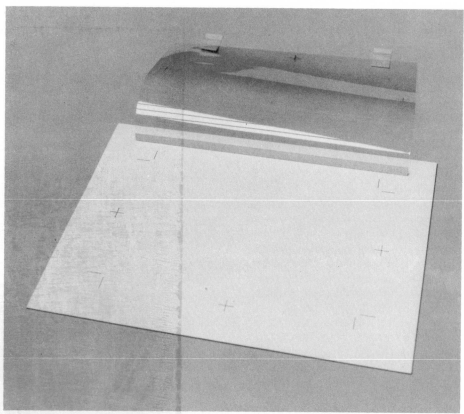

Base mechanical on illustration board with hinged acetate overlay. Register marks on base mechanical and acetate overlay must be in perfect registration.

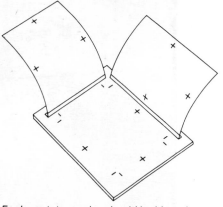

Each acetate overlay should be hinged to different sides of the base mechanical.

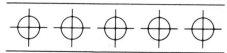

Printed register marks on clear, self-adhesive cellophane tape.

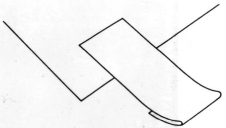

Drafting tape tab attached to acetate overlay.

In the negative-making process, the overlay is backed with white paper and photographed as reflection copy in the same way as the key mechanical. This means that the overlay elements may be comprised of pasted-up copy on white paper, as well as shapes rendered directly on the acetate. Shapes rendered directly on the acetate may be retouched with white paint, since the white paint and the white surface behind the acetate will photograph the same.

Either black or red acetate ink or color film may be used for rendering shapes on acetate. Red is preferred because, being transparent, it permits the underlying copy to remain visible, which is particularly important where accurate register is involved. An acetate ink made especially for masking on overlays, such as Grumbacher Patent Red or Patent Black, works better than general purpose acetate ink. Also, there are several brands of red color film made especially for masking, such as Parapaque, Cellopaque, Transopaque, Formopaque, and Rubylith. Color film is used for large, simple shapes, and ink is used for small, intricate shapes, as well as for adding details or making corrections on color film shapes.

To achieve accurate register with the underlying mechanical, the overlay must be pressed tightly against it. In straight-line work, this is automatically accomplished by the pressure of the T-square and/or triangle. In freehand rendering, it can be accomplished by pressing the handle end of a brush (held in the left hand) against the immediate area being rendered. Use a scrap of paper under the working hand to avoid damaging the acetate or rendering.

Masking ink may be thinned with water, removed from acetate with a water-moistened swab or tissue, and applied by brush or ruling pen. Don't worry about streaks with red masking ink; as long as the coverage is thorough and reasonably dense, it will reproduce as opaque black. It is difficult to rule fine lines accurately on acetate, particularly with masking ink. If much line ruling is involved (apart from outlining shapes), it may be better to use regular India ink on drafting film, which is made especially for ruling, and is also dimensionally stable. The best method, if it is possible to use it, is to rule the lines on paper and then paste them up.

Types of Masking Film. There are two types of color film used for masking. In the first type, such as Cellopaque, the film is laminated to a waxed paper backing sheet with low-tack adhesive. To use it, cut a piece of film slightly larger than the shape to be masked (don't cut through the backing sheet). Peel off and apply to the acetate overlay (or base mechanical). Then press down, trim, and burnish.

In the second type, such as Rubylith, the film is laminated to a 3- or 5-mil (.003″ or .005″) clear acetate backing sheet with low-tack adhesive. The backing sheet serves as an acetate overlay, and is hinged to the mechanical (with the film attached) in the same way as described previously for a regular acetate overlay. The shape to be masked is cut in the film (don't cut through the acetate backing sheet), and the unwanted film is peeled off. Since the film is backed with low-tack adhesive, peeled-off film may be applied in the same way as described for film with paper backing.

The type of masking film used is determined largely by personal preference. However, paper-backed film is more economical and easier to use when the masked areas are small, whereas acetate-backed film is easier to use when the masked areas are large. Paper-backed film also permits the use of frosted or prepared acetate, which is necessary when using non-acetate inks and other mediums on the overlay.

Masking film is usually ruby-red in color, but in some brands it is also available in amber. Both colors photograph as black, the advantage to amber being that it is easier to see through.

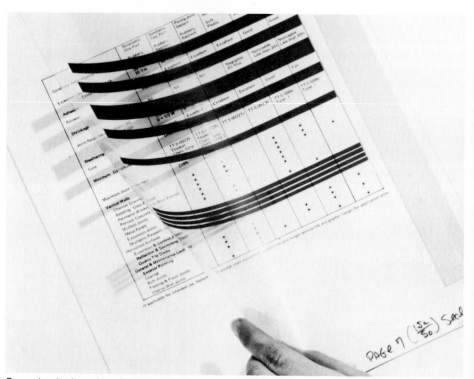

Paper-backed masking film used on acetate overlay for color separation (Formopaque by Formatt).

MULTICOLOR MECHANICALS— FLAT COLOR

As described in the section on Color Printing (page 32), the original copy for flat color printing is black and white, and is assembled on the mechanical in such a way that the printer is able to separate the copy for each printing color. There are various methods of assembling the copy for color separation, and the choice depends upon the type of copy involved and the degree of accuracy required for color register. If more than one method is suitable, the designer usually uses the one that entails the least amount of work for the printer, but if the designer's time is at a premium, he may use the one that is fastest for him, even though it may increase reproduction costs.

It is frequently either necessary or desirable to combine separation methods. For example, while certain colors in a job might best be separated by the key-line method, others might best be separated on an acetate overlay. Usually the most appropriate separation method is suggested by the copy itself. If not, the printer should be consulted.

Loose register. Black overprints background color, blocking it out.

Loose register. Colors do not abut.

Loose register. Overprinted colors create a third color in the overprint area.

Lap register. Blue overlaps red. The width of the overlap should be no wider than 1/64", since overprinting of transparent inks creates a third color.

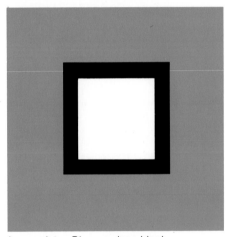

Lap register. Blue overlaps black. The width of the overlap can be generous, since the black blocks out the blue.

Color Register. There are three types of color register: loose, lap, and hairline. In loose register, the colors do not abut; either they are completely separated, or one overprints another. Overprinting is possible when the foreground color is either black or so dark that it completely blocks out the background color. Of course, as explained in Color printing (page 32), overprinting may also be done with a transparent color to achieve a mixture of the foreground and background colors. In either case, since the foreground shape does not need to be dropped out of the background color, there is no problem of color register.

In lap register, the colors abut, but their sizes, shapes, values, and/or hues are such that a substantial overlap is possible without creating an obvious and undesirable third color where they overlap. (A

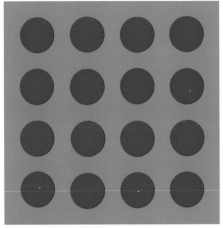

Hairline register. Because of the smallness of the shapes, any more than an infinitesimal overlap will create an undesirable third color.

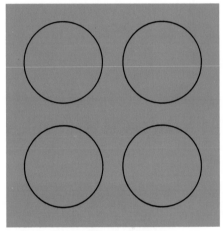

Hairline register. Because of the thinness of the black lines, the blue overlap must be infinitesimal.

certain amount of overlap is necessary with abutted colors. This is to avoid the possibility of a white gap between the colors in the event that the plates print slightly off-register.) The amount of overlap is usually about 1/64" but may be even wider if the second color is black. Be aware, however, that the underlying color will usually make the black more glossy in the overlap area.

In hairline register, the colors abut, but their sizes, shapes, values, and/or hues are such that any more than a hairline overlap will create an obvious and undesirable third color where they overlap. For example, if a small yellow shape overlaps a small blue shape more than a hair, a disturbingly obvious green border will result. Hairline register is also necessary when a color area abuts a very thin line of any color, including black.

Acetate Overlay Separation. This method is generally used for loose and lap register work. It is not suitable for hairline register or very intricate work for two reasons. One is that the acetate is not dimensionally stable enough for hairline register, and the other is that it is extremely difficult to render intricate shapes and/or maintain a consistently fine hairline overlap on an overlay.

In overlay separation, the copy for each color is assembled—in register—on separate sheets, and the printer simply photographs these sheets to make the printing plates. Because the printer's task is minimized, this is the most economical method of color separation, and is therefore used whenever possible.

The copy for the darkest and/or most complicated color (usually black) is placed on the key, or illustration board, mechanical, and the copy for the lighter and/or less complicated colors is placed on the overlays. To insure accurate positioning of overlay copy, guidelines (either graphite or light blue) are usually drawn on the key mechanical. Where colors abut, the lighter color must overlap the darker color.

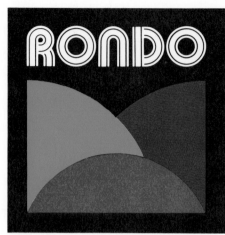

3-color design—black, red, and blue. Violet is an overprint of red and blue tints.

Key-line Separation. This method is used for hairline register and very intricate work. The copy for all colors is placed on the key mechanical, and the printer separates the copy for each printing plate through camera and/or stripping techniques. Key-line separation may also be used for loose and lap register work, but it is usually more expensive than overlay separation.

There are two methods of key-line separation. In the most common method, all shapes, both black and color, are outlined with a thin black line. The black shapes are then completely filled in with black. The color shapes are also filled in, but a narrow, jagged-edged band of white is left where they abut the black or another color of a darker value. In other words, wherever colors abut, one side is filled in and the other side is left with a band of white. (Only the outline itself actually touches the abutting color.) If the abutting colors are equal in value, either side can be filled in.

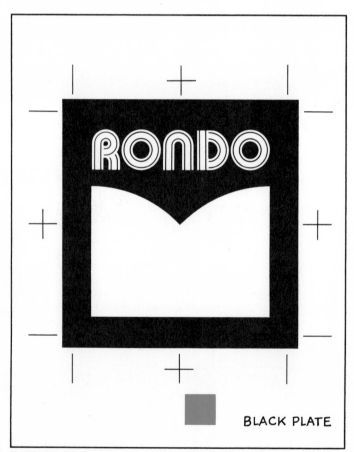

Overlay separation. Black copy is placed on illustration board. Note crop marks, register marks, and color swatches. Also note that the black copy bleeds ⅛" beyond the trim marks. A negative stat of the type is pasted in position with the cut edges blackened.

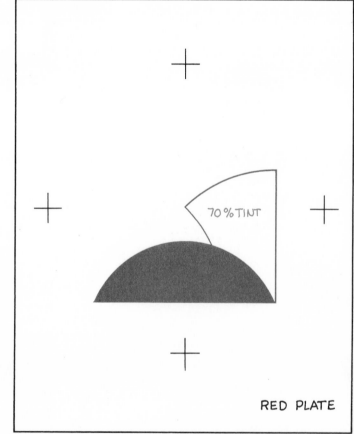

Overlay separation. Red copy is placed on an acetate overlay.

The printer makes as many negatives as there are colors, and on each negative he removes the unwanted colors and completes the shape (if necessary) of the wanted color, thus achieving a separate negative for each color. By photographically spreading or shrinking a color (usually the lighter one), he is able to obtain hairline register.

The other method of key-line separation is to render the black shapes in solid black, and the color shapes in red outlines, with no filling in. As with the previously described method, the printer makes as many negatives as there are colors, and removes or completes shapes as necessary to achieve a separate negative for each color. Since the red "key" lines are common to both abutting colors, their thickness determines the amount of overlap.

In all methods of color separation, colored type on a black or colored background must be separated by the printer. A positive proof is either pasted on the background shape, or, if it obscures key elements of the background shape, it is pasted on an overlay. The printer makes two negatives, one of the type, and one of the background with the type dropped out. Hairline register is achieved by photographically spreading or shrinking one color, usually the lighter one.

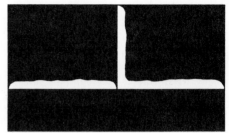

Key-line separation. Black shape is solid black. Color shapes are also solid black except for a jagged-edged band of white between color breaks.

Printed result.

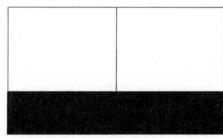

Key-line separation. Black shape is solid black. Color shapes are indicated with thin, red lines.

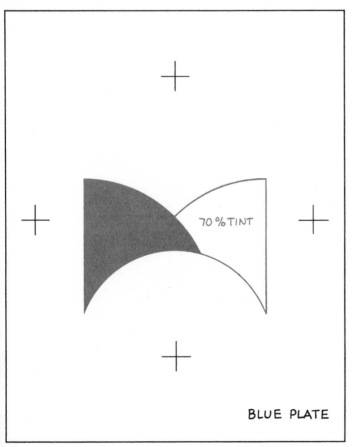

Overlay separation. Blue copy is placed on an acetate overlay.

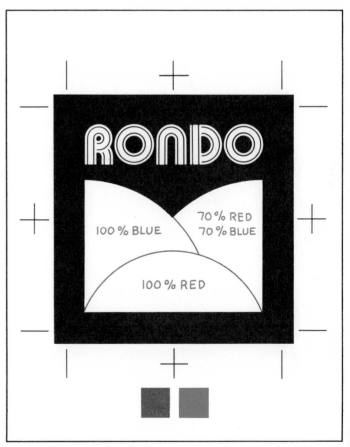

Key-line separation. Black copy is placed on illustration board, and color breaks are indicated with thin, red lines.

SPECIFICATIONS

After the mechanical has been flapped with a tracing paper overlay and heavy paper cover (see Flapping Artwork, page 97), all specifications are added. As explained previously, many of these specifications are written directly on the key mechanical or overlays in black, red, or light blue, depending upon their location. If the specifications are very extensive, they can be written on the tracing paper overlay.

With flat color mechanicals, a swatch of each color is pasted on the key mechanical. Also, a color sketch of the mechanical is drawn on the tracing paper overlay. This is called a color breakdown, and is done with colored pencils or color markers. The colors don't have to match accurately and may be roughly applied, but the color breaks must be clearly delineated. It is usually possible to show all the color breaks in a narrow band that runs horizontally, vertically, or diagonally across the mechanical. This saves a good amount of rendering time.

MULTICOLOR MECHANICALS—PROCESS COLOR

The size and position of the full-color, continuous-tone copy is indicated on the key mechanical in the same way as for black-and-white continuous-tone copy; either with a red holding line, a solid black or red shape, or a photostat.

If any of the accompanying line copy is to be printed in color, the key-line method of color separation is usually employed. Any flat color can be achieved by mixing the process colors in various combinations and tints. The desired color can be specified with a swatch pasted on the mechanical, but the most accurate method is to find the desired color in a process color guide, and list its component colors and percentages on the mechanical.

Portion of 4-color process mechanical showing color specification for type. This mixture of yellow, magenta, and cyan will produce a golden brown.

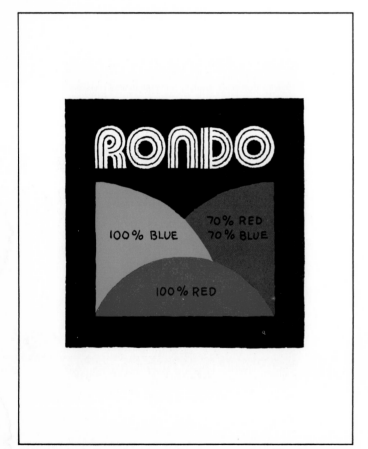

Color breaks indicated on the tracing paper overlay with color markers.

Color breaks indicated in a narrow band on the tracing paper overlay.

Appendix

Glossary

Accordion fold. A series of parallel folds, each folding in opposite directions.

Agate line. Unit of measurement for column depth in newspapers and magazines. 14 agate lines equal 1 inch.

Ampersand. The symbol & used in place of *and.* It is the Latin word *et,* meaning *and.*

Aniline printing. See *Flexography.*

Antique finish. An uncoated, uncalendered, rough paper finish with either a wove or laid texture.

Ascender. The portion of a lower case letter that extends above the x-height.

Asymmetrical type. Lines of type varying in length and staggered over one another.

Author's alteration (AA). In proofreading, any alteration which is not a *printer's error (PE).*

Backbone. See *Spine.*

Backing up. The printing of a sheet already printed on the other side.

Bad break. In type, an incorrect or undesirable hyphenation. Also, a *widow* (which see).

Base line. The imaginary line upon which capitals and most lower case letters stand.

Base mechanical. See *Key mechanical.*

Basis weight. The weight in pounds of a ream (500 sheets) of paper of a basic size. The basic size is different for each grade of paper.

Benday process. A method of applying screen patterns to line plates. Now superseded by *screen tints* (which see).

Binding. The process of joining separate sheets into pamphlet, magazine, or book form. Also, the cover of a book.

Blanket. In offset lithography, the rubber-surfaced fabric which is wrapped around the blanket cylinder, and transfers the image from the plate cylinder to the paper.

Bleed. The portion of a printed image that extends beyond the trim edge of the sheet.

Blind embossing. Embossing (which see) done without ink or metal foil.

Blind keyboard. In phototypesetting, a keyboard which produces only an encoded tape or disc. It has no character display or hard (typewritten) copy output.

Blocking. In letterpress, the mounting of photoengravings on wood blocks to bring them *type-high.*

Blocking out. The operation of eliminating undesirable backgrounds and portions of artwork or negatives by opaquing.

Blowup. An enlargement, as of a photograph, type, etc.

Blueline. A sheet of paper or film printed with light blue (non-reproducing) guidelines. Used for the positioning of copy in the paste-up or stripping operations.

Blueprint. Also called a *blue.* A contact photoprint on paper, made from stripped up negatives or positives, and used as a *pre-press proof* (which see).

Blurb. Summary of a book, usually on the jacket. Also, a *caption.* Also, the balloon and enclosed text in a comic strip.

Body. The piece of metal that carries the relief image of the letter. The body depth is the point size of the type. Also, the viscosity or consistency of printing ink.

Body type. Also called *text type.* Small sizes of very legible type generally used for the main body of text, as opposed to *display type* (which see).

Bold face (BF). A heavy version of a text weight typeface.

Bond paper. A grade of writing, printing, or drawing paper that is strong and durable, and treated to have good writing and erasing qualities.

Booklet. See *Pamphlet.*

Book paper. A general term for coated and uncoated paper used for books, magazines, pamphlets, etc.

Borders. Decorative strips available in type and printed film for making borders around pages and type elements.

Bristol board. In printing paper, a stiff board in many textures, colors, and weights. In drawing paper, a white kid or plate finish paper in many weights. The different weights in drawing bristol are achieved by laminating sheets together (1 ply to 5 ply).

Broadside. A large, printed sheet folded for mailing.

Brochure. See *Pamphlet.*

Brownprint. Also called a *Van Dyke* or *silverprint.* A brown contact photoprint on paper, made from stripped up negatives or positives, and used as a *pre-press proof* (which see).

Built-up lettering. Lettering which is first drawn in pencil and then carefully inked in and retouched, as opposed to *calligraphy* (which see).

Bulk. The thickness of paper, measured by the caliper per sheet or the pages per inch (PPI). Caliper is measured in mils or points. One mil or point is .001".

Bullet. In type, a large, round dot used as a decorative device.

Butted lines. In type, two or more linecast slugs placed in one line to achieve a wider line or column.

Calendered paper. Paper which has been passed between calender rolls on the paper-making machine to achieve a smooth finish.

Caliper. The thickness of paper, measured in thousandths of an inch, and expressed in mils or points. One mil or point equals .001".

Calligraphy. Lettering that is written, usually with a broad-nib pen, as opposed to built-up lettering, which is carefully modeled.

Camera-ready. Finished art or copy that is ready to be photographed for platemaking.

Caps and small caps (C & SC). Two sizes of capitals in the same point size. Small caps are usually the same height as the x-height of the lower case letters.

Caption. The text accompanying photographs or illustrations.

Cast-coated paper. Coated paper with an exceptionally high gloss and excellent ink receptivity.

Center spread. The two center pages in a saddle-stitched pamphlet or magazine.

Centered type. Lines of type of varying length centered over one another.

Character count. The total number of characters in a piece of copy.

Chase. In letterpress, a steel frame in which type and engravings are locked up, either for printing or for duplicate platemaking.

Chipboard. Also called *newsboard.* A heavy, gray, low-grade cardboard, usually used for the backing on pads of paper, packages, etc.

Coated paper. Paper coated with pigment to improve its printability and opacity, and ranging from dull to very glossy.

Cockle finish. Bond paper with a puckered finish, usually with a high rag content.

Cold type. A term originally used to differentiate between metal keyboard composition (hot type) and photographic keyboard composition (cold type). Because there are now so many methods of non-metal composition, keyboard and otherwise, it is no longer a very descriptive term.

Collating. To gather sheets or signatures in their correct sequence, usually by machine. Also called *gathering.*

Collotype printing. Also called *photogelatin.* A printing process that utilizes a photosensitized gelatin plate. Continuous tones can be printed without the use of a halftone screen.

Colophon. Trademark of the publisher of a book. Also, an inscription placed usually at the end of a book listing the editor, designer, typeface, printer, paper, etc.

"Color". The overall tone of type or other graphic elements on a page. "Color" refers to the optical mixture of figure/ground patterns, either black and white or actual color and white.

Color break. The boundary that separates two colors on a mechanical.

Color correction. In process color platemaking, the masking, re-etching, or dot etching of color separations to improve color rendition.

Color filter. A sheet of colored glass, gelatin, or plastic used in photography to absorb certain colors and permit better rendition of other colors.

Color matching system. A system of specifying flat color by using standard printing ink formulas and coded color swatches.

Color process. See *Process color printing.*

Color separation. The separating of full-color art into the four process colors by means of color filters, either photographically or by electronic scanning. Also see *Mechanical color separation.*

Color swatch. A small sample of color attached to the mechanical, to be matched in printing ink.

Color transparency. A full-color photographic positive on film, such as Ektachrome, Kodachrome, etc.

Combination plate. A printing plate that contains both halftone and line copy. Usually refers to *photoengraving* (which see).

Composing stick. A hand-held device used for assembling foundry type.

Composition. See *Typesetting.*

Compositor. A person who sets type.

Comprehensive (comp). A highly-finished layout for presentation.

Computerized composition. Unjustified tape is produced on the keyboard and later run through a computer, which makes end-of-line decisions regarding justification and hyphenation.

Condensed type. A narrow typeface.

Contact print. A photographic print made from a film negative or positive in direct contact with sensitized film, paper, or printing plate.

Continuous-tone copy. Copy that has a full range of gradated tones from black to white, such as wash drawings, photographs, etc.

Contrast. The difference between tones. In high contrast, the tonal differences are great, and in low contrast, the tonal differences are slight.

Conversion systems. Systems for converting metal type and photoengravings to film images for making offset and gravure plates.

Cool colors. Colors which contain enough blue to make them appear cool rather than neutral or warm.

Copy. In graphic design, reading matter (either typewritten or printed) as opposed to art. In printing, anything to be reproduced, including reading matter and art.

Copyfitting. The process of determining the amount of space it will take to set copy in a specific type size and style.

Counter. The white shape inside a letter, such as the bowl of the *b.* Even shapes that are not completely enclosed, such as those in the *H,* are also counters.

Counting keyboard. In phototypesetting, a keyboard which produces a hyphenated, justified tape. The operator makes end-of-line decisions. See also *Non-counting keyboard.*

Cover paper. A general term applied to a variety of heavy printing papers used for covers, direct mail pieces, etc.

Crawling. The contraction of ink or other medium on a surface because of lack of adhesion.

Crease score. See *Score.*

Crop. To eliminate unwanted portions of copy. Cropping is indicated on the original copy with *crop marks.*

Crop marks. Short, fine lines drawn on the copy to indicate the cropped area. Also called *trim marks* when used to indicate the trim size of a printed sheet.

Cut. In letterpress, a line or halftone engraving.

Cut-out lettering. Letters printed on adhesive-backed film, to be cut out and adhered to artwork.

Cut score. See *Score.*

Cyan. One of the four *process ink colors* (which see). Also called *process blue.*

Dampeners. In offset lithography, cloth-covered rollers that distribute the dampening solution.

Dandy roll. On the papermaking machine, a wire-covered cylinder that imparts a *wove* or *laid* texture to the paper, as well as *watermarks.*

Deckle edge. The untrimmed, feathery edges of paper. Text, cover, and other fancy papers are frequently deckle-edged.

Deep-etch plate. In offset lithography, a plate in which the inked areas are etched below the surface, as opposed to a *surface plate.* Deep-etch plates are used for color and long runs.

Densitometer. A light-sensitive instrument designed to measure density, or tonal values, for achieving correct photographic exposure.

Density. In photography, the measurement of tonal values, or relative blackening, of a negative or positive.

Descender. That portion of a letter that extends below the base line.

Diazo. In offset lithography, a sensitized coating used on *presensitized* and *wipe-on* plates.

Diazoprint. A black-and-white direct-positive contact photoprint on paper or film. Used for producing positive proofs from film positives, as in phototypesetting.

Didot. The point system used in most European countries. Also, the name of a typeface.

Die-cutting. The use of sharpened steel rules to cut shapes in paper and board, such as labels, packages, displays, direct mail pieces, etc.

Direct impression composition. See *Typewriter composition.*

Direct mail. Any printed piece designed specifically for mailing.

Direct screening. In process color separation, a halftone color separation negative made directly from the original copy.

Display type. Any bold, decorative, or large size of type generally used for headlines, titles, and other display purposes, as opposed to *body type* (which see).

Distribute. To return type, matrices, and related composition materials to their storage places after use.

Doctor blade. In gravure, a thin, flexible metal blade which presses against the etched plate cylinder and wipes the ink from the nonprinting areas.

Dot. The individual formation or element of a halftone.

Dot etching. Tonal correction of halftone negatives or positives by the chemical reduction of dot sizes.

Double-dot halftone. In offset lithography, a halftone photo made by combining two halftone negatives, the purpose being to extend tonal range. Not to be confused with *duotones,* which require two printing plates.

Double spread. Two facing pages. Also called a *spread* or *two-page spread.*

Drawing paper. Paper or board specifically formulated for drawing and rendering, as opposed to *printing paper* (which see). Also called *studio* or *art* paper.

Drier. A substance added to ink to hasten its drying. Often called a *siccative.*

Dropout halftone. See *Highlight halftone.*

Dropout type. Type dropped out to white on a halftone or screen tint background. When dropped out of a solid background, it is usually called *reverse type.*

Dry mounting. A method of mounting photographs, using an adhesive-coated tissue that bonds under heat and pressure.

Dry offset. See *Letterset.*

Dummy. A mock-up of a package, display, booklet, folder, etc. It may be either blank or graphically rendered.

Duotone. A two-color halftone reproduction made form one-color, continuous-tone copy, such as a black and white photograph. Usually, one plate is printed in dark ink, and the other in light ink.

Duplex paper. Printing paper that has a different color or finish on each side.

Duplicate plates. In letterpress, plates made from locked-up type and/or photoengravings, such as stereotypes, electrotypes, and plastic and rubber plates.

Duplicator. A small printing machine for short-run, low-quality reproduction, such as Multilith, Mimeograph, and Multigraph.

Dye transfer. An opaque, full-color photographic print made from any transparent or reflective copy.

Eggshell finish. An uncoated, uncalendered paper with a finish between that of *antique* and *machine flinish*.

Electronic scanner. An electronic device used for scanning color transparencies and making color separations.

Electrotype. In letterpress, a high-fidelity duplicate plate made from type and/or engravings, and involving molding, casting, and electrolytic plating. Also called an *electro*.

Ellipsis. In type, an intentional omission of one or more words, usually indicated by three dots (...). The plural is *ellipses*.

Embossed finish. Paper with a textured finish resembling woodgrain, linen, leather, etc.

Embossing. Impressing a relief image in paper or other material, either in conjunction with a printed image, or on blank paper *(blind embossing)*.

Em quad. Commonly called an *em*. A unit of space that is the square of the type size to which it belongs. For example, a 12 point em is 12 points in width.

Emulsion. In photography, the photosensitive coating on film paper, glass, etc.

End-of-line decisions. In typesetting, decisions regarding hyphenation and justification. Can be made by the operator or by computer.

End papers. In casebound books, the sheets that attach the covers to the signatures.

English finish (EF). An uncoated, calendered book paper with a finish between that of *machine finish* and *supercalendered*.

Engraving. A printing plate that has been etched or incised. In letterpress, called a *photoengraving*. Also, an intaglio printing process sometimes called *steel-die* or *copperplate engraving*. Also, the act of engraving.

En quad. Commonly called an *en*. A unit of space that is one half the width of an *em* (which see).

Etch. To produce an image on a plate by chemical action. Also, the acid used in etching. Also, in offset lithography, the solution used to help keep non-printing areas of the plate free of ink.

Exposure. In photography, the duration and intensity of light acting upon a light-sensitive coating, or emulsion.

Extended type. A wide typeface. Also called *expanded*.

Face. The printing surface of a metal type, plate, etc. Also, a style of type (shortened from *typeface*).

Facsimile. An exact reproduction. Also, the radio transmission of art and copy through the use of electronic scanners.

Fake color process. Full-color printing done from hand-rendered color separations. In one method, the separations are rendered in tones of black and white, and in another, the separations are rendered in the four process colors.

Felt side. In papermaking, the top side of the sheet, which is usually smoother than the bottom, or *wire side*.

Filler. In papermaking, a substance added to the pulp to increase opacity, improve printability, and make a smoother surface.

Filling in (or filling up). In printing, the filling in of small non-printing areas with ink, such as between halftone dots.

Filter. See *Color filter.*

Finished art. Art or copy to be photographed for reproduction, as opposed to layouts, comps, sketches, etc.

First proof. In type, the first proof taken after type has been set. Also called a *galley proof* (which see). See also *Revise proof* and *Reproduction proof.*

Fixing. The chemical process which renders a photographic image permanent after it has been developed. Also, spraying artwork with fixative.

Flash exposure. The supplementary exposure made in halftone photography to strengthen the dots in the shadow areas of negatives.

Flat. The assemblage of the various film negatives and/or positives on a sheet of goldenrod paper or other supporting material. The flat is used to expose the sensitized printing plate.

Flat color. Also called *match color*. A printing ink color usually mixed to the specifications of the designer, as opposed to *process color* (see *Process inks).*

Flat-tint halftone. A halftone printed over a screen tint of another color. Also called a *fake duotone.*

Flexography. A form of letterpress printing in which the printing plate is made of rubber. Formerly called *aniline printing.*

Flop. To reverse an image from left to right *(mirror image.)*

Flush cover. A book or booklet cover the same size as the enclosed pages, such as in paperbacks. Also see *Overhang cover.*

Flush left (or right). Type set to line up at the left (or right) of the column.

Flyer. Any advertising piece, such as a leaflet, distributed in large numbers.

Folder. A single sheet of paper in which the folds are an integral part of the design.

Folio. Page number. Also, a sheet of paper folded once to make a 4-page signature.

Font. See *Type font.*

Foot. The bottom of a sheet or page. The top is called the *head.*

Form. In letterpress, type, photoengravings, and other matter locked up in a chase.

Format. The size, layout requirements, etc. of a printed piece, page, or publication.

Foundry type. Metal, hand-set type cast at a foundry, as opposed to metal, machine-set type, which is cast from matrices at the time of composition.

Fountain. The ink reservoir on a printing press. Also, the reservoir on an offset press that holds the "water," which is a solution used to dampen the plate and keep the non-printing areas from accepting ink.

Four-color process. See *Process color printing.*

Fourdrinier. A machine for making paper in an endless web.

French fold. A sheet of paper printed on one side and then folded once horizontally and once vertically to produce a 4-page folder.

Frisket. A mask or stencil made of paper, film, or other material to block out or protect portions of plates or artwork.

Fugitive colors. Colors that are not lightfast or permanent.

Full color. See *Process color printing.*

Furnish. The mixture of pulp and additives that is used to make paper.

Furniture. In letterpress, the blocks of wood and strips of metal that are used to fill in blank spaces around type and engravings in a *chase* (which see).

Galley. A flat metal tray used to hold metal type as it is assembled.

Galley proof. In metal typesetting, a rough proof made from type assembled in a galley. Also, the first rough proof in phototypesetting. After errors have been corrected, a *reproduction proof* (which see) is made. If further galley proofs are made after corrections, they are called a *first revise, second revise,* etc.

Gang printing (or ganging up). Printing a number of different jobs, or multiples of the same job, on one sheet.

Gate fold. A sheet or page that folds inward, and opens like a gate.

Gathering. See *Collating.*

Goldenrod. A yellow-orange paper that is used for assembling film negatives and positives for exposure to the printing plate. The completed assemblage is called a *flat.* On a light table, goldenrod is translucent enough to make the positioning of negatives possible, but in the vacuum frame it blocks the passage of actinic light, thus serving as a photographic mask during plate exposure.

Grain. In paper, the predominant direction of the fibers. Paper tears and folds straighter with the grain than across the grain.

Gray scale. A strip containing gray tones from white to black, usually in 10 percent increments. Used to measure the tone or value of grays and colors.

Grippers. On printing presses, metal fingers that clamp onto the paper as it passes through the press.

Gripper edge. As paper feeds into a press, its leading edge is clamped by grippers. An unprinted margin of about ⅜″ (depending on the press) must be provided for the grippers.

Gutter. The inner margin of a page, next to the binding.

Hairline. A very thin line or space. The finest line that can be reproduced.

Halation. In photography, the spreading of light beyond the highlight areas of the image, thus creating a soft, blurry perimeter known as a *halo*.

Half title page. The first page of a book, attached along the binding edge to the *end paper*. Because it doesn't open fully, it usually contains only the title in a small size.

Halftone. A reproduction in which continuous tones have been converted to a pattern of tiny dots of various sizes through the use of a halftone screen.

Halftone screen. A glass or film base screen used to convert continuous-tone copy to halftone copy. The glass screen is ruled with opaque grid lines and is called a *crossline screen*. The film-base screen contains dots that become less dense at their periphery, and is called a *contact screen*.

Hanging indentation. A paragraph in which the first line is flush left, and the remainder of the lines are indented uniformly.

Hanging punctuation. Periods, commas, quotes, and apostrophes "hung" in the margins to achieve a better vertical alignment in a column. Generally used only in columns not exceeding 10 or 15 lines.

Hard copy. In phototypesetting, typewriter-like copy produced during keyboarding in addition to an encoded tape or disc.

Head. The top of a sheet or page. The bottom is called the *foot*.

Heading. One or more words set in a different size and/or style than the body type for emphasis. Also called a *head*.

Headline. The most prominent line of type in a printed piece. The next most prominent line is called a *subhead*.

Hickey. A spot or imperfection on a printed piece due to lint, bits of ink skin, etc. on the plate or offset blanket.

Highlight. In continuous-tone and halftone copy, the lightest areas.

Highlight halftone. A halftone in which the small dots in the highlight areas have been removed, usually by manipulation of the camera exposure, but sometimes by dot etching or retouching. Also called a *dropout halftone*.

Holding lines. Lines drawn on the mechanical to indicate the position of halftones and screen tints. Usually red.

Hot metal composition. Also called *hot type*. Typesetting in which the type is cast in molten metal at the time of composition, such as Linotype, Monotype, etc. Also, any metal composition, both machine-set and foundry type, as opposed to *cold type* (which see).

House organ. A periodical published by a company or organization.

Hue. Hue, intensity, and value are the three properties of color. Hue is the name of a given color, such as red, blue, yellow, etc.

Idiot tape. See *Unjustified tape*.

Image master. In phototypesetting, a disc, grid, drum, etc, that holds the type font or fonts.

Imposing stone. A machined steel surface (formerly stone) on which metal type and engravings are locked up in a chase.

Imposition. The arrangement and positioning of pages or other units of a job so that they fit the press sheet properly.

Impression. The image made by contact of an inked plate or type with paper.

Imprint. A company's name, etc. printed on a previously printed piece.

Indicia. The markings printed in place of stamp, cancellation, postmark, etc. on envelopes in bulk mail.

Indirect letterpress. See *Letterset*.

Indirect screening. In process color separation, a halftone negative or positive made from a continuous-tone, color-separated negative or positive.

Initial. A large letter used to begin a body of copy. Often used at the beginning of a chapter.

Ink fountain. See *Fountain*.

Ink holdout. The ability of paper to limit or prevent the absorption of ink.

Insert. A printed piece which is inserted into another printed piece or publication.

Intaglio. A printing process in which the printing image is depressed below the surface of the plate. *Gravure* and *engraving* are intaglio processes.

Interlinespacing. A term used in photo-

typesetting for *linespacing* or *leading*.

Italic. A slanted letter with cursive, or flowing, strokes. Not to be confused with *oblique*, which is a slanted roman letter, or with *script*, which has connecting strokes between letters.

Jacket. The printed wrapper on a casebound book. Also called a *dust cover*.

Job press. See *Platen press*.

Jog. To align the edges of a pile of sheets by vibration.

Justify. To make lines of type equal in width (flush left and right) by adjusting the space between words.

Kern. In foundry type, that part of a letter which overhangs the type body and rests on the shoulder of the adjacent type, thus making a tighter fit.

Kerning. To space certain letter combinations closer than normal for a better fit. In foundry type, this is done with kerned letters or by cutting the type body. In phototypesetting and photolettering, it is done by backspacing.

Key. To code original copy and its layout or mechanical position with a number and/or letter.

Keyboard composition. Typesetting done by means of a keyboard, such as Linotype, Monotype, phototypesetting, typewriter, etc.

Keyline. A mechanical in which color and screen tint shapes are drawn in red outline on the illustration board rather than on acetate overlays.

Key mechanical, negative, or plate. In color printing, the mechanical, negative, or plate that contains the basic format of the job and is used as a guide for registering the other colors.

Kid finish. A slightly toothy finish commonly used on high quality paper and bristol board.

Kill. To delete unwanted copy. Also, to distribute or dump type after use. Also, to destroy unwanted negatives or plates.

Kraft. A brown paper or board made by the sulfate process.

Kromecote. A brand name for *cast-coated paper* (which see).

Lacquer. A clear, colorless, synthetic coating applied to printed surfaces for appearance and/or durability. Also see *Varnish*.

Laid paper. An uncalendered paper with a watermarked pattern of closely-spaced lines in one direction and widely-spaced lines in the other. Also see *Wove paper*.

Lamination. A clear plastic film bonded to a printed sheet for appearance and/or durability. Also refers to the bonding together of paper and board in papermaking.

Lap. In color printing, the slight overlap that occurs where colors abut. Also see *Register* and *Spreading or shrinking.*

Laydown sequence. The sequence in which colors are printed.

Layout. A hand-rendered design for a printed piece. The four types of layouts are (in order of degree of finish): thumbnail sketches, rough layouts, finished layouts, and comprehensive layouts, or comps.

Leader. A series of dots or dashes set in type.

Lead-in. One or more words at the beginning of a block of copy set in a different typeface.

Leading. (Pronounced *ledding.*) The amount of additional space (measured in points) placed between lines of type. In metal type, this is done with strips of metal called *leads.* Also called *linespacing* or *interlinespacing.*

Ledger paper. A grade of paper similar to bond but heavier and more durable.

Letterfit. The quality of spacing between letters in a typeface design. Good letterfit means that the spacing is both optimum for legibility and consistent with any combination of letters.

Letterpress. A printing process in which the printing image is raised and the non-printing areas are depressed.

Letterset. A printing process in which a relief-image plate is used on a modified offset press. Also kown as *dry offset* or *indirect letterpress.*

Letterspacing. The addition of more space than is normally used between letters.

Ligature. In type, two or three characters specially joined or fitted together, such as *ff, fi, ffl,* etc., the purpose being to improve the letterfit of difficult letter combinations.

Lightface. A lightweight version of a typeface.

Linecaster. A typesetting machine that casts a line of type on one slug, such as Linotype and Intertype.

Line copy. Any copy composed of solid blacks and white with no tonal gradations.

Line engraving. In photoengraving, a printing plate made from line copy, as opposed to a *halftone engraving.*

Line gauge. See *Type gauge.*

Line negative. A tone reversal, on film, of line copy (which see). The line copy is transparent, and the surrounding areas are opaque black.

Line printer. In phototypesetting, a tape-activated printout machine for editing purposes.

Linespacing. See *Leading.*

Lining figures. Typeface numerals which are the same height as the capitals, as opposed to Old Style figures, which vary in height. Also called *Modern figures.*

Lithography. A planographic printing process

in which the printing and non-printing areas of the plate are on the same level, or plane. The plate is chemically treated to make the printing areas ink-receptive, and the non-printing areas water-receptive. Also see *Offset lithography.*

Lockup. In letterpress, type and engravings positioned and wedged securely in a chase.

Logotype (or logo). A specially designed word or name in a particular letter style, always used in the same way. Frequently similar to a *trademark* (which see), but is usually purely typographic.

Long ink. A consistency of printing ink. Long ink is stringy; short ink is buttery.

Lower case. The small letters of an alphabet, as opposed to capitals. Infrequently called *minuscules.*

Machine coated. Paper which is coated on one or two sides on the papermaking machine, as opposed to usually higher-quality *off-machine coated* paper.

Machine composition. In metal type, type-setting done by casting type from molds or matrices, usually by keyboard, as opposed to the hand-setting of type cast at the foundry.

Machine finish (MF). An uncoated, calendered book paper with a finish between that of *eggshell* and *English finish.*

Magazine. In type, the channeled container used to store matrices in Linotype and Intertype machines.

Majuscules. Archaic term for capital letters.

Makeready. The preparatory work necessary to make a press or other machine ready for operation, such as adjusting the feeder, grippers, plate pressure, etc.

Manuscript. The original typewritten copy to be set in type. Also called *copy* or *typescript.*

Mark up. To mark copy with typesetting specifications.

Mask. Paper, film, or other material used to block out selected portions of an image. Also see *Frisket.*

Masthead. The typographic design used for the title of a magazine or newspaper.

Match color. See *Flat color.*

Matrix (or mat). A mold for the casting of type or plates. Also, the master font in photo-typesetting. Plural is *matrices* or *mats.*

Matte finish. A paper finish that is uncalendered and fairly smooth. Also, any finish that is dull rather than glossy, as in photographs.

Mean line. The imaginary line that delineates the tops of lower case letters without ascenders. Also called the *waist line* or *x-line.*

Measure. In typesetting, the pica width of a line or column of type.

Mechanical. A camera-ready assembly con-

taining all copy pasted or rendered in printing position. Also called a *paste-up* or *keyline.*

Mechanical binding. A binding method employing a mechanical device, such as a metal or plastic coil.

Mechanical color separation. The pre-separation of colors by the designer on the mechanical, either with overlays or by keylining.

Middle tones. In continuous-tone and halftone copy, the intermediate tones between highlights and shadows.

Miniscules. An archaic term meaning small, or lower case, letters.

Modern Style type. A style category typified by strong contrast between thick and thin strokes, unbracketed serifs, and symmetrically balanced swells. Bodoni is a typical Modern Style.

Moiré pattern. A third, usually unwanted pattern that occurs when two repetitive patterns are superposed.

Mold. See *Matrix.*

Montage. A composite image made from several separate images.

Morgue. A reference file or department.

Mottled. Spotty or unevenly printed areas.

Mortising. In photoengraving, the operation of cutting out sections of engravings for the purpose of inserting type or other engravings.

Multilith. Brand name for a small, offset duplicator press.

Negative. In photography, a tone reversal of the original on film, paper, glass, etc.

Negative paste-up. The pasting together of two or more photostats in negative form so that the subsequent positive print will be all on one sheet.

Newsprint. Paper made primarily from groundwood pulp and used for printing newspaper.

Non-counting keyboard. In phototypesetting, a keyboard which produces an unhyphenated, unjustified tape. These operations are later performed by a computer. See also *Counting keyboard.*

Oblique. A slanted roman letter. Not to be confused with *italic,* which has a cursive design that is different from its roman counterpart.

Oblong. A book, pamphlet, magazine, etc. that is bound on its short dimension. When bound on its long dimension it is called *upright.*

Offset. Shortened term for offset lithography. Also, the former term for *set-off* (which see).

Offset lithography. Commonly called *offset.* A form of lithography (which see) in which the image is transferred to a rubber blanket, and from there to the paper.

Offset paper. Paper formulated especially for offset printing.

Old Style figures. Typeface numerals which vary in height, as opposed to *lining figures,* which are all equal in height to the capitals.

Old Style type. A style category typified by mild contrast between thick and thin strokes, bracketed serifs, and off-center swells. Caslon is a typical Old Style type.

Opacity. In paper, relating to the *show-through* of printing from the reverse side or next sheet.

Opaque. Non-transparent. Also, to render transparent portions of film non-transparent. Also, the medium used for opaquing.

Optical center. The perceived center, which appears slightly higher than mathematical center.

Optical character recognition (OCR). A system that reads copy electronically and then produces a coded tape.

Orthochromatic. A photographic emulsion sensitive to all light except red.

Outline halftone. See *Silhouette halftone.*

Overhang cover. A cover larger than the enclosed pages, as opposed to a *flush cover* (which see).

Overlay. A transparent or translucent sheet of film or paper hinged over artwork for protection, specifications, or color separation.

Overprinting. Printing over an area that has already been printed.

Overrun. Copies or sheets printed in excess of the specified number.

Ozalid. The company name for a brand of diazoprint, frequently used generically.

Packing. Paper used to underlay the plate, blanket, impression cylinder, etc. to achieve the proper printing pressure.

Pagination. Numbering the pages of a book.

Pamphlet. A book of a few sheets, usually with a paper cover. Also called a *booklet* or *brochure.*

Panchromatic. A photographic emulsion sensitive to all visible spectral colors.

Paper grade. Category or type of paper, based on its application, weight, etc.

Parchment. Goat or sheep skin made into sheets for writing, illuminating, etc. Also, a paper made to simulate parchment.

Paste-up. An assembly of various elements with adhesive, usually rubber cement. Also, another term for *mechanical* (which see).

Pebble finish. A paper finish achieved by embossing.

Perfect binding. A binding method in which the pages and cover are held together by adhesive only.

Perfecting press. A press that prints both sides of the sheet in one pass through the press.

Perforating. The punching of a series of holes or slots in a sheet so that a portion of the sheet can be detached.

Photocomposing. In phototypesetting, a system for composing a complete page layout electronically. In platemaking, a *step and repeat machine* (which see). In photography, the making of a *photomontage* (which see).

Photocomposition. See *Phototypesetting.*

Photocopy. A photographic copy of a print, transparency, or flat artwork.

Photodisplay. See *Photolettering.*

Photoengraving. In letterpress, an etched relief printing plate produced with the aid of photography.

Photogelatin. See *Collotype.*

Photogravure. An infrequently used term for *sheet-fed gravure* printing.

Photolettering. Also called *photodisplay.* A photographic method of setting display sizes of type and lettering on paper or film.

Photomechanical. Pertaining to any platemaking process in which the plate is imaged photographically.

Photomontage. Two or more photographs combined into one image. Also called *composite photography.*

Photoprint. A photographic print made from a film negative or positive.

Photoproof. In phototypesetting, a first, rough, or galley proof used for proofreading.

Photorepro. In phototypesetting, a reproduction-quality proof.

Photostat. A photographic reproduction method in which both negative and positive prints are on paper.

Phototypesetting. Also called *photocomposition.* A keyboard composition system that utilizes photographic, electronic, and mechanical components to produce letter images on photosensitive paper or film.

Photounit. Also called a *phototypesetter.* The unit in a phototypesetting sytem that sets and exposes type on to film or paper.

Pi. Also called *pie.* To spill or mix up metal type.

Pica. A typographic measurement, approximately $1/6$ of an inch. There are 12 *points* in a pica.

Picking. In printing, the lifting of the paper surface because of ink that is too tacky for the strength of the paper. Also see *Tack.*

Pigment. Color particles in ink, paint, etc.

Piling. The sticking or caking of ink on rollers, plate, or blanket during printing.

Pin register. The use of punched holes and special pins on copy, film, and plates to achieve accurate register.

Plate finish. In paper, a smooth, hard finish achieved by calendering.

Platemaking. Specifically, making plates for any printing process. Broadly, the various steps necessary to convert copy to a printing plate.

Platen press. Also called *job press.* In letterpress, a flatbed press that operates in a clamshell movement.

Ply. One of the two or more sheets that are laminated together to form bristol board, etc.

Point. A typographic measurement, approximately $1/72$ of an inch. There are 12 points in a pica (which see). Also, a thickness measurement for paper and board. One point (in paper and board) equals one mil (.001″).

Positive. In photography, a reproduction on film, paper, glass, etc. that matches the tones of the original, as opposed to a *negative.*

Poster. A sheet of paper printed on one side. Designed to be posted and read quickly in passing.

Posterize. To convert a continuous-tone image to two or more flat tones. May be done photographically or by hand rendering.

Preface. A statement by the author that precedes the text of a book, as opposed to the *foreword,* which is usually written by someone other than the author, and the *introduction,* which introduces the text.

Pre-press proof. Proof made from the *flat* on photosensitive paper or film before the plate is made.

Preprinted. Printed material that is printed before, and separate from, the overall job.

Presensitized plate. A printing plate in which the light-sensitive coating has been applied by the manufacturer.

Press proof. In color printing, a proof made from the printing plates, either on a proofing press or at the beginning of the run on the production press.

Press run. The number of sheets or copies to be printed.

Pressure-sensitive. An adhesive coating that sticks without moistening.

Primary colors. The three basic colors from which all colors can be made. In pigment: yellow, red, and blue. In light: red, green, and blue.

Printability. The various paper, ink, and press factors that affect the quality of the printed piece.

Printer's error (PE). An error made by the typesetter, as opposed to an error or alteration made by the author (*AA*).

Printing paper. Paper or board specifically formulated for printing and other production applications, as opposed to *drawing paper* (which see).

Printout. In phototypesetting, the typewriter-like copy produced by a tape-driven line printer.

Process camera. A large camera used to make film negatives and positives for plate-making. Also called a *copy camera* or *graphic arts camera*.

Process color printing. Also called *full-color* or *four-color process printing.* The method of reproducing full-color copy by printing it in the three primary colors plus black.

Process inks. The four special inks used in process color printing: magenta (or red), yellow, cyan (or blue), and black.

Progressive proofs (or progs). In process color printing, proofs made from the four plates, printed separately and progressively overprinted.

Proof. A trial print taken from a printing plate, flat, or type.

Proofreaders' marks. Standard symbols and abbreviations used to make corrections and alterations in copy.

Pulp. The mixture of wood and/or rag fibers from which paper is made.

Punch register. See *Pin register.*

Quad. A piece of type metal, less than type-high, used in spacing words, filling out lines, etc. See *Em quad* and *En quad.*

Quoins. (Pronounced *coins* .) Wedges used to lock up type and engravings in a chase.

Rag paper. High-quality paper made either partly or entirely from cotton fiber.

Ragged right (or left). In type, lines of varying length vertically aligned on one side and thus unaligned on the other. Usually specified as *flush left/ragged right* or *flush right/ragged left.* Such a column is called *unjustified.*

Raised printing. See *Thermography.*

Ream. 500 sheets of paper.

Recto. Right-hand page of a spread, as opposed to *verso,* or left-hand page.

Reflection copy. Opaque copy viewed by reflected light, as opposed to *transmission copy* (which see).

Register. The correct relative position of two or more negatives, printing plates, impressions, etc. so that they align exactly with each other.

Register marks. Small crosses or other marks placed on copy to facilitate the registering of overlays, negatives, printing plates, etc.

Reproduction proof (or repro). A final, high-quality proof made following corrections

indicated on the first or galley proof. It is pasted on to the mechanical and used for reproduction.

Retouching. The correcting or altering of artwork, photographs, negatives, etc.

Reversal film. Film that does not reverse the tones of the original. That is, a positive remains positive, and a negative remains negative.

Reverse. To reverse tonal values, as with a negative.

Reverse type. Type dropped out to white on solid background. When dropped out of a screened background, it is usually called *dropout type.*

Revise proof. In type, a corrected galley proof. May be *first revise, second revise,* etc.

Right-angle fold. A fold that is 90° to a previous fold.

Right reading. An image with the correct left/right orientation. This is as compared to *wrong reading,* where the image is reversed from left to right.

River. Spaces between words that accidentally line up in a number of consecutive lines to form an objectionable "river" of white space that meanders more or less vertically through the column.

Roman. Upright letters of any style, as opposed to *italic.* Less frequently, a typeface more or less based on early Roman letterforms.

Rotary press. A press in which both the impression and printing surfaces are cylindrical.

Rotogravure. Web-fed gravure printing, as opposed to sheet-fed gravure printing, or photogravure.

Rough. A rough layout, usually reproduction size.

Routing. In photoengraving, the cutting away of unwanted metal from non-printing areas of a plate.

Rule. In metal type, a strip of metal that prints as a line. Available in many weights, double and triple lines, dashes, etc. Also, any line used in conjunction with type, whether metal type, phototype, or hand-drawn.

Runaround. Type that is fitted around an illustration, photograph, etc.

Run in. Type to be set without paragraph breaks.

Running head. A title or other heading that runs at the top of every page.

Saddle-wire stitching. A method of binding in which staples are inserted through the spine and clinched in the centerfold. Used for pamphlets and magazines.

Sans Serif type. A style category for any typeface without (sans) serifs.

Scaling. Determining the ratio of enlargement or reduction.

Scanner. See *Electronic scanner.*

Score. To crease paper so that it will fold easily, usually necessary for stiff and/or heavy paper. Very heavy board may also need to be partially cut, and is called *cut scoring.*

Screen. See *Halftone screen.*

Screen angle. In color printing, the angle at which each halftone screen is placed to avoid a *moiré pattern* (which see).

Screen printing. Also called *silkscreen printing.* A printing process that employs a stencil adhered to a fine-mesh screen. Ink is forced through the screen openings with a rubber blade called a *squeegee.*

Screen ruling. The number of lines or dots per inch on a halftone screen.

Screen tint. A flat, unmodulated tint or tone usually achieved by stripping a piece of halftone film on the platemaker's negative. Also called a *Benday tint, halftone tint,* or *flat tint.*

Scribing. The cutting of lines in blackened film emulsion with a scriber. Used for fine ruled forms instead of ruling on the mechanical.

Script type. Type that imitates handwriting and has connecting strokes between letters.

Scum. In offset lithography, an ink film that prints in non-printing areas.

Self cover. A cover of the same paper as the inside pages.

Self mailer. A direct mail piece designed to eliminate the need for an envelope.

Separation. See *Color separation.*

Serif. The short cross-stroke at the end of a letter stroke.

Set-off. Wet ink transferred from one sheet to another when piled after printing.

Set solid. Lines of type set with no leading or additional space between lines.

Sewed soft cover. A book with sewn signatures, but with a soft instead of a hard cover. More durable and expensive than *perfect binding* (which see), which is the usual method of binding soft cover books.

Shadows. In continuous-tone and halftone copy, the darkest areas.

Sheet-fed. A press that prints sheets rather than a *web,* or continuous roll, of paper.

Shooting copy. Copy to be photographed for reproduction. Also, the act of photographing copy.

Short ink. A consistency of printing ink. Short ink is buttery; long ink is stringy.

Shoulder. In metal type, the flat top of the type body surrounding the raised face or printing surface.

Show-through. The paper property which

permits a printed image from the reverse side or next sheet to be seen through the sheet. See also *Opacity* and *Strike-through*.

Side-wire stitching. A method of binding in which staples are inserted from the front to the back of the book, magazine, etc., about ⅛" in from the binding edge.

Signature. One sheet of paper printed on both sides and folded and trimmed in such a way that it results in four or more consecutively-ordered pages in a book pamphlet, etc.

Silhouette halftone. Also called an *outline halftone*. A halftone in which the background has been eliminated.

Silkscreen printing. See *Screen printing*.

Sizing. A material added to paper during manufacture to make it moisture resistant.

Slip sheeting. In printing, inserting blank sheets between printed sheets to prevent *set-off* (which see). In graphic design, inserting a blank sheet between rubber-cemented surfaces to facilitate positioning. The sheet is slipped out during the bonding operation.

Slitting. The cutting of paper into narrower sheets after it has been printed, by means of cutting wheels on the press or folding machine.

Slug. A line of type cast in one piece on a linecasting machine such as Linotype. Also, a strip of metal, 6 points or wider in thickness, used for linespacing. If thinner than 6 point, it is called a *lead*.

Small capitals (SC). Also called *small caps*. Capitals that are the x-height of the lower case letters of the same point size.

Soft cover. Any paper cover, but usually refers to a paperback book.

Sorts. In metal type, individual characters obtained separately on special order, rather than in standard fonts.

Spacebands. Devices in linecasting machines that wedge between words to justify the line.

Spaces. In handset type, pieces of metal, less than type-high, for spacing letters and words.

Spec. (Pronounced *speck*). Short for specifying or specification. For example, to *spec* type means to write the type specifications on the copy.

Spine. The binding side of a book. Also called *backbone*.

Spiral binding. See *Mechanical binding*.

Split fountain. A color printing technique in which two or more colors can be printed in one press run by dividing the ink fountain into compartments.

Spotting. The elimination of small defects in negatives by opaquing.

Spread. Two facing pages. Also called *two-page spread* or *double spread*.

Spreading or shrinking. In color printing, to photographically alter the size of a film image slightly to achieve sufficient *lap* (which see).

Square halftone. A halftone having four straight sides and squared corners, either rectangular or square in shape. Also called a *square-finish halftone*.

Square Serif type. A style category typified by heavy, square-cut serifs.

Stamping. The imprinting of book covers with a relief-imaged die, and usually in conjunction with ink or metal foil. If no ink or foil is used, it is called *blind stamping*.

Steel-die engraving. See *Engraving*.

Step and repeat machine. A machine for making multiple exposures on a printing plate from one master negative, as well as for achieving accurate register of color plates. Also called a *photocomposing machine*.

Stereotype. In letterpress, a duplicate plate made from type and/or engravings, and involving the pouring of molten metal into a paper or plastic mold (mat) of the original. Of lower quality than an electrotype, and commonly used in newspaper reproduction. Also called a *stereo*.

Stock. Paper, board, or other material to be printed.

Straight matter. Body or text type, all the same size and style (but may include italic and/or boldface), set in a column with no unusual variations.

Strike-on composition. See *Typewriter composition*.

Strike-through. In letterpress, the impression of type on the reverse side of the sheet. In all printing processes, the penetration of ink into the paper so that it shows through the paper.

Stripping. The assembling of film negatives and/or positives on a *flat* (which see). The flat is used to expose the sensitized printing plate.

Substance. See *Basis weight*.

Sulphate paper. Made by cooking wood chips in a solution of caustic soda and sodium sulfide. Before bleaching, the pulp can be made into brown kraft paper. After bleaching and further refining, it can be made into fine printing papers.

Sulphite paper. Made by cooking wood chips in a solution of bisulphite of lime. Not as strong as sulphate paper, and therefore not as widely used.

Supercalender. In papermaking, a stack of calenders, separate from the papermaking machine, used to produce a high finish on paper.

Surprinting. Line copy superimposed over screened copy on the same printing plate. Not to be confused with *overprinting*, which involves two printing plates.

Swash type. Capital letters with decorative flourishes.

Swell. In thick-and-thin letters, the swelled shape of curved strokes.

Tack. The stickiness of printing ink. Ink that is too tacky will cause *picking* of the paper (which see).

Text paper. An antique or eggshell finish book paper, frequently with deckled edges, for decorative applications.

Text type. See *Body type*.

Thermography. A printing method that produces raised, engraved-like images.

Three-color process. *Process color printing* (which see) in which the black plate is eliminated.

Thumbnail. A rough, miniature layout sketch.

Tint. A *screen tint* (which see). Also, to add white to a color.

Tipping. The process of pasting end papers or separately printed inserts into or onto a signature, usually before collating.

Tissue overlay. A sheet of tracing paper hinged over artwork for protection and/or marking specifications.

Title page. The page of a book that carries the title, author's name, and publisher's name. Usually page 3.

Titling type. A typeface in which capitals and numerals are cast the full height of the top surface of the type body. There are no matching lower case letters.

Tooth. A slightly rough paper finish.

Trademark. An established symbol for an individual or company. Similar to a logo, but does not necessarily include typography.

Transitional type. A style category with the characteristics of both Old Style and Modern Style typefaces. Typified by Baskerville.

Transmission copy. Transparent copy viewed by transmitted light, as opposed to *reflection copy* (which see). Color transparencies and color negatives are examples of transmission copy.

Transparent copy. See *Transmission copy*.

Transpose. To exchange the positions of letters, words, or lines.

Trapping. The ability of an already-printed ink to accept an overprinted ink.

Trim marks. Short, fine lines drawn on the mechanical to indicate the trim size of the printed sheet. Also called *crop marks*.

Trim size. The size to which a sheet will be cut after printing. Indicated on the mechanical with *trim marks* or *crop marks*.

Typecasting. Setting type by casting it in molten metal, such as by Linotype or Monotype.

Type family. The complete range of sizes and variations of a typeface design, such as roman, italic, bold, condensed, expanded, etc.

Type font. The complete assortment of characters for one size of a typeface, which includes capitals, lower case, figures, and punctuation marks.

Type gauge. A scale containing typographic measurements such as points, picas, and agate lines. Also, a *line gauge*, which contains scales for measuring line depths of columns.

Type-high. The height of a piece of metal type from the foot to the face (.918″). Photoengravings are made type-high by mounting them on wood or metal blocks.

Type series. The complete range of sizes of one specific typeface design. This does not include family-related variations such as italic, bold, etc.

Typesetting. Also called *composition*. The composing of type by any method.

Typewriter composition. Composition for reproduction produced by a special typewriter, such as VariTyper or IBM Composer. Also called *strike-on* or *direct impression* composition.

Typo. A typographic error made by the typographer.

Typographer. A company that specializes in typesetting. Persons who set type are usually called typesetters or compositors.

Unit system. A counting method used in Monotype, phototypesetting, and typewriter composition to determine when a line is ready to be justified. The unit is a subdivision of the em, and the width of each letter is measured in units.

Unjustified tape. In phototypesetting, an unhyphenated, unjustified tape produced by a *non-counting keyboard* (which see). Also called *idiot tape*.

Unjustified type. Lines of type set with equal wordspacing and therefore slightly uneven in length. May be set flush left/ragged right, or flush right/ragged left. See also *Justify*.

Up. As in *two-up, three-up*, etc. The printing of multiple duplicate jobs on one sheet.

Upper case. Capital letters, as opposed to lower case, or small, letters.

Upright. A book, pamphlet, magazine, etc. that is bound on its long dimension. When bound on its short dimension it is called *oblong*.

Vacuum frame. A contact printing frame which uses vacuum to hold the film copy in tight contact with the sensitized film or printing plate during exposure.

Value. The lightness or darkness of a color or tone of gray. It is measured with a *gray scale* (which see) and stated by percentage.

Van Dyke. See *Brownprint*.

Varnish. A clear, colorless coating applied to printed surfaces for appearance and/or durability.

Vehicle. The liquid medium in which pigment is suspended in paint, printing ink, etc.

Vellum finish. An uncoated, uncalendered paper with a slightly toothy finish that is smoother than eggshell finish. Also, a heavy tracing paper.

Velox print. A halftone printed on photographic paper, to be pasted on the mechanical as line copy.

Verso. The left-hand page of a *spread*, as opposed to *recto*, or the right-hand page.

Vignette halftone. A halftone in which the edges fade into the white of the paper.

Viscosity. In printing ink, resistance to flow; the opposite of *fluidity*.

Visual. A *layout* (which see).

Visual display. In phototypesetting, a screen on the keyboard unit, similar to that on an electronic calculator, showing a limited number of words as they are being set. Also, lines of copy displayed on the cathode ray tube of a visual display terminal.

Waist line. See *Mean line*.

Warm colors. Colors which contain enough yellow and/or red to make them appear warm rather than neutral or cool.

Wash drawing. A drawing done with black ink, dye, or watercolor, diluted to various degrees to produce a complete range of tonal gradations.

Washup. The process of cleaning the rollers, plate, ink fountain, etc. of the press.

Watermark. A translucent image in the paper, put in during manufacture by a raised design on the *dandy roll* (which see).

Web. A continuous roll of paper.

Web-fed press. A press that prints from a web, or roll, of paper, rather than sheets.

Weight. The lightness or heaviness of a typeface, such as light, regular, bold, and extra bold.

Widow. A single word in the last line of a paragraph; the last line of a paragraph carried over to the next page; the first line of a paragraph at the bottom of a page; or any other situation where a word or line stands alone. If a widow cannot be corrected in typesetting, the author should alter the copy if possible.

Wire side. In papermaking, the bottom side of the sheet, as opposed to the top or *felt side*. The felt side is usually smoother.

Wire stitching. See *Saddle-wire* and *Side-wire stitching*.

Woodcut. A relief image cut in a block of wood.

Also, the print therefrom. A woodcut is done on the side grain of wood, and a wood engraving is done on the end grain.

Wood type. Hand-set type routed out of wood. Formerly used for sizes too large to be practical in metal. Now largely replaced by photolettering.

Wordspacing. Adding space between words to fill out a line to a given measure *(justifying)*.

Work and tumble. To print one side of a sheet, then turn it over from front to back to print the other side.

Work and turn. To print one side of a sheet, then turn it over from left to right to print the other side.

Wove paper. An uncalendered paper with a soft, smooth finish. Also see *Laid paper*.

Wraparound plate. A flexible letterpress printing plate that is clamped around the plate cylinder like an offset plate.

Writing paper. A grade of bond paper specifically formulated for writing, as opposed to bond paper formulated for printing.

Wrong font (WF). In typesetting, the erroneous inclusion of a letter or letters from another font.

Wrong-reading. An image that is reversed from left to right, and can only be read correctly in a mirror, as opposed to *right-reading*.

Xerography. A copying process that uses static electricity to form an image, such as a Xerox machine.

x-height. The height of lower case letters without ascenders or descenders.

x-line. See *Mean line*.

Abbreviations

AA   Author's alteration.

BF   Bold face.

BM   Between marks.

B&W   Black and white.

C1S or **C2S**   Coated 1 side or coated 2 sides.

Caps   Capitals.

C&SC   Capitals and small capitals.

CRT   Cathode ray tube.

CPP   Characters per pica.

CPS   Characters per second (typesetting speed).

DO   Dropout (as in halftone).

EF   English finish (paper).

HT   Halftone.

Ital   Italic.

LC   Lower case.

M   1,000 sheets of paper.

MF   Machine finish (paper).

Ms   Manuscript. Plural is *mss*.

Neg   Negative.

OCR   Optical character recognition.

p   Page. Plural is *pp*.

PE   Printer's error.

PMS   Pantone Matching System.

Pos   Positive.

PPI   Pages per inch.

Pt   Point.

SC   Small capitals.

SC   Supercalendered (paper).

Sil or **Silo**   Silhouette (as in halftone).

Spec   To specify type, etc.

SQ   Square (as in halftone).

SS   Same size.

TR   Transpose.

U&lc   Upper and lower case.

VDT   Visual display terminal.

Vig   Vignette (as in hafltone).

WF   Wrong font.

Bibliography

Advertising Agency and Studio Skills. Tom Cardamone. Watson-Guptill, New York, 1970.

Basic Typography. John Biggs. Watson-Guptill, New York, and Faber and Faber, London, 1968.

Commercial Artist's Handbook. John Snyder. Watson-Guptill, New York, 1973.

Designing with Type. James Craig. Watson-Guptill, New York, 1971.

Direct Mail Design. Raymond Ballinger. Van Nostrand Reinhold, New York, 1963.

Graphic Arts Encyclopedia. George Stevenson. McGraw-Hill, New York, 1968.

Graphic Design. Tony Hinwood. Drake Publishers, New York, 1973.

Graphic Design and Reproduction Techniques. Peter Croy. Hastings House, New York, 1968.

Graphic Reproduction Photography. J.W. Burden. Visual Communication Books, New York, 1972.

The Graphics of Communication. Arthur Turnbull and Russell Baird. Holt, Rinehart and Winston, New York, 1968.

Handbook of Advertising Art Production. Richard M. Schlemmer. Prentice-Hall, 1966.

Layout. Raymond Ballinger. Van Nostrand Reinhold, New York, 1956.

Lettering for Advertising. Mortimer Leach. Van Nonstrand Reinhold, New York, 1956.

Lettering for Reproduction. David Gates. Watson-Guptill, New York, 1969.

The Lithographers Manual. The Graphic Arts Technical Foundation, Pittsburgh, Pa., 1974.

Pocket Pal. International Paper Co., New York, 1974.

The Practice of Printing. Ralph W. Polk. Chas. A. Bennett Co., Peoria, Illinois, 1952.

Preparing Art for Printing. Bernard Stone and Arthur Eckstein. Van Nostrand Reinhold, New York, 1965.

Production for the Graphic Designer. James Craig. Watson-Guptill, New York, 1974.

Technical Drawing. Giesecke, Mitchell, and Spencer. The Macmillan Co., New York, 1949.

Type. David Gates. Watson-Guptill, New York, 1973.

Type and Typography. Ben Rosen. Van Nostrand Reinhold, New York, 1963.

Typography. Aaron Burns. Van Nostrand Reinhold, New York, 1961.

Art supply catalogs:

A.I. Friedman, Inc.
25 West 45 St.
New York, N.Y. 10036

Arthur Brown & Bro., Inc.
2 West 46 St.
New York, N.Y. 10036

Charrette Corp.
2000 Massachusetts Ave.
Cambridge, Mass. 02140

Alvin & Co., Inc.
Box 188
Windsor, Conn. 06095

Dick Blick Co.
Box 1267
Galesburg, Ill. 61401

Designed by David Gates
Composed in Helvetica by Rockland Typographical Services
Printed and bound by Kingsport Press